Biodiversity

William Dudley, *Book Editor*

Daniel Leone, *Publisher*
Bonnie Szumski, *Editorial Director*
Scott Barbour, *Managing Editor*

CURRENT CONTROVERSIES

Cover photo: © CORBIS

Library of Congress Cataloging-in-Publication Data

Biodiversity / William Dudley, book editor.
    p. cm. — (Current controversies)
    Includes bibliographical references and index.
    ISBN 0-7377-0850-6 (pbk. : alk. paper) — ISBN 0-7377-0851-4
(lib. : alk. paper)
    1. Biological diversity. 2. Endangered species. I. Dudley, William,
1964– II. Series.

QH541.15.B56 B565   2002
333.95'11—dc21
                                    2001033527
                                          CIP

Contents

Chapter 1: Is Declining Biodiversity a Serious Ecological Problem?

Mass Extinction and Biodiversity Loss: An Overview
by David Hosansky   15
Many scientists contend that our planet is faced with the prospect of the
largest wave of plant and animal extinctions since dinosaurs became
extinct 65 million years ago. However, experts disagree about how the
potential loss of Earth's biological diversity will affect the global environment and what governments should do to preserve endangered
species.

Yes: Declining Biodiversity Is a Serious Ecological Problem

Loss of Biodiversity Is a Global Crisis *by Edward O. Wilson*   24
Earth's biodiversity is rapidly diminishing as distinct species of life
become extinct at rates 100 to 1,000 times greater than before the arrival
of humanity. Habitat destruction by human activities is a primary cause of
biodiversity loss. Precipitous loss of biodiversity will have large and negative consequences for the global environment and human welfare.

Declining Biodiversity Can Adversely Affect Local Environments
by the Ecological Society of America   29
Human welfare is ultimately dependent on the viability of Earth's ecosystems and their ability to perform certain processes, such as the use and
recycling of soil nutrients and water to promote plant growth. Declines in
biodiversity may adversely affect the ability of ecosystems to function.
Prudence dictates that biodiversity must be preserved in order to safeguard local and global environments.

Invading Species Threaten America's Biodiversity and Environment
by Joel Achenbach   37
The biological diversity in the United States is threatened by a growing
invasion of non-native species of plants, animals, and microorganisms.
These species can take over local environments and displace—or even
cause the extinction of—native species.

Chapter 3: Are Commercial Farming Practices Harming Agricultural Biodiversity?

Yes: Commercial Farming Practices Are Detrimental to Biodiversity

No: Commercial Farming Practices Are Not Detrimental to Biodiversity

Chapter 4: How Can the World's Biological Diversity Best Be Preserved?

political process. Scientists disagree on whether placing a monetary value on biodiversity would help or hinder conservation efforts.

world's biological diversity. Preserving biodiversity requires not only efforts to stabilize the world's human population, but also a change in attitude so that nature is seen as something to be respected, not manipulated for profit and convenience.

In many of the regions in which biodiversity is imperiled, languages and indigenous cultures are also becoming extinct. The forces of globalization and industrialization endanger both cultural and biological diversity. A biocultural approach that seeks to preserve both realms of diversity is called for.

Foreword

By definition, controversies are "discussions of questions in which opposing opinions clash" (Webster's Twentieth Century Dictionary Unabridged). Few would deny that controversies are a pervasive part of the human condition and exist on virtually every level of human enterprise. Controversies transpire between individuals and among groups, within nations and between nations. Controversies supply the grist necessary for progress by providing challenges and challengers to the status quo. They also create atmospheres where strife and warfare can flourish. A world without controversies would be a peaceful world; but it also would be, by and large, static and prosaic.

The Series' Purpose

The purpose of the Current Controversies series is to explore many of the social, political, and economic controversies dominating the national and international scenes today. Titles selected for inclusion in the series are highly focused and specific. For example, from the larger category of criminal justice, Current Controversies deals with specific topics such as police brutality, gun control, white collar crime, and others. The debates in Current Controversies also are presented in a useful, timeless fashion. Articles and book excerpts included in each title are selected if they contribute valuable, long-range ideas to the overall debate. And wherever possible, current information is enhanced with historical documents and other relevant materials. Thus, while individual titles are current in focus, every effort is made to ensure that they will not become quickly outdated. Books in the Current Controversies series will remain important resources for librarians, teachers, and students for many years.

In addition to keeping the titles focused and specific, great care is taken in the editorial format of each book in the series. Book introductions and chapter prefaces are offered to provide background material for readers. Chapters are organized around several key questions that are answered with diverse opinions representing all points on the political spectrum. Materials in each chapter include opinions in which authors clearly disagree as well as alternative opinions in which authors may agree on a broader issue but disagree on the possible solutions. In this way, the content of each volume in Current Controversies mirrors the mosaic of opinions encountered in society. Readers will quickly realize that there are many viable answers to these complex issues. By questioning each author's conclusions, students and casual readers can begin to develop the critical thinking skills so important to evaluating opinionated material.

Current Controversies is also ideal for controlled research. Each anthology in the series is composed of primary sources taken from a wide gamut of informational categories including periodicals, newspapers, books, United States and foreign government documents, and the publications of private and public organizations. Readers will find factual support for reports, debates, and research papers covering all areas of important issues. In addition, an annotated table of contents, an index, a book and periodical bibliography, and a list of organizations to contact are included in each book to expedite further research.

Perhaps more than ever before in history, people are confronted with diverse and contradictory information. During the Persian Gulf War, for example, the public was not only treated to minute-to-minute coverage of the war, it was also inundated with critiques of the coverage and countless analyses of the factors motivating U.S. involvement. Being able to sort through the plethora of opinions accompanying today's major issues, and to draw one's own conclusions, can be a complicated and frustrating struggle. It is the editors' hope that Current Controversies will help readers with this struggle.

Greenhaven Press anthologies primarily consist of previously published material taken from a variety of sources, including periodicals, books, scholarly journals, newspapers, government documents, and position papers from private and public organizations. These original sources are often edited for length and to ensure their accessibility for a young adult audience. The anthology editors also change the original titles of these works in order to clearly present the main thesis of each viewpoint and to explicitly indicate the opinion presented in the viewpoint. These alterations are made in consideration of both the reading and comprehension levels of a young adult audience. Every effort is made to ensure that Greenhaven Press accurately reflects the original intent of the authors included in this anthology.

"Many scientists believe the twenty-first century will be a crucial time in determining the fate of many of this planet's species."

Introduction

The term "biodiversity"—short for biological diversity—was first used in the 1980s by scientists to refer to the richness of biological variation on Earth or within a particular region. In their book *Saving Nature's Legacy*, ecologists Reed Noss and Allen Cooperrider define biodiversity as

> the variety of life and its processes. It includes the variety of living organisms, the genetic differences among them, the...ecosystems in which they occur, and the ecological and evolutionary processes that keep them functioning, yet ever changing and adapting.

As this definition suggests, biodiversity exists on several levels. Perhaps the most common definition of the term refers to the variety of different *species* on the planet or in a given habitat. Approximately 1.7 million species of plants, animals, fungi, microbes, and other forms of life have been identified and named by biologists, but estimates of the total number of species on this planet vary greatly, from ten million to one hundred million. Scientists are engaged in several efforts around the world to identify and number undiscovered species, and many environmental laws, such as the Endangered Species Act, focus on preventing their disappearance or extinction.

The concept of biodiversity also extends to different levels of biological organization. *Genetic* diversity refers to the genetic variation within the same species. This can cover distinct populations of the same species (rice, for instance, exists in thousands of distinct varieties) or genetic variation within the same population (cheetahs in Africa, for example, lack genetic diversity in that all members are very similar in their genetic makeup). Scientists also refer to *ecosystem* diversity, noting the presence on Earth of a wide variety of natural habitats that contain differing varieties of life and ways in which species interact with each other. The World Resources Institute states that "the breadth of the concept [of biodiversity] reflects the interrelatedness of genes, species, and ecosystems."

Biodiversity at all levels is an important environmental resource. "Our lives depend on biodiversity in ways that are not often appreciated," writes scientist Anthony C. Janetos. He and other observers have described several different ways in which humans rely on biodiversity. On a utilitarian level, humans depend on other species for food, clothing, wood, medicines, and other necessities and comforts of living. Domesticated strains of crop plants and animals are continually interbred with their wild "cousins" to introduce new genetic combinations that can improve yields, drought tolerance, and disease and pest resistance. Endangered species of plants or animals may have properties yet to be discovered that could provide important medicines. In addition to such direct benefits, the world's diverse living creatures working in concert provide important ecological "services" such as air and water purification, climate regulation, erosion control, and providing oxygen in the atmosphere that humans need to breathe. "Biodiversity keeps the planet habitable," concludes biologist Peter Raven. Some ecologists also stress the aesthetic value of a natural world rich with an abundance of varied and often beautiful life-forms.

These important benefits conferred by biodiversity may be at risk, some believe. "Biologists who explore biodiversity see it vanishing before their eyes," writes Edward O. Wilson. Conservationists have classified eight thousand species as endangered, and the true number of species nearing extinction may be much higher. Scientists such as Denis Saunders of Australia's Commonwealth Scientific and Industrial Research Organisation (CSIRO) estimate that seventy-thousand species become extinct each year—almost two hundred species a day. Many argue that the world could possibly lose 50 percent of its species over the next century. These extinctions are primarily blamed on the pressures exerted by a human population that has grown from less than 1.75 billion in 1900 to more than 6 billion in 2000. Human activities such as hunting, fishing, logging, the conversion of natural habitat into farmland and urban areas, and the spread of non-native species into fragile ecological areas are all blamed for species extinction and declining biodiversity. "In both direct and indirect ways," writes ecologist R. Edward Grumbine, "human activities are causing a biodiversity crisis—the largest mass extinction in 65 million years."

Despite widespread agreement within the scientific community on the importance of biodiversity, some areas of contention remain. One concerns the extent of the extinction crisis. Extinction, most biologists agree, is a natural phenomenon that has occurred throughout world history; the question is whether contemporary extinction rates are abnormally high. Some scientists have argued that dramatic estimates in the thousands of species becoming extinct every year are speculative guesses without supporting data and that the number of *documented* extinctions remains relatively small. "The world is not losing species very rapidly yet," argues science writer Dennis T. Avery. Moreover, Avery and others contend that most known extinctions have taken place on islands, which have small populations that are highly vulnerable to extinction and therefore do not necessarily demonstrate the existence of a biodiversity crisis elsewhere.

Disagreement also exists regarding the ramifications of species loss. People who may be concerned about the fate of the panda or blue whale may feel less sense of loss if an undiscovered species of beetle in the tropical rainforest becomes extinct—a far more likely scenario. In many cases, another species may simply replace the ecological niche or function of a species that became extinct.

Introduction

"Losing a species may be tragic," writes author Mark L. Plummer, "but the result is rarely, if ever, catastrophic." Conservationists retort that the cumulative ramifications of loss of biodiversity may very well damage the resiliency of ecosystems.

A third area of controversy revolves around proposed remedies for preventing loss of biodiversity. Since human activities are believed to be the main threat to biodiversity, most proposed solutions—such as setting aside land as wildlife habitat, banning hunting of animals, restricting logging—inevitably result in restrictions on human activities and create economic burdens. Many conservationists believe that these are costs that humanity must shoulder. But some observers argue that due to the scientific uncertainty as to the extent and ramifications of loss of biodiversity, broad conservation measures attempting to restrict human activities might not be warranted or should at least be weighed against other social goals. "Species are menaced to improve roads to hospitals, build university campuses, create affordable housing, make the raw material for newspapers and magazines, and create a host of other social goods," argues Plummer. "When we alter or cancel these projects to benefit nature, we make life harder for human beings."

Humanity faces some critical choices about whether and how to preserve global biodiversity. Many scientists believe the twenty-first century will be a crucial time in determining the fate of many of this planet's species and that actions people take now will have a significant and lasting legacy. The various contributors to *Biodiversity: Current Controversies* discuss the causes, repercussions, and solutions to declining biodiversity. It is hoped that the articles that follow will shed light on one of the truly global issues of our time.

Chapter 1

Is Declining Biodiversity a Serious Ecological Problem?

Mass Extinction and Biodiversity Loss: An Overview

by David Hosansky

About the author: *David Hosansky is a freelance writer specializing in environmental topics. He previously worked as a senior writer for* CQ Weekly *and as a reporter for the* Florida Times Union.

Zoo biologist Edward J. Maruska can remember exploring the rain forests of Costa Rica in the late 1970s, when thousands of shimmering golden toads gathered in ponds of the mist-shrouded Monteverde Cloud Forest Reserve to breed.

But all the toads had vanished by the 1980s. Scientists believe that the spectacular toads, easily recognized by the males' bright orange color, fell victim to disease, changing climate patterns or pollution.

"They were so unique," recalls Maruska, executive director of the Cincinnati Zoo and Botanical Garden. "Then they were gone."

Last sighted by scientists in 1989, the golden toad is among thousands of species that have become extinct in recent years. Humans are wiping out much of the Earth's plant and animal life by paving over open space for homes and factories; clearing forests for cultivation and grazing; polluting the air and water; and introducing non-native species into fragile ecological areas.

Even primates, which belong to the taxonomic group that includes human beings, are not immune. Scientists recently concluded that a West African monkey known as Miss Waldron's red colobus has been wiped out because of deforestation and hunting. The red-cheeked monkey lived in the rain forest canopy of Ghana and the Ivory Coast. It was the first time in several centuries that a primate had become extinct.

In fact, civilization's unrelenting march across unspoiled lands has had such a profound effect on nature that scientists warn we have entered an age of mass extinction the likes of which have not been seen since the demise of dinosaurs some 65 million years ago.

The Earth, scientists say, has experienced wholesale loss of life on such a colossal scale only five times before. Some contend it will bring irrevocable changes for the planet's dominant species—humans—altering everything from food supplies to medical breakthroughs to the weather.

"There's scientific debate about the rate and the extent of species loss, but I don't think there's much remaining debate that we're in a period of mass extinction," says Eleanor Sterling, director of the Center for Biodiversity and Conservation at the American Museum of Natural History in New

> *"Humans are wiping out much of the Earth's plant and animal life."*

York City. "It's absolutely one of the most critical issues that's facing us today."

Biologists cannot quantify the rate of extinction because they do not know the total number of species that exist on Earth—let alone the numbers of mostly unknown animals, plants, fungi and other organisms that are vanishing. But leading scientists believe that based on the pace of destruction of the richest habitats, such as tropical rain forests and coral reefs, the world is losing species at a rate of 100 to 10,000 times the normal, or "background," rate. They warn that 50 percent or more of all species will be gone by the end of the current century.

In the United States alone, the U.S. Fish and Wildlife Service lists 1,233 plants and animals as threatened or endangered. That probably greatly understates the full number of vanishing species because the government lacks the resources to search for all types of endangered organisms. Around the globe, human activities are threatening countless species of frogs, tropical beetles, freshwater fish, birds, flowers and trees as well as familiar mammals such as tigers, gorillas and giant pandas.

"We anticipate we've lost a whole host of species, sometimes before we even documented them," says David Olsen, a conservation biologist with the World Wildlife Fund (WWF). "We know enough about patterns of biodiversity around the world and the loss of natural habitats to say that we are in the midst of a very serious event."

Although not all biologists agree on the extent of the loss, they generally regard mass extinction as one of the gravest issues facing humanity. According to a 1998 poll by the American Museum of Natural History, most scientists in the United States believe that the world is in the midst of a mass extinction. Moreover, they rate it a greater threat to society than more publicized problems such as pollution, global warming and the thinning of the ozone layer.

Scientists believe the loss of so many species of animals, plants and microorganisms could have profound and unpredictable effects on the United States and every other nation. Many plants and animals provide food, fibers and building materials, as well as new medicines. Others regulate the flow of water, influence weather patterns, fertilize crops, prevent topsoil erosion and reduce the amount of carbon dioxide in the atmosphere. Even tiny creatures such as insects, regarded by many as pests, are probably essential for the survival of Homo sapiens by filling critical niches in the global ecosystem.

"So important are insects and other land-dwelling arthropods that if all were to disappear, humanity probably could not last more than a few months," Harvard biologist Edward 0. Wilson wrote in his influential 1992 book, *The Diversity of Life.*

World leaders have responded to the threat of biodiversity loss with a series of international agreements. The 1973 Convention of International Trade in Endangered Species of Wild Fauna and Flora (CITES) has helped preserve well-known species such as elephants and sea turtles. In the United States, the Endangered Species Act (ESA), along with other government measures such as pesticide regulations and passage of the Clean Water Act, are credited with fostering the recovery of several species on the brink of extinction, including the bald eagle.

A series of high-profile conferences, including the 1992 Earth Summit in Rio de Janeiro, Brazil, has helped focus attention on the worldwide loss of biodiversity. In recent years, powerful organizations such as the World Bank have begun to provide grants to developing countries for projects that help restore the environment, and industrialized nations have provided incentives, such as debt forgiveness, to developing countries to preserve biologically important habitat. Some environmental groups promote ecotourism as a way to help local communities profit by limiting harmful development.

> *"Biologists cannot quantify the rate of extinction because they do not know the total number of species that exist on Earth."*

However, ecosystems are threatened by such a multitude of factors that even optitmistic conservationists warn that numerous species are doomed. "We're at the beginning of the [extinction] curve, and the question is whether we'll get it together soon enough to avoid a lot of the loss," says Thomas Lovejoy, chief biodiversity adviser at the World Bank.

The No. 1 cause of extinction, both in the United States and worldwide, is habitat destruction. As people clear forests, drain wetlands and dam rivers, they destroy the homes of countless organisms. The United States, for example, has lost almost half its wetlands since the 18th century, and tropical countries have lost more than half of their rain forests.

The introduction of invasive species such as fire ants and kudzu, which proliferate rapidly and overcome native species, also has increased the pace of extinctions. Island ecosystems are particularly sensitive. In Guam and Hawaii, for example, newly introduced rats, cats and snakes have wiped out many species of native birds.

Pollution, overfishing and hunting also threaten wildlife habitat. And more potential threats loom. Environmentalists now fear global climatic changes could decimate habitats in natural parks before they can migrate to more suitable surroundings.

"We have quite static ways of protecting biodiversity at the moment, drawing boundaries about a population and saying, 'This population is now conserved,'" says the American Museum of Natural History's Sterling. "As the temperature changes, you're going to have an empty preserve and a species that has migrated out."

But while scientists have expressed growing alarm about the rapid disappearance of more and more species, the Museum of Natural History poll indicates the issue of mass extinction has not yet resonated with the general public. Unlike more visible environmental problems, such as air pollution and contaminated drinking water, the loss of obscure beetles and salamanders does not affect the daily lives of most people.

> "World leaders have responded to the threat of biodiversity loss with a series of international agreements."

Furthermore, the business community is reluctant to support government regulations that restrict development to protect plants and creatures that seem to have little significance. That was dramatically illustrated in the late 1980s and early '90s, when loggers heatedly protested plans to set aside forests that were habitat to the rare northern spotted owl.

"Let's prioritize what the real costs are, because our resources are limited," says William L. Kovacs, vice president of environmental and regulatory affairs for the U.S. Chamber of Commerce. "We can spend tens of billions of dollars in trying to protect something that has very little benefit to man."

Complicating the issue, scientists disagree about both the extent and the implications of mass extinction. Biologists, who have identified about 1.75 million species worldwide, estimate the actual total ranges anywhere from 3.6 million to more than 100 million.

Harvard's Wilson believes that more than half of these will be gone by the end of the century unless strong conservation measures are undertaken. He and other biologists have arrived at such estimates by calculating the number of species in biologically diverse habitats—especially coral reefs and tropical rain forests—and the rate at which those habitats are being destroyed by human actions.

"Biologists who explore biodiversity see it vanishing before their eyes," he wrote in a special [Spring 2000] Earth Day edition of *Time* magazine.

But some contend that concerns about extinction are overstated. Michael Gilpin, a University of San Diego biology professor, predicts that future extinctions will be largely confined to obscure organisms in developing countries. "It's not that we're going to lose zebras and wildebeests," he says. "Beetles we're going to lose, but we're never going to know what they are."

Others go as far as to argue that human disruptions of nature actually may be good in the long run. They contend that past extinctions and other disturbances that alter ecosystems created openings for new organisms, often increasing overall diversity. "Without extinction, without a loss of current variety, future variation diminishes," two professors [Julian L. Simon and Aaron Wildavsky] argued in a controversial 1992 article.

However, few in the scientific community take such a sanguine view. Even a skeptic such as Gilpin warns the loss of species deprives the world of genetic diversity, making it harder for scientists to develop new medicines and more disease-resistant strains of crops. "We're burning our genetic library," he says.

Others believe that a mass extinction will result in a natural world dominated by disease-carrying animals that have learned to adapt to human society. What sorts of animals are likely to proliferate if the pace of extinction continues? Sterling predicts "rats and cockroaches," among others.

As policy-makers confront the specter of mass extinction, here are key questions being asked:

Should we preserve endangered plants and animals?

As an aspiring botanist growing up in the San Francisco area, Peter H. Raven enjoyed tromping about and identifying numerous species of local plants. Now he finds many formerly wild areas paved over, and the plants either gone or dying out.

Raven, who is director of the Missouri Botanical Garden and a leading advocate for protecting biodiversity, warns that the same pattern is being repeated around the globe, threatening to impoverish human society on a vast scale because scientists constantly turn to nature to develop new foods, medicines and other products.

"As we lose biodiversity, we lose many opportunities for a rich and sustainable and healthy life," Raven says. "It's biodiversity that makes this a living planet. Most of the species that are likely to be lost in the coming century have never been seen by anybody. We will never be able to exploit their potential."

Raven and other conservationists cite three major reasons why it is critical for world leaders to do everything possible to preserve fast-disappearing species:

• Plants and animals provide humans with essentials such as food, clothing, shelter and medicine. Food supplies could dwindle if not for wild plants that can be crossbred with cultivated varieties to provide hardier crops. For example, a wild species of Mexican maize, nearly extinct when found in the 1970s, has been used to develop disease-resistant corn.

> *"The issue of mass extinction has not yet resonated with the general public."*

Similarly, endangered plants have helped to spur pharmaceutical breakthroughs. The potent anti-cancer drug Taxol, for example, is derived from the bark of the Pacific yew tree. A study by the National Institutes of Health and other agencies concluded that about 40 percent of the most commonly prescribed drugs are developed from natural sources.

• Living organisms stabilize the environment. Scientists are finding that forests, wetlands and other ecosystems play a major role in regulating water drainage, preventing landslides and soil erosion, and even influencing rain patterns and other types of weather. When the environment is degraded, catastrophe may occur, Environmentalists point to Haiti, now virtually deforested and gradually turning into a desert.

• Society has ethical and aesthetic obligations to preserve the environment. In essence, conservationists—and some religious leaders—argue, every organism has an intrinsic beauty and a place in the world that should not be disturbed by human actions. In fact, some go so far as to say that human beings can never feel at home in a world scarred by environmental degradation.

"Our brains are formed around biodiversity," says Raven of the Missouri Botanical Garden. "A lot of our art is based on it. We are related to it."

"If we don't pay more attention to these issues, then the consequences down the road for ourselves and our future generations will be very significant," says Mark Schaefer, president of the Association for Biodiversity Information, a conservation research organization.

Perhaps surprisingly, some skeptics argue that preservation efforts, by disrupting natural processes, actually can damage the environment. They point out that extinction, after all, is a vital part of evolution: Certain species vanish, and others take their place. "I would make the argument that species live and die and evolve," says the Chamber of Commerce's Kovacs. "Whether you like it or not, you and I are part of evolution. At some point of time, our ancestors died out and changed."

> **"Scientists disagree about both the extent and the implications of mass extinction."**

Some also question whether the government should continue to stress the protection of species in an age when technological breakthroughs are allowing scientists to develop genetically modified crops that are resistant to disease and adverse weather. Scientists are even beginning to try to recover species through cloning.

Business leaders also are concerned about the cost of protecting endangered species. They point out that the construction of roads, hospitals, housing developments and other structures have been blocked for relatively trivial environmental concerns, sometimes at the cost of human health.

In 1998, for example, senators battled over building a single-lane gravel road through Alaska's Izembek National Wildlife Refuge, disrupting a pristine habitat but giving residents of Cold Bay, an isolated fishing village, year-round access to a healthcare facility. In the end, lawmakers decided to leave the preserve intact while agreeing to spend $37.5 million on an all-weather airport building and other facilities for the community.

Kovacs says the government should pay more attention to the needs of society, even if environmentalists protest. "Human beings are species too," he says, "and they have some rights on the planet."

Are environmental laws helping rare species?

A boater on the Potomac River just outside Washington, D.C., can expect to see something that would have been remarkable just three decades ago: pairs of nesting bald eagles. The majestic birds, which nearly vanished from the conti-

> **"Business leaders . . . are concerned about the cost of protecting endangered species."**

nental United States in the 1960s, have staged a strong comeback thanks to the 1970 federal ban on the highly toxic pesticide DDT and the 1973 Endangered Species Act.

"The return of the bald eagle is a fitting cap to a century of environmental stewardship," President Bill Clinton declared at a [1998] White House ceremony celebrating the comeback of the bird that has symbolized the nation for 200 years.

Although the bald eagle remains comparatively rare because of the destruction of its habitat, it nevertheless symbolizes the success of environmental laws. Other successes include the grizzly bear, the gray whale and the gray wolf.

The Endangered Species Act is part of a network of environmental laws that preserve habitats and rare species. The 1972 Marine Mammal Protection Act restricts the hunting of seals, polar bears and other marine mammals; the 1972 Clean Water Act helps rehabilitate waterways and restore many species of fish, and the 1964 Wilderness Act protects remote areas from road building and other development that can fragment habitat and isolate species.

Congress in 1990 took a step toward stopping the introduction of non-native species, which can wipe out native species by preying upon them or outcompeting with them for food, by passing the Non-Indigenous Aquatic Nuisance Act. The law established a task force that coordinates federal efforts to keep out non-native aquatic species, such as the zebra mussel, which is notorious for proliferating in the pipes of drinking water systems, hydroelectric plants and industrial facilities, constricting water flow and affecting heating and cooling systems.

The Endangered Species Act, however, is the only U.S. law targeted specifically at helping rare animals and plants. Policymakers are divided on whether it has been successful.

Since its passage, more than 1,200 species in the United States have been listed as either endangered or threatened. Of that number, just 11 species have recovered sufficiently to be taken off the list; nine were removed because of improved data, such as the discovery of additional populations; and seven have become extinct.

Based on these results, the law's critics brand it a failure. "It hasn't really been effective in achieving its goals," says Duane Desiderio, assistant staff vice president of the National Association of Home Builders. "It's become little more than an act with a list."

He contends that environmentalists are more intent on stopping development by "adding more and more species to the list" than they are on fostering the recovery of rare organisms.

Environmentalists, however, say that many more animals and plants would be extinct today if it were not for the law. For example, the number of black-footed ferrets—a Western weasel that feeds on prairie dogs—had dwindled to18 in the mid-1980s before the government stepped in and helped nurture the population back to several thousand.

"If you look at it in terms of preventing extinctions and getting species to a point where at least there is a chance to bring them back, then on that level it's been effective," says Christopher Williams, senior program officer for wildlife conservation policy at the WWF. . . .

The law originally was conceived to help majestic animals such as the bald eagle. But, to the exasperation of developers, it often is imposed instead to protect rodents and insects such as the Delhi fly and the Indiana bat—even though few people appear concerned about such species.

"Should you stop an entire road or an entire hospital that serves a region just because you've found some flies that scientists say they can't find any use for?" asks Kovacs of the Chamber of Commerce. "The program has gotten ridiculous. The environmentalists have really lost control of their common sense."

But environmentalists say it is essential to protect all species, even the most obscure, to preserve an ecosystem. "Each plant or animal, of course, has its own unique set of genes. Once that organism is lost, so is that unique genome," says Schaffer of the Association for Biodiversity Information. "We simply don't know where the next critical bacterium or fungi or plant may be found that contains some unique chemical substance encoded in its gene.". . .

Will humans survive the current wave of extinctions?

Ever since biologists began studying the extinction of species, they have pondered how long humans will endure. Since animal species typically survive for a few million years, and Homo sapiens evolved only about 100,000 years ago, the odds would appear to be good that humans will be around for quite awhile.

However, if extinctions occur at up to 1,000 times the normal rate in the 21st century, could human beings disappear as well? The reassuring answer from most biologists: Not likely. To be sure, humans have the capability of destroying themselves through nuclear or biological warfare, and some scientists even speculate that machines or genetically engineered versions of humans could take over the world.

> *"Environmentalists say it is essential to protect all species . . . to preserve an ecosystem."*

But, apart from such extraordinary scenarios, the laws of nature suggest that humans are well-positioned to survive a mass extinction.

"We are by far the most widely distributed . . . species on the planet and, with our technology, I believe the most unassailable," University of Washington geologist and paleontologist Peter D. Ward wrote in a 1997 book on extinction, *The Call of Distant Mammoths.* "We are the least endangered species on the planet."

Plant and animal species most vulnerable to extinction usually are few in number, live in a limited area and lack the ability to adjust to change. In contrast, there are more than 6 billion people who live throughout the world and eat all types of food. It is hard to picture a natural scenario—even repeated volcanic eruptions, massive flooding or global climate change—in which the Earth's environment is so altered that people can no longer survive, paleontologists say.

However, some experts warn that the loss of biodiversity could undermine the well-being of society because it may become harder to grow crops and develop new medicines and other products.

"I can't see a scenario where the destruction of biodiversity is going to drive human beings to extinction," says Raven of the Missouri Botanical Garden, "but I see a world that is dull, gray, homogenized and bleak, with many fewer possibilities for developing new products and with many fewer interesting things to do. As we lose biodiversity, we lose many opportunities for rich and sustainable and healthy lives."

Raven and other scientists also believe that the Earth may not be able to sustain its population, which is expected to reach anywhere from 7.3 billion to 10.7 billion by 2050, according to United Nations projections. In particular, they say that people in wealthy countries like the United States have to consume less or risk depleting the world's resources. "If everybody in the world were consuming at the level of the United States, we would need about three planets like Earth to support them," he says.

> *"The laws of nature suggest that humans are well-positioned to survive a mass extinction.*

Others, however, reject such bleak scenarios. They believe that, thanks to advances in genetics, scientists will be able to develop better crops and more effective medicines despite the loss of wild species. Indeed, they speculate, genetically modified organisms may even help speed up habitat restoration.

The debate may be moot. Scientists are not certain of what prompted previous mass extinctions, but they know that the causes must have been cataclysmic. If a massive asteroid were to strike the Earth—which may have wiped out the dinosaurs 65 million years ago—humans could perish along with most other plants and animals.

University of Chicago statistical paleontologist David M. Raup estimated the odds of a significant asteroid or comet striking Earth during a person's 75-year lifespan at 1 in 4,000. Although that may indicate that humans are pretty safe, Raup writes that experiencing a "civilization-destroying impact" would appear to be a far greater possibility than dying in an airplane crash.

"We don't know," Raup concludes, "whether we chose a safe planet."

Loss of Biodiversity Is a Global Crisis

by Edward O. Wilson

About the author: *Edward O. Wilson, a noted authority on biology and the evolution of behavior, is a research professor at Harvard University and the author of many books.*

Known as the biosphere to scientists and as the creation to theologians, all of life together consists of a membrane around earth so thin that it cannot be seen edgewise from a satellite yet so prodigiously diverse that only a tiny fraction of species have been discovered and named. The products of billions of years of evolution, organisms occupy virtually every square centimeter of the planet's surfaces and fill nearly every imaginable niche.

Biologists estimate that more than half the species occur in the tropical rain forests. From these natural greenhouses, many world records of biodiversity have been reported—425 kinds of trees in 2.5 acres (1 hectare) of Brazil's Atlantic forest and 1,300 butterfly species from a corner of Peru's Manu National Park, both more than 10 times the number from comparable sites in Europe and North America. At the other extreme, the McMurdo Dry Valleys of Antarctica, with the poorest and coldest soils in the world, still harbor sparse communities of bacteria, fungi and microscopic invertebrate animals.

A few remarkable species, the "extremophiles," have achieved astonishing feats of physiological adaptation at the ends of habitable Earth. In the most frigid polar waters, fish and other animals flourish, their blood kept fluid by biochemical antifreezes. Populations of bacteria live in the spumes of volcanic thermal vents on the ocean floor, multiplying in water above the boiling point. And far beneath Earth's surface, to a depth of 2 miles (3.2 km) or more, dwell the SLIMES (subsurface lithoautotrophic microbial ecosystems), unique assemblages of bacteria and fungi that occupy pores in the interlocking mineral grains of igneous rock and derive their energy from inorganic chemicals. The SLIMES are independent of the world above, so even if all of it were burned to a cinder, they would carry on and, given enough time, probably evolve new life-forms able to re-enter the world of air and sunlight.

Earth's biodiversity (short for biological diversity) is organized into three levels. At the top are the ecosystems, such as rain forests, coral reefs and lakes. Next down are the species that compose the ecosystems: swallowtail butterflies, moray eels, people. At the bottom are the variety of genes making up the heredity of each species. How much biodiversity is there? Biologists have described a total of between 1.5 million and 1.8 million species. Yet this impressive achievement is only a small beginning. Estimates of the true number of living species range, according to the method employed, from 3.6 million to more than 100 million.

Least known are the smallest organisms. By repeated sampling, biologists estimate that as few as 10% of the different kinds of insects, nematode worms and fungi have been discovered. For bacteria and other microorganisms, the number could be well below 1%. Even the largest and most intensively studied organisms are incompletely cataloged. Four species of mammals, for example, have recently been discovered in the remote Annamite Mountains along the Vietnam-Laos border. One of them, the saola or spindlehorn, is a large cowlike animal distinct enough to be classified in a genus of its own. Earth, as far as life is concerned, is still a little-known planet.

Biologists who explore biodiversity see it vanishing before their eyes. To use two of their favorite phrases, they live in a world of wounds and practice a scientific discipline with a deadline. They generally agree that the rate of species extinction is now 100 to 1,000 times as great as it was before the coming of humanity. Throughout most of geological time, individual species and their immediate descendants lived an average of about 1 million years. They disappeared naturally at the rate of about one species per million per year, and newly evolved species replaced them at the same rate, maintaining a rough equilibrium. No longer. Not only has the extinction rate soared, but also the birthrate of new species has declined as the natural environment is destroyed.

The principal cause of both extinction and the slowing of evolution is the degrading and destruction of habitats by human action. While covering only 6% of Earth's land surface, about the same as the 48 contiguous United States, the rain forests are losing an area about half the size of Florida each year. Damage to intact forests, which occurs when they are broken

> *"Biologists who explore biodiversity see it vanishing before their eyes."*

up into isolated patches or partly logged, or when fires are set, threatens biodiversity still more. With other rich environments under similar assault, including coral reefs (two-thirds degraded) and salt marshes and mangrove swamps (half eliminated or radically altered), the extinction rate of species and races is everywhere rising.

Not all doomed species disappear immediately. Most first suffer loss of their ranges and gene pool to dangerously low levels, eventually descending to join what biologists call the "living dead." Throughout the world, 976 tree species, for example, are classified as critically endangered. Two are down to three or four surviving individuals and three others to only one. I have been grimly compiling what I call the Hundred Heartbeat Club of animal species—those consisting of a hundred or fewer individuals, hence that number of heartbeats away from total extinction. The club's more familiar members include the Javan rhinoceros, Philippine eagle, Hawaiian crow, Spix's macaw and Chinese river dolphin. Other endangered species lined up for early admission are the giant panda, Sumatran rhinoceros and mountain gorilla.

Paleontologists recognize six previous mass-extinction events during the past half-billion years (the number was until recently believed to be five, but now another, from early Cambrian times, has been added). The last and most famous, which occurred 65 million years ago and was caused by a giant meteorite strike off the present-day coast of Yucatan, ended the age of dinosaurs. These catastrophes followed a typical sequence. First, a large part of biodiversity was destroyed. There was a bloom of a small number of "disaster species," such as medleys of fungi and ferns, that survived and reproduced rapidly to fill the habitable spaces emptied of other life. As more time passed, a few "Lazarus species" reappeared in localities from which they had been wiped out, having been able to spread from isolated pockets difficult to detect. Then, very slowly, across 2 million to 5 million or more years, life as a whole evolved again to its full, original variety.

"Researchers of biodiversity agree that we are in the midst of the seventh mass extinction."

Researchers of biodiversity agree that we are in the midst of the seventh mass extinction. Even if the current rate of habitat destruction were to continue in forests and coral reefs alone, half the species of plants and animals would be gone by the end of the 21st century. Our descendants would inherit a biologically impoverished and homogenized world. Not only would there be many fewer life forms, but also faunas and floras would look much the same over large parts of the world, with disaster species such as fire ants and house mice widely spread. Humanity would then have to wait millions of years for natural evolution to replace what was lost in a single century.

In the long term, I am convinced, the quenching of life's exuberance will be more consequential to humanity than all of present-day global warming, ozone depletion and pollution combined. Why? For practical reasons, if nothing else. Humanity's food supply comes from a dangerously narrow sliver of biodiversity. Throughout history, people have cultivated or gathered 7,000 plant species for food. Today only 20 species provide 90% of the world's food and three— maize, wheat and rice—supply more than half. Tens of thousands of species of the world's still surviving flora can be bred or provide genes to increase production in deserts, saline flats and other marginal habitats.

Natural pharmaceuticals offered by biodiversity are also underutilized. Only a few hundred wild species have served to stock our antibiotics, anticancer agents, pain killers and blood thinners. The biochemistry of the vast majority—millions—of other species is an unfathomed reservoir of new and potentially more effective substances. The reason is to be found in

> *"There are reasons to be warily optimistic that biodiversity may be salvageable."*

the principles of evolutionary biology. Caught in an endless arms race, these species have devised myriad ways to combat microbes and cancer-causing runaway cells. We have scarcely begun to consult them for the experience stored in their genes.

If the future enhancement of agriculture and medicine is not thought enough to merit conservation, then consider survival. The biosphere gives us renewed soils, energy, clean water and the very air we breathe, all free of charge. The more species that compose wild communities, the more stable and resilient becomes the planet as a whole.

Then consider ethics. More and more leaders of science and religion now pose this question: Who are we to destroy or even diminish biodiversity and thus the creation? Look more closely at nature, they say; every species is a masterpiece, exquisitely adapted to the particular environment in which it has survived for thousands to millions of years. It is part of the world—part of Eden if you prefer—in which our own species arose.

The profligacy of the 20th century has led humanity into a bottleneck of overpopulation and shrinking natural resources. Through this bottleneck humanity and the rest of life must now pass. By the end of the new century, if we are both lucky and wise, we will exit in better shape than we entered, with the population peaked around 8 billion or less and a gradual decline begun. People everywhere will have acquired a decent quality of life, with the expectation of more improvement to come. One of the defining goals of the century must also be to settle humanity down before we wreck the planet. To that end it is important to accept the challenge and responsibility of global conservation—and to do so right now, before it is too late. We will be judged by the amount of biodiversity we carry through the bottleneck with us.

There are reasons to be warily optimistic that biodiversity may be salvageable. Whether it happens in time depends fundamentally on the shift to a new ethic, which sees humanity as part of the biosphere and its faithful steward, not just the resident master and economic maximizer. That change of heart has begun in most countries among a few farsighted leaders and a growing part of the general public, albeit very slowly.

Success also depends on attention to sustainable management of the environment, including protection of biodiversity. Conservation experts now give top priority to "hot spots," pockets of wild nature that contain high concentrations of endangered species, which give hope that a great deal can be accomplished in a short span of time. From the coastal sage of California to the rain forests of West Africa, the hottest of the terrestrial hot spots occupy only 1.4% of the world's land surface yet are the exclusive home of more than a third of the terrestrial plant and vertebrate species. Similarly, from the streams of Appalachia to the Philippine coral reefs, aquatic hot spots occupy a tiny fraction of the shallow water surface. This much of the world can be set aside quickly without crippling economic or social consequences. More difficult but equally important are the preservation and long-term nondestructive use of the remaining fragments of the old-growth forests, including the tropical wildernesses of Asia, Central Africa and Latin America.

None of this will be easy, but no great goal ever was. Surely nothing can be more important than to secure the future of the rest of life and thereby to safeguard our own.

Declining Biodiversity Can Adversely Affect Local Environments

by the Ecological Society of America

About the author: *The Ecological Society of America, founded in 1915, is a private organization of scientists that works to promote ecological science. It publishes periodic* Issues in Ecology *reports to inform the public and political leaders about environmental issues.*

One of the most striking features of the earth's biota is its extraordinary diversity, estimated to include about 10 million different species. One of the most conspicuous aspects of contemporary global change is the rapid decline of this diversity in many ecosystems. The decline is not limited to increased rates of species extinction, but includes losses in genetic and functional diversity across population, community, ecosystem, landscape, and global scales. The term "biodiversity" refers collectively to all these aspects of biotic diversity. The wide-ranging decline in biodiversity results largely from habitat modifications and destruction, increased rates of invasions by deliberately or accidentally introduced non-native species, over-exploitation and other human-caused impacts.

On a global scale, even at the lowest estimated current extinction rate, about half of all species could be extinct within 100 years. Such an event would be similar in magnitude to the five mass extinction events in the 3.5 billion year history of life on earth. On local and regional scales, biodiversity declines are already pronounced in many areas, especially where natural ecosystems have been converted to croplands, timber plantations, aquaculture and other managed ecosystems. The diversity of these managed ecosystems is often low, and species composition very different, compared with those of the natural systems they have replaced.

What are the consequences of such declines in biodiversity and how might they affect human welfare? The earth's living organisms contribute to human

Reprinted, with permission, from "Biodiversity and Ecosystems Functioning: Maintaining Natural Life Support Processes," by the Ecological Society of America, *Issues in Ecology*, 1999.

welfare in a variety of ways. First, humans derive from them goods and products essential to life, including food, medicine, and industrial products, genetic resources for crop breeding, and natural pest control services. Such benefits can be viewed as the market values of biodiversity because they are readily tied to our economy and often can be assigned a dollar value in the marketplace. Second, biodiversity has nonmarket values that can be expressed in terms such as knowledge, aesthetic, existence and other values. These non-market values of biodiversity are difficult to quantify, but are, for many, sufficient justification for preserving biodiversity independent of market values.

A third category of value, ecosystem services, is the focus of this report. The organisms that live, grow, reproduce, and interact within ecosystems help to mediate local and regional flows of energy and materials. Energy flow refers to the capture of light energy by green plant or algal photosynthesis and its dispersal as chemical energy throughout the food web to plant- or algal-feeding animals, predators, and eventually decomposers. The flow of materials involves the recycling of carbon, nitrogen, phosphorus and other elements between living organisms and the air, water, and soil. These biologically mediated energy and materials flows contribute to many ecological or life support services that benefit human welfare such as greenhouse gas regulation, water treatment, erosion control, soil quality control, and plant growth. Ecosystem services can also include cultural benefits, such as religious, aesthetic, recreational, or inspirational values that humans derive from ecosystems.

"Studies have shown that ecosystems are indeed sensitive to changes in the numbers and kinds of species found in their communities."

Determining whether biodiversity per se is important to ecosystem functioning has been difficult, partly because many of the factors such as habitat conversion that reduce local biodiversity also directly affect many ecological processes, masking the more subtle impacts of species loss on functioning. Recent studies, however, have begun to shed considerable light on the issue. These studies have shown that ecosystems are indeed sensitive to changes in the numbers and kinds of species found in their communities. In this report, we provide an overview of ecosystem functioning, review the distinction between taxonomic biodiversity (i.e., species numbers) and functional biodiversity, and evaluate the current status of research concerning ecosystem responses to changes in biodiversity.

Ecosystem Functioning

Ecosystem functioning reflects the collective life activities of plants, animals, and microbes and the effects these activities—feeding, growing, moving, excreting waste, etc.—have on the physical and chemical conditions of their environment. (Note that "functioning" means "showing activity" and does not imply that organisms perform purposeful roles in ecosystem-level processes.) A functioning ecosystem is one that exhibits biological and chemical activities characteristic for its type. A functioning forest ecosystem, for example, exhibits rates of plant production, carbon storage, and nutrient cycling that are characteristic of most forests. If the forest is converted to an agroecosystem, its functioning changes.

Ecologists abstract the essential features of an ecosystem into two compartments, the biotic and the abiotic. The biotic compartment consists of the community of species, which can be divided functionally into plant producers, the consumers that feed on producers and on each other, and the decomposers. The abiotic compartment consists of organic and inorganic nutrient pools. Energy and materials move between these two compartments, as well as into and out of the system. Ecosystem processes are quantified by measuring rates of these movements (e.g., plant production, decomposition, nutrient leaching or other measures of material production, transport or loss). Ecosystem functioning, in turn, is quantified by measuring the magnitudes and dynamics of ecosystem processes.

Ecosystem functioning results from interactions among and within different levels of the biota, which ecologists describe as a "nested" hierarchy. For example, green plant production on land is the end product of interactions of individual plants nested within populations; interactions among populations nested within a single species; interactions among a variety of species nested within a group of functionally similar species; and so on up to the level of interactions between different types of ecosystems nested within landscapes.

Biodiversity: Species, Functional Types, and Composition

Although every organism contributes to ecosystem processes, the nature and magnitude of individual contributions vary considerably. Research in biodiversity places much emphasis on the uniqueness of individual species and their singular contributions to ecosystem services. Yet most ecosystem processes are driven by the combined biological activities of many species, and it is often not possible to determine the relative contributions of individual species to ecosystem processes. Species within groups such as grazing mammals, large predators, perennial grasses, or nitrogen-fixing microbes may therefore be functionally similar despite their uniqueness in genes, life history, and other traits.

Groups of species that perform similar roles in an ecosystem process

> *"Research in biodiversity places much emphasis on . . . individual species and their singular contributions to ecosystem services."*

are known as functional types or functional groups. Species may also be divided into functional types based on what they consume or by trophic status (e.g., their place in the food web as producers, decomposers, predators). Within trophic groups, species may be further divided according to life history, climatic or nutrient needs, physiology or other biological traits. Researchers may place a species into several different functional categories depending on the ecosystem process they are studying.

Because species can vary dramatically in their contributions to ecosystem functioning, the specific composition or identity of species in a community is important. The fact that some species matter more than others becomes especially clear in the case of "keystone species" or "ecosystem engineers" or organisms with high "community importance values." These terms differ in usage, but all refer to species whose loss has a disproportionate impact on the community when compared to the loss of other species. For example, a species of nitrogen-fixing tree, *Myrica faya,* introduced to the Hawaiian islands has had large-scale effects on nitrogen cycling, greatly increasing the amount of this essential plant nutrient in soils where the tree invades. The nitrogen-fixing lupine *Lupinus arboreus* also enriches soils and, as a consequence, encourages invasions of weedy grasses. Among animals, moose (*Alces alces*) through their dietary preferences greatly reduce soil nitrogen levels and also influence the succession of trees in the forest. Beavers, too, through their feeding and dam-building not only alter soil fertility and forest succession but increase the diversity of ecosystems in a landscape. Even termites play critical roles in soil fertility and other ecological processes in many arid grasslands.

On the other hand, there are some examples where additions or losses of particular species have had little effect on ecosystem processes.

Ecosystem Responses to Changes in Biodiversity

Since [nineteenth-century evolutionary theorist Charles] Darwin, prominent biologists have hypothesized about the relationship between biodiversity and ecosystem functioning. More recently, concerns about increasing loss of biodiversity and questions about resulting degradation of ecosystem services have stimulated unprecedented observational, theoretical, and experimental studies.

Observational Studies. It might seem that observational studies comparing one ecosystem type with another, or comparing similar ecosystems at different locations, could provide ready answers to questions about the impacts of species richness on ecosystem processes. But these studies have invariably proven problematic. For example, an ecosystem such as a tropical forest or a coastal wetland may vary from one site to another not only in species number and composition, but also in physical and chemical conditions such as soil type, slope, rainfall, or nutrient levels. Comparing different ecosystems is likely to yield an unclear result because the response to variations in biodiversity cannot easily be distinguished from responses caused by variations in environmental and other factors. It is possible, though difficult, to control statistically for such potentially confounding factors.

Experimental Studies. Experimental studies, if well-designed, can minimize the confounding factors that plague observational studies. Experiments can provide insights not only into the relationships between biodiversity and ecosystem functioning but also into the possible mechanisms behind the relationships. Studies to date have ranged from large outdoor experiments and trials in large controlled environment facilities to modest-sized pot experiments and tests in small laboratory microcosms. This research has attempted to address two different questions about the link between biodiversity and ecosystem functioning. First, how are levels of ecosystem functioning affected by changes in biodiversity, particularly species richness? Second, how are the dynamics of ecosystem functioning, particularly the resilience and stability of processes, affected by changes in biodiversity? The following two sections review the experimental and theoretical results that shed light on these questions.

> *"Results from many experimental studies . . . demonstrate that ecosystem productivity increases with species richness."*

Biodiversity and Levels of Ecosystem Functioning. Results from many recent experimental studies conducted in North America and Europe demonstrate that ecosystem productivity increases with species richness. These studies range from large outdoor experiments to controlled laboratory experiments conducted in growth chambers, greenhouses, or small containers. Outdoor experiments such as those conducted in grasslands on nutrient-poor serpentine soils at Stanford, California and on prairie grasslands at Cedar Creek Natural History Area, Minnesota, work with plant communities similar to those found in nature, but researchers vary the number of plant species from one experimental plot to another. This approach is also used in the BIODEPTH experiments, in which seven European countries have established outdoor plots that range in plant diversity from low species numbers to the average numbers typically found at each site. More precise experiments using growth chambers have been conducted by researchers at Imperial College of London, Silwood Park, England and Centre d'Ecologie Fonctionnelle et Evolutive, Montpellier, France. More recent laboratory experiments in Europe and North America have begun to examine the impact of other components of biodiversity, such as the diversity of soil microorganisms, on plant production and the role of bacteria, predators, and herbivores in freshwater microbial communities.

All of these studies show that ecosystem functioning is decreased as the number of species in a community decreases. Declines in functioning can be particularly acute when the number of species is low, such as in most managed ecosystems including croplands or timber plantations. In addition, recent experimental studies in grasslands indicate that the effects of biodiversity on production can depend on both the number of functional groups present and the identity of the plant species (i.e., on community composition). Other studies have shown that loss of functional groups from a food web, or reductions in the number of species per trophic group (producers, consumers, decomposers) can also cause declines in ecosystem functioning. Finally, another study has shown that some species of plants may be more or less productive or show no response at all to changes in the diversity of their communities, even though total community productivity is, on average, lower at lower diversity.

Studies on plants have been particularly revealing and support results from recent theoretical models which predict that decreasing plant diversity leads to lower plant productivity. These models predict that diversity and composition are approximately equal in importance as determinants of ecosystem functioning. Two possible mechanisms have been identified to explain why levels of ecosystem functioning increase with increasing biodiversity. First is the "sampling effect": When the pool of species available in a region contains individual species that vary in productivity and other contributions to ecosystem functioning, then species-rich ecosystems have a higher probability of containing species with high levels of functioning. Second is the "complementarity effect": This occurs when increasing diversity results in increasing numbers of species that are complementary rather than competitive in their use of resources, exploiting different niches, such as rooting depths, and allowing more effective use of available resources.

Biodiversity and Ecosystem Stability, Predictability and Reliability. Few experimental studies of the impact of biodiversity on stability have been attempted, largely because stability is a long term attribute of a system and testing for it requires either long-running experiments or experiments with short-lived organisms. In the one available long-term ecological field study, however, reductions in plant species richness also lowered the resistance of grassland production to drought. Predictably—lower year-to-year fluctuations in community productivity—was also significantly lower at lower diversity. In addition, studies of microbial communities in small experimental chambers have also shown that fluctuations in ecosystem functions such as productivity can be greater when species richness is reduced. Thus, the loss of diversity causes a loss of ecosystem stability.

Several mechanisms could account for these results. One mechanism comes from the ability of competing species to replace or compensate for one another and thus minimize, at higher diversity, the ups and downs in functioning. Another mechanism is

> *"Plant production, nutrient use, . . . soil fertility, and the . . . stability of ecosystem processes can falter in the face of reductions in biodiversity."*

the "portfolio effect," a theory which suggests that cumulative properties such as ecosystem functioning show less severe fluctuations in systems with many species, much the way investment portfolios of varied stocks have lower long term variance than portfolios of one or a few kinds of stocks.

Summary. Three points emerge from this growing body of research. First, declining species richness can lead to declines in overall levels of ecosystem functioning. This is especially pronounced at lower levels of diversity. This finding is particularly relevant to current ecological change, since most ecosystems are being transformed into managed systems which typically contain only a few dominant species, whereas the natural ecosystems they replaced typically contained tens to hundreds of species.

Second, at least one species per functional group is essential to ecosystem functioning. Having more than one species per functional group may or may not alter overall levels of ecosystem functioning, but it may nevertheless insure against loss of functioning in times of disturbance if species within functional groups are able to replace or compensate for one another.

Third, the nature of an ecosystem's response to declining biodiversity is dependent on community composition, that is, on which species are lost and which remain. Research to date, however, has not identified any clear rules allowing us to predict in advance the impacts of the loss of any particular species on ecosystem processes.

Although these three points have been repeatedly observed in a wide variety of experiments, there is still debate about the mechanisms behind them. Research into the link between biodiversity and ecosystem functioning is a new discipline and much work remains to be done.

Questions for Future Research

Research to date strongly supports the idea that ecosystem functioning is sensitive to changes in local species identities, community composition and diversity. Although current studies are limited in scope, they do demonstrate that plant production, nutrient use, nutrient leaching, soil fertility, and the predictability and stability of ecosystem processes can falter in the face of reductions in biodiversity. Despite this progress, several areas of uncertainty remain to be investigated.

What are the effects of changes in biodiversity at scales other than species or functional groups? Most studies involving biodiversity and ecosystem functioning have focused only on changes in the number and variety of species and/or functional groups. Yet many important ecological processes occur at the landscape level, and current studies strongly suggest that landscape-level alterations of biodiversity affect ecosystem functioning. There is a need for experimental research that manipulates biodiversity at both larger and smaller (e.g., genetic) scales.

Is current knowledge applicable to all ecosystems? Studies to date have examined primarily isolated ecosystems. Future experiments across multiple ecosystem types will be needed to test whether findings from lakes or grasslands, for example, can be applied more widely. This approach is already being tested in BIODEPTH, a pan-European biodiversity-ecosystem functioning experiment that may serve as a model of the kind of experiments needed. At eight field sites across Europe, BIODEPTH researchers have created grass-herb ecosystems with varying levels of biodiversity drawn from local species pools. Results of these studies will expand to the landscape level our understanding of the relationship between biodiversity and such ecosystem processes as production, decomposition and nutrient retention.

How important is diversity at all levels of the food web to ecosystem functioning? With the exception of some studies conducted inside laboratory growth chambers, most experiments to date have considered only plant species diversity and not variations in the numbers of herbivores, carnivores, parasites, decomposers and other players in the food web. Yet these creatures not only comprise the most numerous portion of the earth's biota but are also significant players in the flow of materials and energy. Experiments that involve multiple levels of the food web are critical to expanding our understanding of the ecological consequences of biodiversity loss.

How will other global changes interact with changing patterns in biodiversity and ecosystem functioning? Currently, few experiments are explicitly examining interactions among such factors as increased atmospheric carbon dioxide, increased ultraviolet-B radiation, increased nitrogen deposition, global warming, habitat fragmentation, and changing patterns of biodiversity. Experiments considering all these factors at once are impractical. Yet one project that examines interactions of three of these factors is currently in progress at Minnesota's Cedar Creek Natural History Area. The experiment, BIOCON, manipulates plant diversity, carbon dioxide, and nitrogen in experimental grassland plots.

What are the economic consequences of ecosystem responses to changing biodiversity? Currently, economic valuations have focused on market values of either ecosystem services or biodiversity. Future analyses which integrate both biodiversity and ecosystem functioning may provide a better understanding of the potential economic impacts of biodiversity loss.

A Prudent Strategy

Unprecedented changes are taking place in the ecosystems of the world, including species losses through local extinctions, species additions through biological invasions, and wholesale changes in ecosystems that follow transformation of wildlands into managed ecosystems. These changes have a number of important effects on ecosystem processes. Recent evidence demonstrates that both the magnitude and stability of ecosystem functioning are likely to be significantly altered by declines in local diversity, especially when diversity reaches the low levels typical of managed ecosystems. Although a number of uncertainties remain, the importance of ecosystem services to human welfare requires that we adopt the prudent strategy of preserving biodiversity in order to safeguard ecosystem processes vital to society.

Invading Species Threaten America's Biodiversity and Environment

by Joel Achenbach

About the author: *Joel Achenbach is a staff writer for the* Washington Post *newspaper.*

Cruising westward at 300 feet, the helicopter is heading straight for the end of civilization. You can see it just ahead. It's a line across the surface of the Earth—a levee, built years ago to hold back the swamp. Now it works in reverse, restraining the developers. Beyond the levee there are no shopping malls, no houses, no roads, just a wet prairie full of alligators, lily pads and saw grass.

And there's something new, something growing, spreading—a pale-green substance that seems to be crawling all over the tree islands that speckle this portion of the Everglades. The pilot takes the chopper down for a closer look. You can see it, sure enough: lygodium. Old World climbing fern.

It has gone berserk. It's like the Blob. The islands are caving in at the center, crushed by the dense, matted blanket of vegetation. The willows, the hollies, the cabbage palms—they're being buried alive.

"You wouldn't see any of this three years ago," testifies the chopper pilot, Jim Dunn.

David Viker, deputy manager of the federally managed swamp, says, "It looks like a green bomb went off."

What exactly is this virulent organism? It's a houseplant. In the right context, it's a lovely little fern.

Lygodium is the classic invasive species: an organism that's been transported by human beings to habitats where it has no natural enemies. The counterattack against this intruder is just one isolated battle in what is becoming a major war from the Everglades to Rock Creek Park, from Hawaii to your own back yard. The scale of the conflict is planetary.

There are bombs detonating everywhere.

There have always been invasive species, but ecologists and government officials say the situation has become riotous. One study estimated that exotic species, including diseases, cost the nation more than $130 billion a year. There is an emerging sentiment that this could be the next great environmental crisis, that without serious countermeasures we will find ourselves living in what the nature writer David Quammen has called the "Planet of Weeds."

In 1999 President Bill Clinton signed an executive order requiring all federal agencies to address the problem of invasives. The order created a new entity called the Invasive Species Council. . . . But for all the bureaucratic sparks, there are no platoons of weed-whacking commandos taking to the hills with machetes.

For the general public the issue remains relatively obscure. People grasp the dangers posed by bulldozers and acid rain. It's not as easy to understand the menace of, say, Eurasian milfoil.

The issue also suffers from its scattered nature. The invaders range from bacteria to vines to feral pigs. Broadly defined, invasive species come from every kingdom of life. A few examples:

- Domestic honeybees are under attack from the invasive Varroa mite and from aggressive "killer" bees that have arrived from South America.
- West Nile virus, blamed for seven deaths in 1999, has reappeared among birds and mosquitoes in New York. Central Park was closed one night this past week to allow aerial spraying of pesticide.
- The Asian tiger mosquito arrived in the United States in the mid-1980s and now plagues the Washington area. It bites all day long.
- The fabled sagebrush of Nevada is being replaced by cheat grass, an invader from Europe that is explosively flammable.
- Miconia, a plant with razor-edged leaves, has arrived in Hawaii and formed impenetrable stands over thousands of acres.
- More than 5,000 prize maple trees in New York and Chicago have been cut down after infestations by the Asian longhorn beetle.
- The Asian swamp eel has turned up in canals in South Florida and may soon start devouring small fish in the Everglades.

The invaders are characterized not so much by their exotic origins as by their virulent behavior, the way they overrun natural defenses. They are, by nature, insidious. When they get loose, they tend to have perfect camouflage. Weeds are green.

Invasive species have been pestering America for more than a century. Starlings from Europe were released in Central Park in the late 1800s by a

> *"The invaders range from bacteria to vines to feral pigs."*

Shakespeare fan who wanted to introduce to America the birds mentioned in the plays. The great American chestnut tree was wiped out by an Asian fungus first detected in New York in 1904.

What's new is the scale and pace of the invasion. Global economic trade has put life in a blender. Sometimes the mode of transportation is the ballast water of a ship that has crossed the ocean and plied the St. Lawrence River to Lake Ontario. Sometimes it might be the treads of a hiker's boot, the perfect slot for an exotic seed. Living things are opportunistic. The ancient barriers—oceans, rivers, mountain ranges—have been breached.

Life is flying around everywhere.

"The blending of the natural world into one great monoculture of the most aggressive species is, I think, a blow to the spirit and beauty of the natural world."

The grim assessment came from Secretary of the Interior Bruce Babbitt as he walked one morning near the Potomac River, not far from his home in Northwest Washington. The Potomac gorge is crawling with invasive vines and weeds—stuff like porcelain berry and mile-a-minute weed. Babbitt may have incited chuckles when he warned of the dangers of purple loosestrife, but he's dead serious.

"There's a brand-new one coming up from Mexico called buffel grass," he said, navigating a trail along a creek near Fletcher's Boathouse. "It is now crossing the border into the Sonoran Desert. It carries fire wonderfully. They're actually pulling it up by hand in Organ Pipe Cactus National Monument."

The buffel grass invasion could doom the saguaro cactus, the great emblem of the Sonoran Desert. Over time, the distinct desert environments of North America could look more and more alike. Repeat that situation all over the planet and you have a recipe for a homogenized world.

> *"Harvard biologist E.O. Wilson argues that invasives will cause more extinctions than ordinary pollution."*

Bill Gregg, a U.S. Geological Survey plant ecologist, likens the disappearance of native species to lost knowledge: "We're burning the library, slowly," he says.

Gregg says the issue of invasives began to heat up in the 1980s, when the population of zebra mussels exploded in the Great Lakes and clogged industrial intake pipes. Other explosions followed. Asian longhorn beetles began arriving as stowaways in wooden crates from China. The link between invasives and economic globalization became obvious. Gregg points out that China and the United States have similar climates and geography, and could easily provide each other with a tremendous supply of weeds and pests.

However bad the problem is now, everyone expects it to get worse. Harvard biologist E.O. Wilson argues that invasives will cause more extinctions than ordinary pollution. Robert F. Doren, a science administrator with the National Park Service, doesn't hesitate to sound the alarm: "Because of the breakdown of ecological barriers, we are now entering the sixth great extinction in the history of the planet."

The extinction problem is most severe on islands, such as Hawaii, home to dozens of endangered birds and plants. Hawaiian officials guard night and day against the arrival of the brown tree snake, which might sneak aboard military flights from Guam.

The snake arrived in Guam several decades ago and has wiped out almost all of the birds on the island. It routinely climbs power lines and triggers electrical blackouts. It has a history of biting children in their sleep.

For the Weed Warriors, invasives are not an esoteric matter. The Weed Warriors are people like Carole Bergmann, Jayne Hench, Michelle Grace and Claudia Donegan, who live in Montgomery County and regularly attack the monstrous vines along Sligo Creek. They sense that the issue is finally getting traction.

"Citizens just started calling, unsolicited, saying something is taking over the forest in our parks," says Hench, a supervisor with the county parks department.

The weed patrol has found numerous tall trees completely smothered, humbled by a rampaging invader called porcelain berry. "It's like a bad horror movie," says Grace.

Most noxious weeds were once desired for a specific function. Tens of millions of kudzu seedlings were planted by the Civilian Conservation Corps in the 1930s. Kudzu fought erosion. Now it's the prototypical gone-crazy weed. Multiflora rose was planted decades ago as a kind of living barbed-wire; now farmers have to bulldoze it out of their fields.

You could find plenty of invaders in your back yard: dandelions, garlic mustard, Japanese honeysuckle, Oriental bittersweet. The economists who study the cost of invasive species don't include the hours people spend on hands and knees yanking weeds from their gardens. English ivy is another invader: It looks great on an old brick building, but turn your back and it scampers into the woods.

Jil Swearingen, a National Park Service biologist, is tracking a long list of Washington area invaders, including common mugwort, smooth bromegrass, paper mulberry, Asiatic sand sedge, spotted knapweed, sticky chickweed, celandine, field bindweed, hound's-tongue, jimson weed, Chinese yam, Indian strawberry, viper's bugloss, lesser stitchwort, and so on.

Some of these pose no serious threat. Others could be time bombs. Bill Gregg says that if you detect an invader early enough, you can remove it mechanically, by force. Wait too long and you have to attack it with chemicals, hardly the most environmentally friendly solution.

"I think metastatic cancer is the strongest analogy," he says.

Mark Sagoff is the naysayer.

"One man's weed or pest is another man's palm tree," he says.

Sagoff is a professor at the Institute for Philosophy and Public Policy at the University of Maryland, and he demands deeper thinking about the war against weeds. He points out that native species can run amok, too, like the wild grape that grows in his own back yard. Deer, too, are native, and increasingly an urban pest.

"No one has shown that exotics are more likely than natives to be harmful," Sagoff wrote recently.

He says there's no such thing as the "balance of nature." Ecosystems change. There's no single way an ecosystem "ought" to be. Sagoff argues that the fight against invasive species sometimes echoes the anti-immigrant rhetoric of America's past. Invasives are accused of "sexual robustness, excessive breeding, low parental involvement with the young, a preference for degraded conditions and so on," Sagoff wrote.

But he isn't completely complacent. He acknowledges that historically significant ecosystems are being altered, and says there may be legitimate aesthetic reasons to object to the change, in the same way that the French might protest the opening of a new McDonald's.

> *"South Florida . . . is particularly susceptible to biological pollution."*

Ecologists say Sagoff's view of invasives doesn't take sufficient account of the rate of change. "People sometimes say this is just speeded up evolution. That's not the case," says Gordon Brown, who works on invasives for the Interior Department. "It's too accelerated."

Tim Flynn, a Hawaiian botanist, points out that Hawaii is so isolated that for most of its history a new species arrived only once every 10,000 years or so. A seabird, having miraculously survived the journey across thousands of miles of ocean, might show up with a seed in its guts. "It has to be a constipated bird," Flynn said. . . .

South Florida, lacking a killer freeze, is particularly susceptible to biological pollution. The Brazilian pepper has completely covered two large areas in the middle of Everglades National Park. The only way to get rid of it is to bulldoze everything, scrape away the limestone bedrock and cart it all away in trucks.

Melaleuca is probably the most hated invader, an ornamental tree that long ago escaped into the Everglades. It forms impenetrably dense stands that can only be knocked back with heavy doses of herbicide. The worst thing you can do is try to burn it. The leaves contain a highly flammable oil, and when a stand burns, the intense heat wipes out every other form of life nearby. The tree, meanwhile, emits millions of seeds, which take root all through the fire zone. The ultimate irony is that, in its native Australia, the melaleuca is an endangered species.

Lygodium, originally sold in nurseries, may turn out to be more diabolical than melaleuca. Its tiny spores can fly for miles in a windstorm. The oldest patches are in southern Martin County, where it pillars up from the forest floor, riding cypress trees to the sky. Dead, whitened tree trunks poke through the flourishing lygodium like skeletal fingers. The weed gradually drifted west and hopped the levee into the Loxahatchee National Wildlife Refuge, where it has proliferated only in the last decade. Aerial surveys revealed 39,000 acres in South Florida infested with lygodium in 1997. By 1999, the figure had risen to 100,000 acres.

The antidote may be yet another exotic species, an Australian moth that feeds on the fern. Biologists are still studying the moth to make sure it won't go berserk itself.

In the meantime, refuge managers attack lygodium with herbicide and machetes. At one point the refuge officials hired some college students to hack away at the fern, but their thrill at having an outdoorsy summer job vanished quickly in the steam of the swamp.

"They lasted about a week," said Mark Museus, the refuge manager. "They didn't want to work in 90-degree weather up to their chests in water with snakes and alligators all around."

Heavy rains flooded a plant nursery near the boundary of Everglades National Park in the fall of 1999. When the waters receded, workers sloshed their way through the nursery, trying to clean up. Then they felt something around their ankles and boots. Something slithering. The creatures were tubular and moved like serpents.

Asian swamp eels.

Bill Loftus, a government biologist, says they were probably dumped in canals by Asian immigrants who wanted to create a food source. But the eels don't stay in one place. They don't even have to stick to water—they can wriggle across a moist road.

"This guy can burrow right into the muck and survive there," Loftus said.

He was standing by an eel-infested canal that runs westward toward the park. Loftus worries that if the eels get into the Everglades, they'll eat shrimp and small fish, and disrupt the food supply of migratory birds.

But maybe they won't.

"Ecology is sort of an inexact science," he said.

The world is a laboratory, and this experiment has little scientific supervision. No one can keep track of all the variables, all the new inputs, the stuff dropping unexpectedly through the skylight and into the bubbling vat of life.

"It's an irreversible experiment. That's the problem. With no control," says Loftus.

Tim Flynn, the Hawaiian biologist, finds it hard to be optimistic: "Sometimes it almost feels like a lost cause."

Among the newest invaders in America is an aquatic fern called giant salvina. It has been found in nine states from Florida to the far West. It grows on the surface of lakes and ponds and can form mats three feet thick.

"It will kill everything beneath it," says biologist Randy Westbrooks. "It's bad news. Bad news."

And in early July 2000 the federal government said it had found an invasive algae, Caulerpa taxifolia, among eel grass in waters off the coast of Southern California. The algae is toxic to sea life. It ruined thousands of acres of underwater habitat in the Mediterranean Sea in the 1980s.

Where did it come from? Aquariums. The algae looks good in a fish tank. Officials suspect that it mutated after exposure to ultraviolet aquarium lights.

Declining Biodiversity Is a Serious Crisis in Hawaii

by William Allen

About the author: *William Allen is a science writer for the* St. Louis Post-Dispatch.

Tourists walking the beaches, streets and parks of resort towns [in Hawaii] . . . see an impressive array of lush vegetation and a kaleidoscope of birds.

Exotic-looking papaya and banyan trees, beautiful blossoms of bougainvillea and the sweet smell of jasmine are everywhere. Canaries, cardinals and Saffron finches flitter about.

But this perfect tropical paradise holds a dark secret: None of these plants or animals is native to Hawaii.

Contrary to the myth, when vacationers come to the Hawaiian Islands, they unknowingly enter a zone of mass extinction, not Eden.

An Ecological Catastrophe

The real Hawaii has become the biggest ecological catastrophe in the United States—the nation's capital of species extinction and endangerment, scientists say.

And this disaster is playing out in the tropical jewel of the United States unnoticed by the American public.

Hawaii, the nation's leader in biological diversity, is well on its way to becoming an archipelago of the "living dead." That's a term biologists use to describe a species of animal or plant that still has a few individuals alive but which almost surely will go extinct soon.

Invasion by non-native species, economic development, suburban sprawl, even environmental destruction by hooved animals—all these have added up to devastation for native animals, plants and the ecological connections that bind them, scientists say. In turn, this threatens the fragile tapestry of life on the islands, its supply of fresh water, its soil and its economic future.

For years, researchers warned about the impact of wild pigs, goats, mongooses and other alien animals imported on purpose or by accident. These creatures have sucked out the natural life of the islands like movie space aliens that take over a human body, feed on it and kill it.

Only a few years ago, scientists here still talked hopefully of reviving nature by applying the techniques of restoration ecology. But some now speak of "hospice ecology"—taking care of species while they inevitably slip into extinction.

Like a doctor trying to save a fatally injured person in a hospital emergency room, some of these scientists are reluctantly awakening to the fact that their patient cannot be saved.

> *"Hawaii . . . is well on its way to becoming an archipelago of the 'living dead.'"*

"Depressing—that's an optimistic way to frame it," said Rick Warshauer, a biologist with the U.S. Geological Survey's biological resources division on Hawaii. He coined the term hospice ecology. "What we're dealing with is whole suites of organisms disappearing."

Said Peter Van Dyke, manager of the Amy B.H. Greenwell Ethnobotanical Garden, on the Kona coast of Hawaii: "It's very frustrating. It's happening before your eyes. It's a problem accepting that and living with it."

Many biologists share this view privately but fear that publicly communicating it could deflate any hope of progress. Others remain hopeful but sober about the looming threats.

"The library is burning," said Rob Robichaux, a biologist at the University of Arizona. "This is a national and international treasure. So it's crucial to save and restore it."

Signaling the seriousness of the downward trend, the St. Louis–based Center for Plant Conservation in 1992 established a field office in Hawaii, its only such office outside Missouri. The center, based at the Missouri Botanical Garden, conserves rare native plants of the United States.

Of the center's six conservation "hot-spots," Hawaii ranks first. The others are California, Florida, Texas, Puerto Rico and the U.S. Virgin Islands.

Scientists concerned about the problem in Hawaii say there is another reason for broader concern. They see the islands as a harbinger of things to come on the mainland, where extinction occurs at a slower rate.

"When it comes down to it, we're all on little islands," Van Dyke said. "It's what's in store for all of us."

Through millions of years of evolution, the isolated Hawaiian Islands have been a virtual biodiversity factory. Their wide range of habitats—with different weather conditions, altitudes and soil type—fueled the creation of many new species from the few that washed or flew ashore from other lands thousands of miles away.

Early Polynesian settlers began to damage the natural environment. That damage increased after the English explorer Captain James Cook opened Hawaii to the West in 1778. The natural rate of native-species extinction jumped.

The extinction rate has risen a thousand-fold since Cook landed, biologists say. That was partly because humans cut the forests and damaged other ecosystems. But the rise also was caused by "barnyard beasts gone wild," as Warshauer put it.

Barnyard beasts refers to pigs, goats and sheep brought to the islands by Westerners. The animals went feral, or wild, learning to live off the natural landscape. These ungulates, or hooved animals, had no natural enemies in Hawaii. So they multiplied and devoured forests, eating native plants and rooting up soil.

More non-native species came, destroying habitat, killing off vulnerable native species and spreading across the islands. Of the 20,000 or so kinds of animals and plants in Hawaii, nearly a third aren't native species.

The extinction rate on Hawaii is unsurpassed in the United States. With less than 1 percent of the U.S. land mass, Hawaii is home to about 360 endangered and rare species—more than 30 percent of the nation's total.

Lost Species

More than 1,000 native Hawaiian species are known to have gone extinct since humans arrived.

Among other measures of the crisis, according to recent reports:
- With rare exception, Hawaii's native forest birds no longer exist below 4,000 feet in altitude—on any of the islands.
- More than a dozen forest-bird species currently listed as endangered are either extinct or near extinction.
- About 600 of the roughly 1,300 native plants meet the criteria for listing as a federal endangered species, but only 282 of them have been listed. Experts attribute the delay to the magnitude of the crisis and budget cuts in federal agencies.
- Of those 282 listed endangered plant species, 133 have only 20 or fewer individuals left in the wild. Many hang in only one small location.
- Maps of the islands show a dramatic decline in natural habitat. For example, less than one-tenth of Hawaii's original dry tropical forest remains. This forest, a natural haven for birds, is scattered in small pockets.
- Populations of pigs, deer, sheep and other feral ungulates are increasing.

Spider Web of Destruction Keeps Growing

The small dirt hole in the forest didn't look like much, but it was a good place to begin to understand extinction in Hawaii.

This hole, high on the eastern slope of Mauna Loa volcano on the Big Island, was much like a hundred others visible in this patch of forest and the millions of others around all the Hawaiian Islands.

The hole looked like someone had dug through the layer of grass and small plants with a single deep thrust of a shovel, then turned over a foot-square chunk of dark brown earth. The shoveler appeared to have gone through the forest haphazardly digging holes and piling up clumps of grass and dirt.

These holes—and the feral pigs that rooted them out—are killing native animals and plants, biologists say. If Hawaiian nature is a critically wounded patient, introduced non-native organisms are the rapidly spreading infection. Here's how it works. Pigs make the holes while searching for edible parts of native plants. Not only does this kill the plant, it opens the ground for invasion by non-native weeds. The aggressive weeds keep pushing, eliminating habitat for native plants and blocking natural processes of forest regeneration.

> *"The extinction rate on Hawaii is unsurpassed in the United States."*

The holes trap small pools of rainwater, providing prime breeding spots for non-native mosquitoes. The mosquitoes spread diseases that kill native forest birds.

The reason these birds survive only above 4,000 feet is that mosquitoes don't live any higher, researchers say.

Even without pigs, holes, mosquitoes and disease, the birds have been devastated by the destruction of most of their forest food plants and habitat by humans and non-native ungulates. And they've come under more direct assault by non-native rats, cats and mongooses.

This story is repeated over and over across Hawaii for all kinds of species. The decline of each species has a multiplier effect through the ecosystem.

A drop in a plant species can cause a decline in a bird species. For example, on Hawaii, the pailila, a bird that relies on seeds of the mamane tree, became endangered when feral sheep and goats devastated a mamane-naio forest on Mauna Kea.

Likewise, plants suffer when birds decline.

"The birds are major pollinators," said Jack Jeffrey, a biologist with the U.S. Fish and Wildlife Service in Hilo. "We're losing the birds, and so we're losing the plants."

Said George Waring, a biologist at Southern Illinois University at Carbondale who conducts research in Hawaii: "It's a chain-reaction. One thing leads to another, leads to another, leads to another. It's never easy to say what the impact of any single effect is going to be. It's like a spider web that goes in every direction."

Government Solutions

A potential solution to the crisis in Hawaii is to get rid of the feral ungulates, biologists say. But that's not fair, hunters say. The state imported many of the game animals in the last century specifically for recreational hunting.

The state plays a pivotal role in the fate of native species by still placing a higher value on introduced game species than on its programs to save native flora and fauna, biologists say. The small but politically well-connected group of hunters fights any attempt to restrict the range of pigs, goats and other game.

Cattle still are allowed to graze on state land leased to ranchers, even if the land is home to endangered plants.

Referring to cattle grazing on one such parcel with two dozen federally endangered plants, biologist Jon Giffin told a reporter for the newsletter *Environment Hawaii*: "If I were to go over and pull up those plants, I'd be arrested under state law. But if a cow does it, it would be OK."

With few exceptions, no place in Hawaii can be saved or restored unless it is surrounded by a strong fence, biologists say. Even more worrisome, new waves of high-jumping deer and mouflon sheep are spreading through the islands even where fences keep other hooved animals out.

A Planet of Weeds

Biologists point out that nature itself will never disappear from Hawaii. Even if all native species go extinct, they will be replaced by some new combination of non-native plants and animals that in many cases will make the landscape appear just as alive as it was before. Just different.

Unless steps are taken to reverse the trend, that is the destiny of the entire planet, not just Hawaii, they say. As nature writer David Quammen wrote: "Virtually everything will live virtually everywhere, though the list of species that constitute 'everything' will be small." Quammen calls the Earth of the future the "Planet of Weeds."

Game management and hunting in Hawaii are probably here to stay, biologists say. But many argue that non-native, non-sensitive areas on state land should be set aside for game and hunting and that the animals should be contained.

Many experts believe that while programs to propagate endangered plants and birds are important, more money should be spent on protecting wild populations and habitat before species become threatened.

"What we think is common today will be endangered in 10 to 20 years, if not already gone," said Marjorie Ziegler, an analyst with the Earthjustice Legal Defense Fund in Honolulu. "It's that critical. In my opinion, everything native is threatened—it's just a matter of where on the endangerment-extinction continuum they are."

The political solutions needed to address such issues may take years to develop. The question is, what will be lost in the meantime?

"A lot of these things don't have years," said Van Dyke. "They have months."

The Extent and Ramifications of Loss of Biodiversity Are Difficult to Assess

by Rowan B. Martin

About the author: *Rowan B. Martin is an environmental consultant in Zimbabwe, Africa, and a former official with the Zimbabwe Department of National Parks and Wildlife Management.*

In most popular accounts, the measure of biological diversity is based on species numbers; therefore, rates of extinction and the listing of endangered species are treated as measures of the trends in biological diversity. . . . The actual number of species that are properly named and recorded is uncertain, and there is no single database that lists them all. . . .

Of the total numbers of species on the globe, the mammals make up about 0.2 percent and the birds about 0.5 percent. However, of all taxonomic groups, the mammals display the greatest diversity, ranging from the pygmy shrew with a body weight of 1.5 grams (g) to the blue whale with a body weight of some 120,000 kilograms (kg). The topic of biological diversity is fraught with subjectivity and the fate of "furry or feathery animals" will probably continue to dominate judgments of biodiversity above any formal scientific measures in the future.

How many species are there? Here, we enter the realms of extreme speculation. Insects make up about 75 percent of all known species and recent work in the neotropics suggests that there are very high numbers of species yet to be recorded. . . . [Robert M.] May (the well-known biologist/mathematician of Oxford University) has reviewed a large number of estimates critically [see Table A], and he considers that [Kevin J.] Gaston's estimate is probably closest to the truth, with the final number of species on earth likely to be closer to 5 million than to 10 million.

Table A. Estimates of the Total Number of Species

Author	Date	Number (millions)
Noel Simon	1983	6–7
P.H. Raven	1985	3–5
I.D. Hodkinson	1982	3–5
J.L. Erwin	1983	~30
Kevin J. Gaston	1991	5–10

Source: Robert M. May, *Biodiversity and Global Change,* 1992.

The cataloging of species is done by taxonomists. May notes that taxonomists (on whose expert opinions the foundations of biodiversity depend) are mismatched with regard to geography and species. Although there are over 3 million invertebrate species, there are approximately 10 vertebrate taxonomists for every plant taxonomist and approximately 100 vertebrate taxonomists for every invertebrate taxonomist. Additionally, only about 6 percent of practicing taxonomists are based in developing countries where the bulk of species are found. May pleads for 'quick-and-dirty' techniques to redress the deficiency and strongly recommends the creation of a central database as a repository for information about species.

The main proponents of high projected rates of species extinctions are Norman Myers, Paul Ehrlich and Anne Ehrlich, and Edward O. Wilson. While conceding that it is very difficult to make estimates because of confounding factors, Wilson nevertheless projects that the current rates of species extinctions are between 1000 and 10,000 times that which existed before human intervention. [John] Tuxill and [Chris] Bright are apparently using Wilson's estimates when they claim in a recent [1998] edition of the Worldwatch Institute's *The State of the World,* that "at least 1,000 species are lost a year." More recently, [Jessica] Hellman et al. have projected that "at least 10,000 species are going extinct per year, or one per hour." Even these rates of loss pale into insignificance when compared with the Chief Scientist of the International Union for the Conservation of Nature (IUCN) Jeffrey McNeely's statement that ". . . if present trends continue, some 25% of the world's species will be lost in the next 25–50 years," or May's statement that "it is reasonable to suggest that something like half of all terrestrial species are likely to become extinct over the next 50 years, if current trends persist." Assuming some 10 million species on the globe, at linear rates of extrapolation, McNeely's figures translate into 50,000 to 100,000 species per year and May's into 75,000 species per year (assuming terrestrial species amount to 75 percent of all species).

Are these figures believable? The wild variation . . . suggests that they are not based on sound scientific estimates or are made to sound worse than they are. Extinction rates such as 1000 species per year certainly sound dramatic. Another way of putting it might be that we are losing 0.01 percent of the species on earth per year or, at linear rates of extrapolation, we can expect to have lost 1 percent of the total complement of global species in the next 100 years. That, however, does not sound as alarming. Despite these ominous numbers, there is a paucity of real data to support these various assertions.

Closer to home, these high estimated rates of species loss do not accord with my own experience of the Southern African region. Southern Africa makes up approximately 3 percent of the global land area and, on a crude basis, we should expect 3 percent of all global extinctions to happen in this region. My considerations are limited to a few vertebrate classes for which it is possible that news of an extinction would reach me. In Table B, I make rough estimates of the global number of species of mammals, birds, reptiles, and amphibia that may exist (increasing the number roughly according to the information given by May on rates of discovery of new species in the various classes of vertebrates). On a simple pro rata basis (which is highly challengeable), if 10,000 species (from all classes, using Hellman et al.'s latest estimate) are going extinct annually and the total number of species (of all classes) is 5.9 million (my scaling up), then the expected rates of extinction given in the third column are based on the proportions that each of the listed classes forms of the total number of species on earth. The final column estimates the number of those extinctions expected to take place in Southern Africa (again, on a pro rata and linear basis) over a period of 35 years (3 percent of the global area multiplied by 35 years), which is approximately the time I have been involved in field work in the region.

Table B. Expected Extinctions in the Southern African Region in a Period of 33 Years Based on the Global Extinction Rates of Edward O. Wilson

Order and Estimated Global Number of Species	Estimated Global Rate of Extinction (spp/year)	Expected Number of Extinctions in Southern Africa in 35 Years (rounded)
Mammals		
5,000	0.85	1
Birds		
10,000	1.69	2
Reptiles		
7,500	1.27	1
Amphibians		
5,000	0.85	1

The fact that I am unaware of *any* extinctions that may have taken place in the region over the period from 1963 to date neither proves nor disproves the estimates. However, it might suggest that some authors are deliberately alarmist in their estimates. . . .

The majority (approximately 75 percent) of global extinctions in recent times have occurred on islands. Stephen Edwards, Head of the International

Union for the Conservation of Nature's (IUCN's) Sustainable Use Initiative, shows that the frequency of known extinctions from 1900 to 1990 exhibits neither an upward nor a downward trend. Although in the past extinction rates of plants have been lower than those of animals, this may change in the future because invasions of alien plants are increasing competitive pressures. Invasions, which displace local species, have been responsible for a large proportion of all the extinctions known to have occurred during the recent historical period.

"How many species are there? Here, we enter the realms of extreme speculation."

The extent of the loss of species and the consequences for human welfare are difficult to assess. Many biologists have reached the reluctant conclusion that not all species are of equal weight in their impact on ecosystem functions and processes, and the concept of "functional" and "interstitial species" clearly has relevance. Certain extinctions have had no impact on life as we know it. The sea cow—a huge mammal over 7 meters in length, which lived in the Bering and Medny Island waters—became extinct around 1750 A.D. Sokolov remarks that ". . . available evidence suggests that no calamitous, or at least, very noticeable, changes occurred. . ." as a result of the extinction. The population fluctuations of the sea otter in the same period and locality had ". . . no substantial effect in terms of loss of biological diversity on the functioning of the marine coastal ecosystem." Similarly, the reduced whale populations around the globe have had no marked effects on the biosphere.

The evidence so far indicates that much of the utilitarian rhetoric about the potential value of species as yet undescribed and the likely damaging effects of species loss on human prospects for survival are clearly overstatements. Extinctions are a natural process and it is incorrect to assume that all change is negative.

Some researchers offer grave figures for the numbers of species in danger of extinction (Table C) based on the recently updated World Conservation Union IUCN Red List of Threatened Animals (1996). The number of species in each IUCN category is entirely dependent on the questionable criteria adopted to define probabilities of extinction over various time spans. The lay reader is given the impression by IUCN Red List that there are generally agreed scientific criteria for deciding what an endangered species is. There are no such absolutes.

For example, the Minimum Viable Population (MVP) needed to ensure the persistence of a population for a certain length of time is a statistical construct based on genetic and demographic properties of the population and environmental factors that may act upon it. Genetic variation and demographic effects can be predicted with some degree of precision, but assumptions about environmental variability are fairly unreliable. The Effective Population Size (N_e) used in MVP calculations is the number of effective breeding animals in any population, which could be *as few as 10 percent* of the actual population, and obviously varies by species. The typical criterion used is that population size should

Table C. Conservation Status of the Higher Orders of Animals Based on the 1996 IUCN Red Data List*

Order	Immediate Danger of Extinction	Vulnerable to Extinction	Nearing Threatened Status
Mammals	11	14	14
Birds	4	7	9
Reptiles	8	12	6
Amphibians	10	15	5
Fish	13	21	5

Source: IUCN Red Data List, Date for reptiles, amphibians, and based on partial surveys.

*All values are percentages

be large enough to ensure a probability of extinction less than a given threshold (e.g., less than a 1 percent likelihood in 100 years).

There has been an historical trend toward increasing MVPs:

1960s MacArthur and Wilson put forward numbers between 25 and 50 individuals.

1980s The 50/500 rule was derived from genetic analyses: It was thought that an effective population size of 50 would provide some protection against short-term loss of fitness due to inbreeding, whereas a population of 500 would prevent loss of genetic variation over a longer term.

1990s We are now in the era of MVP hyperinflation (10,000 to 1 million) based on effects of random fluctuations in the environment. The practical implications of such figures do not bear inspection. If these figures were applied to mountain lions, an area larger than that of the United States would be required for effective conservation.

Definition of Biological Diversity

So what is biological diversity? The Convention on Biological Diversity (CBD) has defined biological diversity as:

> The variability among living organisms from all sources including, inter alia, terrestrial, marine and other aquatic ecosystems and the ecological complexes of which they are part; this includes diversity within species, between species and of ecosystems. (Article 2, CBD)

Biodiversity is not an entity or a resource—rather it is a property, a characteristic of nature. Species, populations, and certain kinds of tissues are resources, but not their diversity as such. Counting species may be a convenient indicator of biological diversity, but it is not an absolute measure of the diversity present at any given site. For example, a grass sward with 20 different grass species is not as diverse a habitat for wildlife as a woodland that has five grass species, five herbaceous species, five shrub species, and five tree species. The first habitat will support a limited community of grazing animals; the second provides habitats for both grazers and browsers and a collection of birds, insects, and other *taxonomic* groups. Unfortunately, all too often, species numbers are the only measure used to describe the status of the world's biota.

The fact that 4 years after its [1993] inception, the CBD has not yet come up with an agreed system for classifying and measuring biological diversity is an indication of the complexity of the construct.

It is entirely human to see the world's biodiversity as being divided into the simple categories of plants, animals, and microorganisms. However, if we seek to measure the extent to which organisms are differentiated genetically (i.e., how far and how much they have evolved over the history of life on earth), then counting simple numbers of species (or the numbers of individuals in species populations) will not achieve this.

Biologists use DNA and RNA sequences to construct phylogenetic trees (cladograms), which depict the points of separation of the phyla making up to-day's classification of living organisms. These points of separation may be the most objective measure of diversity: Put into metaphor, there may be less diversity among thousands of species living on one branch of the tree than there is between the major phyla represented by the larger boughs of the tree.

An objective measure for biodiversity might be one that reflects the increasing phylogenetic divergence (cladistics) of the organisms present at any particular site, but the scientists suggesting it [in *Biodiversity Measurement and Estimation*] concede "it will elicit a wringing of hands and even apoplexy from those who might have to apply it." Simply counting species is an easier, even if less accurate, way of defining the biodiversity of a particular site.

The emphasis on species as the basic building blocks of biological diversity is probably the commonest approach among laypersons and scientists. While recognizing that biodiversity can be quantified in many ways, the noted English biologist May argues for counting species for the simple practical reasons that it is easier to raise money for species and easier to make species the targets for preservation. However, the biological diversity of an area is much more than the number of species it contains. Consider some of the subtleties that using species as the measure of biological diversity misses:

- All species, by their presence or absence, do not contribute equally to biological diversity. [Michael A.] Huston from the Oak Ridge National Laboratory has developed the concept of *structural and interstitial* species: Structural species are those key species that determine the physical structure of ecosystems and influence the environment for the many other, generally smaller, interstitial organisms (e.g., if an oak tree is present at a site, then a whole subset of fauna and flora will also be present). The implication is that not all species are of equal weight in their importance to biological diversity.

- Species with complex life cycles may [writes V. Grant] contribute "two [or more] doses" of biological diversity during their lifetimes (e.g., a frog in its tadpole stage and adult stage). Thus, the time of sampling of sites can influence the outcomes of biodiversity assessment.

- The *grain*, or patch size, of sampling systems will affect outcomes of biodiversity assessments based on species. Surveys that include only higher-level organisms are likely to present a very different picture from those that sample microorganisms and, indeed, if every bacterium species were to be accorded equal weight with the elephant in biodiversity compilations, then the importance of the pachyderm would be minimal.

> *"The extent of the loss of species and the consequences for human welfare are difficult to assess."*

- Comparisons between sites of the species present in like groups (e.g., vascular plants) may show valid differences in biological diversity, but such comparisons are less useful when a number of phyla are lumped together (e.g., reptiles and amphibia along with vascular plants). It is essential not to "mix apples and pears" in biodiversity assessments.

Even at the species level, complete counts of organisms are impractical. Cheap, quick solutions are needed to quantify biological diversity over the global landscape. The continued focus on species for measuring biodiversity suggests a certain inner comfort with familiar terrain. Repeated assessments of the species present at a single site may provide information of changes taking place at that site but do not explain the changes or provide meaningful comparisons with other sites. The larger danger inherent in a preoccupation with species numbers is a "failure to see the woods for the trees" (i.e., the relationships between species and the contributions that species make to the functioning of the ecosystem).

Ecosystems

The Convention on Biological Diversity (CBD) is moving toward adopting an ecosystem approach for the conservation and sustainable use of biodiversity. The CBD has developed 12 principles that characterize the ecosystem approach to measuring biodiversity. Perhaps Principle 5 is the most relevant:

> Principle 5: A key feature of the ecosystem approach includes conservation of ecosystem structure and functioning.

> Rationale: Ecosystem functioning and resilience depends on a dynamic relationship within species, among species, and between species and their abiotic environment. The conservation of these interactions and processes is of greater significance for the long-term maintenance of biological diversity than simple protection of species.

Since the late 1970s, the major nongovernmental organizations . . . have advocated a shift in focus from species conservation to ecosystem conservation. They recognize the dangers of frittering away scarce conservation funds on missions to save species where the causes of their decline lie at the ecosystem level. Whereas fluctuations in species' presence and numbers within ecosystems are normal and part of the dynamics of the larger system, it is the constant functioning and resilience of whole ecosystems that human managers should logically strive to maintain.

Notwithstanding all of the assertions that biodiversity is a characteristic of relationships between and within genes, species, and ecosystems, the tendency to lapse back into regarding species as the fundamental building blocks of biological diversity remains dominant. This tendency is shared even by the most eminent of scientists and suggests that the fundamental concept of biological diversity is problematic. . . .

Points to Remember

Briefly, . . . significant points . . . are:

1. Biodiversity is a property or characteristic of living organisms that captures the essence of their variability derived from evolutionary history. It is difficult to define unequivocally.
2. There is no agreed system for the classification or quantification of biological diversity at the genetic, species, or ecosystem levels.
3. No theories adequately explain biodiversity. . . . Most of the scientific research is directed at explaining species diversity rather than biological diversity per se.
4. There is considerable divergence among scientists about the status of the biodiversity of the world's species and ecosystems:
   a. Uncertainty reigns over the number of species that have actually been taxonomically described, and even greater uncertainty over the number of species that remain to be identified.
   b. There is a paucity of data on the numbers of species that have become extinct this century. The majority of extinctions have occurred on islands, and there are weaknesses in attempts to extrapolate from small areas to global scales. Theoretically derived rates of extinction remain to be verified with real data, and the manner in which figures have been presented appears designed to be alarmist.
   c. Those losses of species that have been clearly documented do not appear to have dire implications either for ecosystem functioning or for human survival.
   d. The most recent figures on numbers of endangered species are more an artifact of new criteria used than they are indicative of any sudden change in the rate of loss of biodiversity. The criteria on minimum viable populations for species are controversial.
   e. The loss of forest cover and the decrease in species population sizes of marine organisms is a cause for concern. The implications of these losses for biological diversity are, however, difficult to predict, despite alarmist predictions to the contrary.

The Importance of Biodiversity to Ecosystem Health Is in Dispute

by Lila Guterman

About the author: *Lila Guterman is a reporter for the* Chronicle of Higher Education.

If environmentalists were to write down their Ten Commandments, one of the sacred principles would surely be, "Honor thy species." The green movement takes as a truism that ecosystems are healthier when they contain many species of plants and animals. Ecological scientists have even coined a term for this riot of life: biodiversity.

Though the idea now seems natural to environmentalists, scientists have long wondered whether an abundance of species truly improves the health of ecosystems and the way they work. Experiments to test that link were not completed until the mid-1990's, when some large-scale, much-heralded studies seemed to provide a positive answer. In 1999, the Ecological Society of America enshrined the importance of biodiversity to ecosystems in a report intended for educators and policymakers. The report concluded that, because ecosystems are vital to human welfare, we must "adopt the prudent strategy of preserving biodiversity in order to safeguard ecosystem processes vital to society."

It sounded harmless enough. But the publication of the article touched off a firestorm of debate that had been smoldering within ecology.

A group of scientists charged that the society's report ignored a different viewpoint held by many. The studies cited by the report, the scientists said, were flawed and didn't justify the conservation recommendation. Diversity is worth saving for moral, aesthetic, and even economic reasons, the critics said, but it might not make ecosystems healthier or more efficient.

The altercation went public when, in a letter in the July 2000 issue of the *Bulletin of the Ecological Society of America*, eight ecologists bluntly charged that the report was "biased" and "little more than a propaganda document"; made "indefensible statements"; and set a "dangerous precedent" for scientific societies by presenting only one side of the debate, even though the report seemed to represent the entire 7,600-member society.

They wrote, "Our concern is that unjustifiable actions are being made to protect this single rationale for biodiversity conservation, and that scientific objectivity is being compromised as a result."

Today, the controversy encompasses issues beyond scientific disagreement.

Some scientists claim that the eminent researchers who lead the movement to link biodiversity to ecosystem health, including John H. Lawton at the Imperial College of Science, Technology, and Medicine's Silwood Park campus, in England, and David Tilman at the University of Minnesota-Twin Cities, have exerted so much influence in the field that the major journals are silencing the critics.

The backing of the environmental movement amplifies the message of those renowned researchers, and may even distort the conclusions they draw from the data, the skeptics charge. "Ecological scientists need to be very, very careful to clearly separate the results of experiments from feelings about what should be," says William K. Lauenroth, a professor of rangeland-ecosystem science at Colorado State University, and one of the letter's authors.

"What these guys are saying is, a system works better if it's got 20 species in it rather than five," says Phil Grime, director of the department of comparative plant ecology at the University of Sheffield, in England, and an author of the letter. "Of course the conservation lobby want to hear this."

The controversy began quietly, as many scientific debates do. In the mid-90's, researchers published the results of field and laboratory experiments to show that greater species diversity meant improved stability or productivity in a plant community, both taken as signs of greater ecosystem health. The papers concluded that extinctions may be threatening ecosystems, which are fundamental to life on earth.

In 1994, Mr. Lawton, his colleague Shahid Naeem, and several other ecologists at Imperial College published a paper in *Nature* on model ecosystems they had established in indoor chambers. The researchers set up some plots with few species and others to which they added species. They found that the plants in chambers with more species tended to produce more biomass, the sum total of living matter in the plants. An accompanying commentary in the journal called the paper "the first unambiguous documentation of the effects of biodiversity on ecosystem processes."

> *"Scientists have long wondered whether an abundance of species truly improves the health of ecosystems and the way they work."*

But critics asserted that flaws had tainted the experiments and biased the results. Some quick library research on the plants in the British experiment pointed to a major problem, says Michael A. Huston, an ecologist at Oak Ridge

National Laboratory and the most outspoken critic of the biodiversity experiments. "As they increased diversity, they were adding larger plants. All their results were inevitable," since larger plants produce more biomass.

It wasn't the only time that skeptics would find a flaw in a study. That same year, in the same journal, Mr. Tilman's research group described how the worst drought in 50 years affected an experiment on the Minnesota prairie. The plots with higher species diversity had resisted the drought better than those with fewer species. But the more-diverse plots also had received less fertilizer in an earlier experiment, so it wasn't clear which factor produced the result.

In 1996, Mr. Tilman reported in *Nature* on a study that eliminated that confounding factor. He seeded 147 plots, each about 100 feet square, with between one and 24 species, randomly chosen from plants native to the prairie. After two years, he found that the more-diverse plots produced more vegetation.

Again *Nature* published a commentary praising the work, and again critics chafed, pointing out that the more-diverse plots had a greater likelihood of containing large plants. That "sampling effect" is nothing but an artifact of the experimental design of randomly choosing species, Mr. Huston and other scientists say. The experiments don't model reality well, they charge, because natural ecosystems do not contain random assemblages of species, nor are extinctions random. David A. Wardle, an ecologist with Landcare Research, a government research institute in Lincoln, New Zealand, goes even further in his critique: "Use of a random-effects model is, to be blunt, simply a nonsense."

Mr. Huston wrote a rebuttal, but *Nature* rejected it. He sent a copy to Mr. Tilman and later published it in the less-prominent journal *Oecologia*. "I didn't pay that much attention to his initial complaints, thinking that they were misplaced, frankly," Mr. Tilman says. But Mr. Huston has kept copies of correspondence in which Mr. Tilman advised him to "calm down, put aside your obvious disdain for me, re-read your [rebuttal] paper, and throw it away."

Mr. Tilman and others believe the sampling effect is actually a mechanism by which biodiversity could affect ecosystem function, and say that some environments may indeed be random communities of plants. Even if it weren't, he says, new results on his prairie plots suggest that the sampling effect is not driving the link between diversity and productivity.

What might be happening instead?

The plants may complement each other, he says. When resources such as nutrients and water are limited, if different species exploit them in different ways, adding more species can lead to more efficient exploitation, and thereby greater productivity, he says.

One way to prove that plants are doing that is by looking for a phenomenon called overyielding. If a diverse plot produces more living matter than its single-most-productive component species, grown in monoculture, then the plants must complement each other.

An experiment published in November 1999 in *Science* claimed to have found just that, at least in certain locations. The huge, $1.7-million effort involved plots seeded randomly, like Mr. Tilman's, at eight sites in Europe. Researchers at several of the sites had planted monocultures of all of the species in the diverse plots, and a few of them found overyielding. But Mr. Huston led a group of scientists' rebuttal, published by *Science* in August 2000, which said that the overyielding occurred only when scientists added a single, important plant—a legume, which made the nutrient nitrogen available to other plants— and was not an effect of increasing species diversity per se.

"It's very common in science to have different interpretations of the same data," says Andy Hector, the lead author of the European report and a colleague of Mr. Lawton's at Imperial College. He says he is re-analyzing the data in light of some of the criticisms.

The debate reaches beyond the technical issues to charges of prejudice made by those who question the link between biodiversity and ecosystem function. Mr. Huston sees evidence of that partiality in the Ecological Society of America report that sparked the current controversy. "It's essentially consistent with the conspiracy theory that there's a small group of people that's manipulating the publication and publicity process to push this specific agenda and promote these specific experiments," Mr. Huston says. He says he was not surprised that the report ignored the alternative interpretations of the experiments, since the lead author on the panel of 12 was Mr. Naeem, who is now at the University of Washington, and Mr. Tilman was an author and the editor of the series of reports. "Of the 25 papers that were cited [in the report], 18 of them were by the people who had actually written the article," says Sheffield's Mr. Grime.

"There are quite a lot of experiments that have used different designs to Tilman and Naeem that do not show the results they get," says Mr. Wardle, of Landcare Research. "These studies don't have the same sort of conservation appeal, and therefore do not get the publicity." What's more, he points out, the most productive natural ecosystems are not the most diverse.

Mr. Wardle even accuses major journals of bias toward papers that purport to link biodiversity to ecosystem function. "I'm skeptical about who gets to referee them," he says. "How did they get published?" asks Mr. Grime. "There are senior figures in science who are associated with them."

The skeptics also object to the generalizations made in many of the research papers and in the report, which imply that the results support conserving biodiversity. Mark W. Schwartz, an associate professor of environmental science and policy at the University of California at Davis, says the experiments are not conclusive enough and have been performed on too few ecosystems to translate into general conservation strategies. He says, "If we grab onto the idea before there's actually support for it, we're going to be making mistakes and leaving ourselves vulnerable to people who oppose conservation and say, what's the evidence for that?"

Not surprisingly, Mr. Tilman disagrees. "The least these results suggest is, it would be foolish to lose diversity from ecosystems," he says. Mr. Naeem agrees: "We can't bring back species once they go extinct."

But both say that much more work needs to be done in other ecosystems before a general law linking biodiversity to ecosystem function could be accepted. Most of the experiments so far have been performed on grasslands.

Mr. Tilman expresses surprise at the implication that journals are excluding the opposing view, saying that Mr. Wardle, Mr. Huston, and Mr. Grime have all published papers or letters in *Science* in recent years.

He and several of the authors of the report for educators and policymakers defend it. "The report was written in a cautious tone to try to reflect what we know and don't know," says Mr. Tilman.

"To tell you the truth, as panel chair, I found the report to be a fairly weak document, given the irreversibility of biodiversity decline," says Mr. Naeem. But he says he argued for inclusion of a diagram, which was later cut, showing different relationships between biodiversity and ecosystem health found in other experiments.

One of the report's authors, David U. Hooper, an assistant professor of biology at Western Washington University, says he was generally pleased with the result but still felt that the alternative viewpoints received too little emphasis. "It was intended as a consensus document. Obviously, we missed. It wasn't," he says. "That was unfortunate, because I don't think it would have taken a lot of tweaking."

In response to the uproar, the Ecological Society of America has changed some of the policies surrounding reports of this type. "We took all the steps we can to minimize any conflicts of interest in the future," says Diana H. Wall, an ecologist at Colorado State University, who was president of the society when the report and letter in response were published.

> *"Some scientists claim that . . . major [scientific] journals are silencing the critics."*

She also says that future reports will bear a disclaimer saying they are not position statements representing the entire society. Mr. Hooper and Peter M. Vitousek, a professor of population biology at Stanford University, are organizing a panel of scientists with varying viewpoints to draft a position paper to represent the society.

In fact, Mr. Naeem and Michel Loreau, a French ecologist involved in the European research, have organized a meeting in Paris in December 2000 to bring the combatants together to discuss the issues. All involved are cautiously optimistic about resolving the items of contention between scientists who have debated in print but rarely, if ever, met face-to-face. "There's an inherent resistance to allow anything to challenge one's own carefully guarded point of view," says Lonnie W. Aarssen, a professor of biology at Queen's University at Kingston, in Ontario, Canada. "There have been a lot of great debates in ecology over the years, and eventually the dust settles and . . . people start learning from what happened during the debate. I think that'll happen with this, too."

Invading Species May Be Beneficial to America's Ecosystems

by Ronald Bailey

About the author: *Ronald Bailey is the science correspondent for* Reason, *a libertarian magazine and author of* ECO-SCAM: The False Prophets of the Ecological Apocalypse.

"That kind of information is dangerous," scolded Jodi Cassell. Cassell, who works with the California Sea Grant Extension program, was speaking at a symposium on "Alien Species in Coastal Waters: What Are the Real Ecological and Social Costs?" at the February 2000 American Association for the Advancement of Science (AAAS) meeting in Washington, D.C. She wasn't alone in her alarm. "We have members of the press here," warned a member of the audience. "I am very concerned that they might think that his view is the dominant view."

The target of this shushing was Mark Sagoff, a philosopher from the University of Maryland who has worked with Maryland's Sea Grant program to determine how the Chesapeake Bay's unique ecology defines a sense of place. Sagoff's sin? He'd had the temerity to point out the benefits that the much-loathed zebra mussels had brought to the Great Lakes.

Zebra Mussels

Introduced via discharged ballast water from European freighters in the mid-1980s, zebra mussel populations have been exploding in the Great Lakes. Tens of thousands of the tiny, striped shellfish can occupy a square meter of any hard surface—like rocks, docks, and boat hulls. Observers initially feared that zebra mussels would clog water-intake pipes for municipalities and power plants and perhaps out-compete native shellfish for food. However, it turns out that the things are voracious "filter feeders." They strain algae and nutrients

Reprinted, with permission, from Ronald Bailey, "Bio Invaders!" *Reason*, August/September 2000. Copyright 2000 by the Reason Foundation, 3415 S. Sepulveda Blvd., Suite 100, Los Angeles, CA 90034. www.reason.com.

like fertilizer runoff from the lakes' waters. As a result, zebra mussels have played a significant role in improving water quality by clearing the lakes of polluting organic matter.

"There has been a striking difference in water clarity improving dramatically in Lake Erie, sometimes six to four times what it was before the arrival of the zebra mussels," according to the U.S. Geological Survey's Nonindigenous Aquatic Species Database. "With this increase in water clarity, more light is able to penetrate deeper allowing for an increase in macrophytes (aquatic plants). Some of these macrophyte beds have not been seen for many decades due to changing conditions of the lake mostly due to pollution. The macrophyte beds that have returned are providing cover and acting as nurseries for some species of fish." What's more, zebra mussels provide food and habitat for all sorts of native fish and ducks.

Having Sagoff point out such positive developments was more than his colleagues on the AAAS panel could bear. To them—and to most professional ecologists—zebra mussels are simply "bad." So too, say ecologists, are all other "non-native" or "invader" species that set up shop in ecosytems different from the ones in which they originated.

A Burning Question

Why ecologists feel this way is no small matter. It is one of the hottest questions in contemporary ecology, and one which has tremendous policy implications: Should massive regulatory steps be taken to make sure "non-native species" are kept out of any given ecosystem? This is the same issue that the signatories to the Convention on Biological Diversity [were] hashing out in Nairobi, Kenya, in Fall 1999. The convention, an international agreement negotiated during the 1992 Earth Summit, is the first comprehensive global treaty to address all aspects of biological diversity, including genetic resources, species, and ecosystems. The results from Nairobi could well be the start of a global system for controlling non-native species. Delegates from 168 countries, including the U.S. (which has signed but not ratified the convention), are considering the "Guidelines for the Prevention of Biodiversity Loss Caused by Alien Invasive Species" devised by the World Conservation Union (WCU) earlier in 2000.

Among other things, these guidelines want to apply the very problematic "precautionary principle" [re-

> *"We have reaped enormous benefits from non-native species."*

quiring positive proof of no harm] to the introduction of alien species. The WCU provisions call for sanctions against people or companies that intentionally introduce species without the prior authorization of national "biosecurity" agencies. They further recommend establishing "appropriate fines, penalties or other sanctions to apply to those responsible for unintentional introductions through negligence and bad practice." The activities of transport companies would "be subjected to appropriate levels of monitoring and control" by the biosecurity bureaucracies. In other words, a decision to regulate non-native species will likely end up regulating international trade, too.

The two basic positions regarding the debate over non-native species were laid out in clear relief at the AAAS meeting. So were the essentially aesthetic underpinnings of those who would devote huge resources to keeping "invaders" out of a given ecosystem. Panelist David Pimentel, an ecologist at Cornell, estimated that efforts to clear zebra mussels from municipal and city water-intake pipes, boat hulls, and docks cost about $200 million a year. Pimentel noted that he and his colleagues have "conservatively" estimated that the 50,000 non-native species introduced into this continent were costing the American economy $137 billion per year. Jodi Cassell and like-minded audience members were clearly worried that if the Sagoffs of the world go around talking about the benefits as well as the costs of non-native species, they might undermine efforts to extirpate invader species from our shores.

Sagoff countered by pointing out that even Pimentel admits that the vast majority of introduced species do not have adverse costs. Pimentel's "50,000" is just a big scare number, noted Sagoff. "Besides, more than 60 percent of insect pests are native. So why single out non-natives in toting up the costs?"

"Acknowledging the potential benefits of non-native species doesn't necessarily preclude efforts to regulate them—or local species."

There's another important point worth making on behalf of the invaders: We have reaped enormous benefits from non-native species. Ninety-nine percent of crop plants in the United States are non-native, as are all our livestock except the turkey. "There is no basis in either economic or ecological theory for preferring native species over non-native species," said Sagoff. He further challenged his fellow panelists to name any specifically ecological criterion by which scientists can objectively determine whether an ecosystem whose history they don't know has been invaded or not. Are invaded ecosystems less productive? No. Are they less species-rich? No. And so on. Tellingly, the panelists had to agree that there is no objective criterion for distinguishing between "disturbed" ecosystems and allegedly pristine ones.

Despite that inability, the Convention on Biological Diversity's Subsidiary Body on Scientific, Technical, and Technological Advice stipulated in 1999 that "it is important to differentiate between natural invasions and human introductions of species."

Why? From a strictly ecological point of view, should we care whether a species arrives on a piece of driftwood or on a cargo boat? Why not just regard the introduction of non-native species as fascinating experiments? *Science* magazine estimated in 1999 that 99 percent of all the biomass—that is, the total of all living matter—in some parts of the San Francisco Bay belongs to non-native species. Yet native species continue to live in the Bay. University of California at Davis evolutionary biologist Geerat Vermeij concluded in a 1991 *Science* article: "Invasion usually results in the enrichment of biotas [the total flora and fauna] of continents and oceans." In layman's terms, introducing species tends to raise the total number of species living in a given ecosystem, not decrease it.

Most recorded extinctions are of species confined to oceanic islands which cannot compete with introduced continental species or humanity's habitat changes. For example, the brown tree snake came to Guam from New Guinea or the Solomon Islands during World War II. (They apparently hitched a ride on either Allied or Japanese ships or planes.) The birds and lizards of Guam were not adapted to snake predators and so were decimated by this alien species. However, continental species are better able to weather invasions. Even the Convention on Biological Diversity's Subsidiary Body concedes, "There are no records of global extinction of a continental species as a result of invasive species."

Of course, that isn't to say that non-native species don't sometimes cause economic harm. Take the case of the American chestnut. There was a time when it was said that an enterprising squirrel could travel from Maine to Georgia on the interlocking branches of chestnut trees. Yet an introduced fungus killed off nearly all of them before 1950.

The loss of American chestnuts was economically damaging, but the ecological costs are much less clear. The disappearance of such a dominant tree species from the Appalachians might have been expected to have had far more major consequences for the survival of other species in the ecosystem than it apparently has had. If the fungus had arrived before European settlers, it is unlikely that the absence of chestnuts would even have been noted.

On the other hand, James Kirkley, a biologist at the Virginia Institute for Marine Sciences, once told me that he would be happy to seed the Chesapeake Bay with Asian oysters. Why? Because overfishing and two fierce diseases have decimated native oysters so that oyster populations are less than 1 percent of their original levels. As a result, Chesapeake Bay waters have become much murkier. Asian oysters are very similar to native ones but resist disease more successfully. "The worst thing that could happen is that the Asian oysters would spread like wildfire," said the biologist. "Which is exactly what we would want them to do." In this case a non-native species would be filling an ecological niche that has been opened by disease.

Acknowledging the potential benefits of non-native species doesn't necessarily preclude efforts to regulate them—or local species, for that matter. Even Sagoff argues that "good reasons exist for controlling known pests, whether native or exotic. Good reasons exist for taking pride in local flora and fauna." As he told me in an interview, "No good reason, economic or ecological, can be given, however, for waging an expensive battle against exotic species as such."

Value Judgments

The preference for native over non-native species is essentially "a religious one," says Sagoff. That doesn't mean it isn't valid, but it does mean that ecologists and environmentalists can't simply justify their preference for native species on the basis of economic fiddling that willy-nilly lumps together basically benign alien species along with bad actors. Nor should ecologists attempt to justify their prejudices through recourse to "objective" science. An argument against alien species "must be explicitly an aesthetic one or historical one," he says. "Ecology should not attempt to become a normative science."

Arguments over which landscapes are to be preferred are at the heart of a lot of political and environmental debates today: suburban development vs. greenbelts; old-growth forests vs. forests managed for logging; wetlands vs. farmland, etc. They should be recognized for what they are and debated on their proper terms, as value judgments that are rooted not in science, but in aesthetics. The fact is that tastes vary. Some people love to look at fields of amber grain and to hear the gentle lowing of cows in a barn. Others prefer prairie grasses dotted with wildflowers and the rude huffing sounds of bison. Ecology will not and cannot tell us which landscape is "better" or should be favored. The most beautiful landscape or ecosystem, like beauty itself, is in the eye of the beholder.

Chapter 2

What Are the Leading Threats to Biodiversity?

Chapter Preface

Most of the observable causes of decline in biodiversity, according to ecologists, stem either directly or indirectly from human activities. These include hunting (which is believed to have caused the extinction of many species since prehistoric times), introducing non-native or alien species to new environments, and converting former wildlife habitat into farms or urban areas. *Homo sapiens'* impact on the world's biodiversity is a direct result of its success in colonizing much of the planet's area and appropriating its natural resources. "Human beings have become a hundred times more numerous than any other large land animal in the history of life," asserts biologist Edward O. Wilson. Humanity's success in exploiting and changing the natural environment, Wilson argues, invariably results in "reducing many other species to rarity or extinction."

Most proposed solutions to restoring biological diversity thus require limitations on human activity. But some controversy remains regarding what main threats should be curtailed. Is human population growth itself a central problem, or is resource consumption by consumers in wealthy nations like the United States the primary issue? Should fossil fuel burning be discouraged, or is the alternative of dams and hydroelectric power even worse? Should efforts be directed at preventing urban sprawl or at encouraging biodiversity in suburban back yards? The articles in this chapter address these and other questions in examining some of the leading threats to global biodiversity.

Past and Present Human Actions Contribute to Loss of Biodiversity

by Dorothy Hinshaw Patent

About the author: *Dorothy Hinshaw Patent is a zoologist and the author of numerous nature books for children and young adults.*

Throughout human history, people have changed their environment to make it more suitable for human life. This ability to alter our environment, to create habitats in which we can thrive, is the secret of our success as a species. We can stitch clothing and build houses that protect us from the extremes of climate. We produce weapons that make us masters of the hunt. We grow foods that feed us well, and we raise domesticated animals that provide us with meat. As a result, humans are the only species to inhabit every continent on Earth, including Antarctica.

But our ability to alter the environment comes at a price to the planet. Every time people have colonized a new region, they have brought about the extinction of large numbers of native species. Our destructiveness to the environment is not a new habit—it has always been with us. It's just that in modern times, we have become especially effective at devastation.

Human Settlement and Extinction

Evidence is strong that when people settle a new land, they drive many species into extinction. Humans (Polynesians from the north, called Maoris) arrived in New Zealand about a thousand years ago. At that time, about thirteen different species of flightless birds called moas made New Zealand their home. The smallest was turkey-sized, while the largest was a giant weighing at least 500 pounds (230 kg). These birds were especially interesting from an evolutionary point of view, since they occupied the ecological niches filled in other places by medium-sized to large mammals. There were no mammals in New

Zealand, so the birds evolved to fill their roles.

When the Maori people arrived, they feasted on the moas. The birds were easy prey. They could not fly, and they had evolved in the absence of powerful predators such as humans. Within a few hundred years, the Maoris extinguished what had taken evolution millions of years to produce. There were many other victims as well. Twenty other land bird species, flightless insects, and a number of unique frogs also disappeared.

Hunting wasn't the only cause of these extinctions. The people cut down trees, destroying forest homes for animals, and they burned the land. Rats arrived with them and made fast work of the eggs of ground-nesting birds and small land animals.

Extinction in Polynesia

The story is the same in other places. The Polynesian islands stretch through the southern Pacific Ocean from north of New Zealand across to the Hawaiian Islands, over 2,000 miles from the shore of North America. The larger islands are volcanic in origin and provide unique opportunities for evolution. These islands were conceived in fire and molten rock far from land. At first, they were devoid of life. Over time, wind and water gradually broke the rock into sand and pebbles, producing an environment in which plants could take root.

But life arrives at such places only by chance. Wind and weather bring random plant seeds, insects, and birds to the empty shores. Once there, some of these colonists become established. Over the millennia, unique species of insects, spiders, birds, other animals, and plants evolved on Polynesian islands and others far from land to fill the various ecological niches. Since most mammals lack the wings to make the long journey, they don't show up on oceanic islands far from continental shores, except for sea mammals such as seals. Island creatures are especially vulnerable to extinction when humans arrive, since they have no defenses against large predators.

The Polynesian people settled the islands like stepping stones, over a period of about three thousand years, starting at the western end with Fiji, Tonga, and Samoa, and arriving in Hawaii about 300 A.D. When they reached a new island, they found new species of birds, many of them flightless, all of them unused to being hunted. Since the islands often lacked good farmlands, the birds were the easiest food to obtain. When the people had killed off most or all of the endemic species—

"Evidence is strong that when people settle a new land, they drive many species into extinction."

those found only in that place and nowhere else—some of them launched their canoes and headed eastward toward new tropical paradises.

The list of extinctions they left in their wake could go on and on—unique kinds of pigeons, starlings, doves, and many other kinds of birds. All through the islands lived different species of flightless rails. Each island had its own unique kinds, but today they survive only in New Zealand and on tiny Henderson Island.

The Hawaiian Islands were the last refuge for these seafaring people. The islands were also the largest of the Polynesian islands except New Zealand. Before people arrived, Hawaii was home to endemic birds such as an eagle much like the American Bald Eagle; several short-winged, long-legged owls; and a flightless ibis. Strange ducklike birds with huge legs, tiny wings, and powerful beaks appear to have filled the same ecological niche as the giant tortoises of the Galápagos Islands off the coast of South America. The Polynesian settlement of the Hawaiian Islands resulted in the extinction of as many as fifty-five such unique bird species.

When the Polynesians arrived they brought along some domesticated animals, including pigs. Over time some pigs became wild. The Polynesian pigs were small. Europeans later brought large pigs which bred with their smaller cousins to produce a destructive animal. These wild pigs uproot plants from the forest floor and have destroyed much endemic plant life. Some Hawaiian parklands are now being surrounded by fences to protect native plants, such as the silversword on Maui, from the pigs.

By the time Captain Cook arrived in 1778, all the big endemic birds had disappeared in Hawaii, but around

> *"Modern humans are even more destructive than their ancestors."*

fifty species of interesting small birds still survived. In the ensuing two centuries, a third of these have also become extinct. The coming of European settlers brought similar further losses of biodiversity to the other Polynesian Islands.

Large Mammals Disappear from America

Before humans arrived in North America after crossing the Bering Strait from Siberia, a fabulous variety of large mammals lived on the grassy plains. Wild horses—a different kind than lived in Eurasia—three kinds of mammoths, numerous antelope, camels, and a now-extinct bison species all shared the land.

Unlike flightless Polynesian birds, these animals were hunted by powerful predators such as saber-toothed tigers and dire wolves. A wide assortment of scavenging birds thrived on the meat left on carcasses when the large mammals died, including now-extinct condors, storks, and eagles.

Even though they were being hunted by four-footed predators, the mammals were not ready for two-leggeds using weapons like powerful spears. While some scientists believe climatic changes brought about the extinction of many of these species, evidence is strong that humans were the cause here, as elsewhere. The disappearance follows the path of human settlement of the continent, and charred bones of the now-extinct species have been found with the charcoal of ancient cooking fires. If climatic change were the cause, why are the species of grasses, butterflies, and wildflowers the same today on the prairies as they were before human settlement? The disappearance of the mammals also brought about the extinction of many of the scavenging birds, for their main source of food disappeared along with the mammals.

Humans and Extinction Today

Wherever humans settle, they bring with them destroyers of native wildlife and plants—the habit of hunting; domesticated animals such as goats, that consume native vegetation and trample birds' nests; rats, that eat eggs and insects; and deforestation and fire, which can destroy entire habitats.

Modern humans are even more destructive than their ancestors, however. Today, in addition to the continuation of all these classic causes of extinction, we produce massive quantities of poisonous chemicals. These chemicals pollute the land and water and destroy native species of plants and animals. For example, the pesticide DDT was once used all across America to control insect pests. Then fish-eating birds such as pelicans and bald eagles began to disappear. Fortunately, scientists were able to link the population crashes of these birds with high levels of DDT that accumulated in the bodies of the fish they ate. When DDT entered the birds' bodies, it interfered with eggshell formation. The shells were so thin and fragile that they broke before the chicks could hatch. This discovery led to the banning of DDT in the United States. At first, no one knew if the bird populations could recover. But fortunately, with government attention and protection, birds like brown pelicans and bald eagles have been increasing in population, and the bald eagle is no longer considered endangered over most of the country.

We do not know what effects the many chemicals used in our industrial world may have on living things, including ourselves, but ominous evidence is developing. For example, scientists are very worried about the falling life expectancy of Russians. Between 1991 and 1994, the life expectancy for a Russian man fell from sixty-four years to fifty-seven years. Life expectancy for an American man in 1994 was seventy-two. Environmental abuse appears to be a strong factor in this alarming development. During the Communist years, factory workers and farmers were exposed to unregulated doses of pesticides and other hazardous chemicals. Nuclear weapons were openly tested, unsafe nuclear power plants were in operation, and toxic substances flowed into rivers. In addition to men dying young, deadly birth defects in Russia are more than four times as common as in the United States. Such problems take many years to develop, but once the effects are felt a great deal of damage has already been done and clean-up is very costly. While the United States and Canada have much better regulation of dangerous substances than did the Soviet Union, what is happening in Russia can serve as a warning not to brush off concerns about the cumulative effects of many potentially harmful chemicals in our air, soil, and water.

We also alter the environment in other ways undreamed of by early peoples, such as building giant dams that prevent salmon from swimming upstream to lay their eggs. Salmon that once swarmed through rivers in the Pacific Northwest are now almost extinct. We also build homes, highways, and shopping malls that destroy the habitats of species with limited ranges. Without homes, the species quietly die out.

The human population is exploding almost worldwide, putting pressure on natural environments to give way to the need for firewood, agricultural lands, and homesites. Human greed often gets in the way of long-range thinking. In developing nations, wealthy timber companies cut down the forests. In some countries, large ranches then take over the land to raise their cattle. When the land is exhausted, people move on, leaving behind a useless, ugly, degraded environment devoid of diversity. Here in North America, timber companies clearcut our national forests, leaving a devastated landscape that cannot support the life that the forests once sheltered.

Human Poverty

Human poverty in this overpopulated world is a major cause of endangered species. When a poor person in Africa or Asia can make as much money from one rhinoceros horn as he would earn in many years of hard labor, the temptation to hunt and kill illegally is very strong. We need to help the world's poor find ways to benefit economically from their environments without destroying them.

We need also to change the way we think about our place in the world and learn how to live in a sustainable fashion with nature. Ultimately, we depend on nature to sustain ourselves. Our food supply, our water, our air, our health, and much of our pleasure in life all begin with Earth and the diversity of life our planet supports.

We must preserve wildlands, especially those that harbor the greatest biodiversity. And when we do alter natural environments, we must do so in thoughtful ways that cause as little harm as possible to natural systems.

Habitat Loss Threatens Biodiversity in the United States

by David S. Wilcove, David Rothstein, Jason Dubow, Ali Phillips, and Elizabeth Losos

About the authors: *The authors are all environmental researchers and activists. David S. Wilcove is affiliated with the Environmental Defense Fund. David Rothstein is a professor at Northeastern University Law School. Jason Dubow works for the Nature Conservancy. Ali Phillips is with the Wilderness Society. Elizabeth Losos is with the Smithsonian Tropical Research Institute.*

On April 28, 1987, a biologist hiking through the remote Alakai swamp on the island of Kauai paused to listen to the sweet, flutelike song of a distant bird. He recognized the song as belonging to a Kauai 'o'o (*Moho braccatus*), a sleek chocolate-brown bird native to these woods. He was surely aware of the significance of this particular song, for during the past four years this particular 'o'o, the very last of its kind, had been the object of much attention among scientists and conservationists. But he could not have known that he was about to become the last person ever to hear it. The next time biologists visited the Alakai swamp, the 'o'o was gone, and yet another American species had moved from the realm of the living to the realm of the dead.

The causes of the Kauai 'o'o's extinction are reasonably clear, although the precise role each factor played in the species' demise is debatable. Much of the bird's forested habitat was destroyed for agriculture, leaving only a relatively few safe havens on steep slopes or in wet, inaccessible places. Most of these places, in turn, were eventually overrun with alien species, including feral pigs that destroyed the native vegetation, as well as plants and songbirds transported to Hawaii from around the world. The introduction of mosquitoes to Hawaii, which occurred in 1826 when the crew of a sailing ship dumped the mosquito larvae—infested dregs from their water barrels, created additional problems for

Hawaii's beleaguered birds. The mosquitoes became a vector for the spread of avian malaria and avian pox, diseases that were probably carried by the introduced birds. The native avifauna, presumably including the 'o'o, lacked resistance to these diseases, and many species quickly succumbed. Soon, only the forests at higher elevations, where cold temperatures kept the mosquitoes at bay, offered a disease-free environment for the native birds. Eventually, however, the mosquitoes reached even these forests, including the Alakai swamp, abetted by feral pig wallows, which created pools of stagnant water ideal for breeding mosquitoes. Thus a combination of factors, including habitat destruction, alien species, and diseases, contributed to the demise of the Kauai 'o'o.

Horsemen of the Environmental Apocalypse

As the loss of the Kauai 'o'o demonstrates, the accelerating pace at which species in the United States—and around the world—are declining is anything but natural. Biologists are nearly unanimous in their belief that humanity is responsible for a large-scale assault on the earth's biological diversity. The ways in which we are launching this attack reflect the magnitude and scale of human enterprise. Everything from highway construction to cattle ranching to leaky bait buckets has been implicated in the demise or endangerment of particular species. The "mindless horsemen of the environmental apocalypse," as E.O. Wilson terms the leading threats to biodiversity, include habitat destruction, introduction of alien species, overexploitation, and diseases carried by alien species. To this deadly quartet we may add yet a fifth horseman, pollution, although some might consider it a form of habitat destruction.

> *"The accelerating pace at which species in the United States . . . are declining is anything but natural."*

Surprisingly, there have been relatively few analyses of the extent to which each of these factors—much less the more specific deeds encompassed by them—is responsible for endangering species. In general, scientists agree that habitat destruction is currently the primary lethal agent, followed by the spread of alien species. Apart from several notable exceptions . . . few quantitative studies of threats to species have been conducted. More such studies are needed to provide conservationists, land stewards, and decision makers with a better understanding of the relationships between specific human activities and the loss of biodiversity. . . .

An Overview of Threats to Imperiled Species

To obtain an overview of the leading threats to biodiversity in the United States, we assessed nearly 2,500 imperiled and federally listed species to determine which were affected by the five broad threat categories described above—habitat destruction, alien species, overharvest, pollution (including siltation), and disease (caused either by alien or native pathogens). . . .

We were able to obtain information on threats for 1,880 imperiled and listed species, or three-quarters (75%) of the plants and animals that met our criteria for inclusion in this study.

There are some important limitations to the data we used. The attribution of a specific threat to a species is usually based on the judgment of an expert source, such as a U.S. Fish and Wildlife Service employee who prepares a listing notice, or a state natural heritage program biologist who monitors imperiled species in a given region. Their evaluation of threats facing that species may not be based on experimental evidence or quantitative data. Indeed, such data often do not exist. . . .

Ranking the Threats

Habitat destruction and degradation, not surprisingly, emerge as the most pervasive threat to U.S. biodiversity, contributing to the endangerment of 85% of the species we analyzed. Competition with or predation by alien species is the second-ranked threat overall, affecting nearly half (49%) of imperiled species. About one-quarter of imperiled species (24%) are affected by pollution, less than a fifth (17%) by overexploitation. and 3% by disease.

Different groups of species vary in their vulnerability to these broad-based threats. Habitat degradation and loss remain the top-ranked threat for all species groups in terms of the number and proportion of species they affect. Alien species, however, affect a significantly higher proportion of imperiled plants (57%) than animals (39%). Certain animal groups, most notably birds and fishes, also appear to be as broadly affected by alien species as plants are. For all aquatic groups—amphibians, fishes, freshwater mussels, and crayfishes—pollution ranks ahead of alien species and is second only to habitat loss as a cause of endangerment. Our finding that a large number of aquatic species are threatened by pollution may reflect our including siltation in the definition of pollution.

Significantly higher proportions of Hawaiian birds and plants are threatened by alien species than are birds and plants on the mainland. This finding is consistent with numerous other studies suggesting that island ecosystems are especially vulnerable to harm by alien species. Similarly, a much higher proportion of Hawaiian birds than continental birds is threatened by disease. By contrast, nearly the same proportion of Hawaiian and continental plants is affected by disease.

A Closer Look at Habitat Destruction

Given the primacy of habitat loss and degradation as a threat to biodiversity, a deeper understanding of this threat is necessary to help inform conservation efforts. For assessing the relative importance of different forms of habitat loss and degradation, we defined 11 major categories: (1) *agriculture,* including agricultural practices, land conversion and water diversion for agriculture, pesticides and fertilizers; (2) *livestock grazing,* including range management activities; (3) *mining, oil, gas and geothermal exploration and development,* including roads constructed for and pollutants generated by these activities; (4) *logging,* including impacts of logging roads and forest management practices; (5) *infrastructure development,* including navigational dredging, and construction and maintenance of roads and bridges; (6) *military activities;* (7) *outdoor recreation,* including swimming, hiking, skiing, camping, and off-road vehicles; (8) *water development,* including diversion for agriculture, livestock, residential use, industry, and irrigation; dams, reservoirs, impoundments, and other barriers to water flow; flood control; drainage projects, aquaculture; navigational access and maintenance; (9) *pollutants,* including siltation and mining pollutants; (10) *land conversion* for urban and commercial development; and (11) *disruption of fire regimes,* including fire suppression. . . .

Ranking the Types of Habitat Loss

The most overt and widespread forms of habitat alteration are, as might be expected, the leading threats to endangered species as measured by the number of species they affect [see graph]. Agriculture affects the greatest number of listed species (38%), followed by commercial development (35%). Water development ranks third, affecting 30% of endangered species. Not surprisingly, the impacts of water development are felt most acutely by aquatic species. Indeed, 91% of endangered fish and 99% of endangered mussels are affected by water development. Dams and other impoundments alone affect about 17% of listed species.

Outdoor recreation ranks fourth, harming a surprisingly large number of endangered species (27%) and affecting a significantly higher proportion of plants than animals (33% versus 17%). Within the category of outdoor recreation, the use of off-road vehicles is implicated in the demise of approximately 13% of endangered species.

Livestock grazing threatens about 22% of endangered species, ranking fifth among causes of habitat degradation. Again, this land use activity is particularly harmful to plants, affecting 33% of listed plant species, a fig-

> *"Habitat destruction and degradation . . . emerge as the most pervasive threat to U.S. biodiversity."*

ure significantly higher than the 14% of listed animals harmed by grazing. Pollutants affect about 20% of species, followed by infrastructure development (17%). Within the category of infrastructure development, roads alone affect 15% of species, confirming their reputation as a leading threat to biodiversity.

Alteration of ecosystem processes is increasingly being recognized as a significant threat to biodiversity. Disruption of fire regimes, for example, affects 14% of listed species. About half of these species are threatened by fire suppression, and the others are vulnerable to controlled or uncontrolled fires.

Logging and mining have contributed to the decline of 12% and 11%, respec-

Importance of Forms of Habitat Degradation

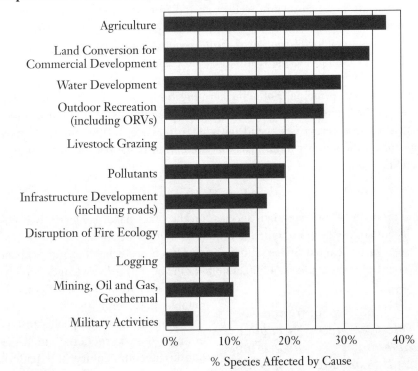

% Species Affected by Cause

tively, of the endangered species we considered. Both of these activities are especially serious threats to freshwater mussels, probably because they result in increased amounts of silt and, in the case of mining, toxic pollutants in rivers. Finally, military activities, such as training maneuvers and bombing practice, affect about 4% of listed species. . . .

Changes in Threats over Time

As human activities and customs change over time, so too do the types and degree of threats to biodiversity. During the eighteenth and nineteenth centuries, unregulated market hunting for meat, eggs, pelts, and feathers took a major toll on many wild bird and mammal populations, endangering some and leading to the extinction of others, such as the great auk (*Pinguinus impennis*). The shift away from reliance on game food, combined with passage and enforcement of wildlife management and protection laws, has reduced the importance of overexploitation as a threat to imperiled species. Overcollecting does remain a serious threat to some rare plants, reptiles, and invertebrate animals. Because our study does not distinguish between historical and contemporary threats, however, it is not well suited to tracking these changes over time. For example, the relatively large percentage (17%) of species we document as being affected by overexploitation includes a variety of animals that were once hunted but are now reasonably well protected from this threat. These include such high-profile endangered species as the whooping crane (*Grus americana*), and California condor (*Gymnogyps californianus*). Similarly, pesticide pollution is listed as the primary threat to the bald eagle (*Haliaeetus leucocephalus*) and North American populations of the peregrine falcon (*Falco peregrinus*), even though the principal pollutant harming both species—DDT—has been banned in the United States since 1972. (DDT continues to be used in other countries where peregrines spend the winter, however.) Thus our study may overestimate the number of animals that are currently harmed by overexploitation and pollutants.

Alien Nation

The problem of invasive alien species, on the other hand, is clearly worsening. There are no accurate figures on the total number of alien species now established in the United States, although the Office of Technology Assessment (OTA) has estimated at least 4,500, a number the agency acknowledges is probably an underestimate. What is indisputable, however, is that the cumulative number of alien species in this country has skyrocketed since the late eighteenth century; this pattern holds for all types of species, from plants to insects to vertebrates. Given that the cumulative number of alien species is increasing steadily, one may confidently predict that alien species will pose an ever increasing threat to our native flora and fauna.

"The most overt and widespread forms of habitat alteration are . . . the leading threats to endangered species."

A somewhat more complicated question is whether the rate of alien introductions has increased over time, which would indicate a rapidly worsening situation for imperiled species. The data from published studies are ambiguous on this point. Reviewing the numbers of alien terrestrial vertebrates, fish, mollusks, and plant pathogens added to the United States per decade over the past 50 years, the OTA found no consistent increase for any of the groups. The greatest numbers of terrestrial vertebrates and fish were added during the 1950s and 1960s, while the 1970s saw the greatest increase in the numbers of mollusks and plant pathogens. On the other hand, a detailed study of alien species invasions of San Francisco Bay shows that there have been more introductions in recent years than in earlier periods.

Many factors influence the rate at which alien species are introduced into the United States, so the lack of a consistent increase in that rate should not be surprising. Species can be brought into the country and released intentionally, or their release can occur as an unintentional by-product of cultivation, commerce, tourism, or travel. Each new development in the field of transportation creates new opportunities for the transport of alien species, from the first sailing ships to reach U.S. shores, to the building of the nation's road and highway system, to the advent of jet airplanes. As transportation technology changes, so do the opportunities for alien stowaways.

Empty cargo ships arriving in the United States used to carry dry ballast in the form of rocks and soil, which was then off-loaded around wharves to provide cargo space. Numerous insects and plants were accidentally introduced to the United States in this dry ballast, including such problem species as fire ants (*Solenopsis invicta* and *S. richteri*) and purple loosestrife (*Lythrum salicaria*). Today, ships use water for ballast instead of dry material, thus ending the spread of alien species via dry ballast. However, the release of ballast water into U.S. waterways has been implicated in the introduction of at least eight alien species since 1980, including the zebra mussel (*Dreissena polymorpha*), which has rapidly become one of the principal threats to the nation's imperiled freshwater fauna. Finally, the public's growing infatuation with ornamental plants, tropical fish, and tropical birds has led to numerous unintentional releases of alien species, including over 300 plants in California alone.

Population Growth

As the human population of the United States continues to grow, an increase is likely in the frequency of biodiversity threats associated with urbanization, such as infrastructure development, water development, and land conversion. Comparable increases in the proportion of species affected by agriculture are also a possibility. There is, in fact, good reason to suspect that a growing human population in the United States will disproportionately affect the nation's imperiled species. . . . Analyses of imperiled species distributions . . . indicate that many of the imperiled species in the United States are clustered in a relatively small number of areas. Comparing imperiled species hot spots with a projection of population density in the year 2025 reveals several regions likely to experience increasing conflicts between development and endangered species protection. Hawaii, California, and Florida are especially important areas for endangered species, and human populations in all three states are projected to increase well beyond the national average. Whereas the population of the United States as a whole is expected to grow by 14% between 1995 and 2010, the populations of Hawaii, California, and Florida are projected to increase by 27%, 27%, and 22%, respectively (U.S. Bureau of the Census 1995).

Climate Change

Climate change, while not regarded as a current threat to any of the species we assessed, is almost certain to become one in the foreseeable future due to increasing concentrations of greenhouse gases from fossil fuel use, land use changes, and agriculture. Climate models developed by the Intergovernmental Panel on Climate Change predict a 0.9–3.5°C increase in global mean temperature over the course of the next century. Attendant to that increase will be a rise in sea levels of 15–95 centimeters and significant changes in the frequencies of severe floods and droughts.

These climate changes are likely to affect a broad array of imperiled species. The Nature Conservancy, for example, estimated that 7–11% of North America's vascular plant species would no longer encounter a suitable climatic regime ("climate envelope") within their present ranges in the event of a 3°C increase in temperature. Due to their small ranges and weak dispersal abilities, imperiled plants would be disproportionately affected. [L.E.] Morse et al. estimate that 10–18% of rare plants . . . could be excluded from their climate envelope due to climate change.

Likewise, [H.B.] Britten et al. noted that relictual populations of the critically endangered Uncompahgre fritillary butterfly (*Boloria acrocnema*), living atop a few peaks in the San Juan Mountains of southwestern Colorado, were extremely vulnerable to unusual weather events. They further hypothesized that a regional warming trend, as might occur due to global climate change, could eliminate all of the butterfly's habitat, essentially pushing it off the mountains and into extinction. Indirect support for this hypothesis comes from a study of another butterfly, the Edith's checkerspot (*Euphydryas editha*). Parmesan (1996) censused populations of this butterfly throughout its known range—Baja California, the western United States, and western Canada—and found significant latitudinal and altitudinal differences in the proportion of populations in suitable habitat that had become extinct. Populations in Mexico were four times more likely to have vanished than those in Canada, a north-south gradient in survival that is consistent with the predicted impacts of global warming on species' ranges.

An Accumulating Management Debt

The major findings of this essay confirm what most conservation biologists have long suspected: Habitat loss is the single greatest threat to biodiversity, followed by the spread of alien species. However, the discovery that nearly half of the imperiled species in our country are threatened by invasive aliens—coupled with the growing numbers of alien species—suggests that this particular threat may be far more serious than many people have heretofore recognized. The impact of alien species is most acute in the Hawaiian Islands, as demonstrated by the fact that virtually all of the archipelago's imperiled plants and birds are threatened by alien species, compared to 30% and 48%, respectively, for imperiled mainland plants and birds.

Pollution, including siltation, ranks well below alien species as a threat to imperiled species in general, but among aquatic organisms, it nearly equals or exceeds alien species. . . . The pollutants affecting the largest numbers of aquatic species are agricultural pollutants, such as silt and nutrients, that enter lakes and rivers as runoff from farming operations. These nonpoint source pollutants have proved to be exceedingly difficult to regulate and control.

Finally, our analysis of biodiversity threats underscores the serious management challenges that conservationists face in their efforts to save imperiled species. A high proportion of imperiled species is threatened either by fire suppression within their fire-maintained habitats or by the spread of invasive alien species. Both types of threats must be addressed through hands-on management of the habitat, such as pulling up invasive plants and trapping alien animals or using prescribed fire to regenerate early successional habitats. Although the Endangered Species Act prohibits actions that directly harm listed animals and, to a lesser extent, listed plants, it does not require landowners to take affirmative actions to maintain or restore habitats for listed species. Thus, a landowner is not obliged to control alien species, undertake a program of prescribed burning, or do any of the other things that may be absolutely necessary for the long-term survival of a majority of our endangered species. In fact, it may be possible for a landowner to rid himself of an endangered species "problem" by literally doing nothing and waiting until the habitat is no longer suitable for the species in question.

> *"As human activities and customs change over time, so too do the types and degree of threats to biodiversity."*

Even those landowners who care deeply about endangered species and wish to protect those on their property face a daunting burden. The cost of undertaking these management actions can be considerable and, at present, is usually not tax-deductible. With a growing list of species in need of attention and less money to spend per species, the U.S. Fish and Wildlife Service cannot hope to cover the necessary management costs for most of the plants and animals it aspires to protect. Nor can it count on the goodwill of landowners to contribute their own money or labor for actions that they are not obligated to perform and that ultimately may result in restrictions on the use of their property. As a nation, therefore, we are incurring a growing "management debt" associated with our efforts to protect imperiled species. Addressing this problem will require that the regulatory controls of the Endangered Species Act and other wildlife protection laws be supplemented with a wide array of incentives to reward landowners who wish to manage their property to benefit endangered species.

Halting the threats to biodiversity will require a combination of strategies and approaches that are appropriate for both the public estate and private lands. Only with a clear understanding of the nature of the threats facing imperiled species can we intelligently design conservation programs that are capable of preventing the imminent loss of a large fraction of the nation's natural heritage.

Global Climate Change Threatens Biodiversity

by Adam Markham and Jay Malcolm

About the authors: *Adam Markham is author of* A Brief History of Pollution *and a former environmental consultant with the World Wildlife Fund, an international conservation organization. Jay Malcolm is a professor of forestry at the University of Toronto, Canada.*

Global warming represents a rapidly worsening threat to the world's wildlife and natural habitat. The increase of global temperatures seen in the late 20th century was unprecedented in the last 1000 years. Professor Tom Crowley of Texas A&M University predicts that in the 21st century "the warming will reach truly extraordinary levels" surpassing anything in the last 400,000 years. New World Wildlife Fund (WWF) research indicates that the speed with which global warming occurs is critically important for wildlife, and that the accelerating rates of warming we can expect in the coming decades are likely to put large numbers of species at risk. Climate change may lead to the disappearance or transformation of extensive areas of important wildlife habitat—many species will be unable to move fast enough to survive.

Species in the higher latitudes of the northern hemisphere, where the warming will be greatest, may have to migrate. Plants may need to move 10 times faster than they did at the end of the last ice-age. Very few plant species can move at rates faster than one kilometer per year, and yet this is what will be required in many parts of the world.

The worst affected countries are likely to be Canada and Russia, where the computer models suggest that, on average, migration rates in excess of one kilometer per year will be required in a third or more of terrestrial habitats. High migration rates will particularly threaten rare, isolated or slow-moving species but will favor weeds and pests that can move, reproduce or adapt fast. The kudzu vine and Japanese honeysuckle are examples of nuisance plants in the US that will likely benefit from global warming.

Conditions today make it far harder for species to move to new habitat than it was thousands of years ago. The last time the climate warmed anywhere near as fast as it is predicted to do this century, was 13,000 years ago when sabre-toothed tigers and wooly mammoths still roamed the earth and humans had just begun to populate the Americas. At that time the whole of human society probably numbered in the tens of millions and all were hunter-gatherers. Farming and cities did not yet exist. Now, the human population has swelled to six billion and vast swathes of habitat across the globe have been lost to urban development and agriculture. Any plant or animal that needs to move must contend with roads, cities and farms. The WWF study shows that human barriers to climate-induced migration will have the worst impact along the northern edges of developed zones in central and northwestern Russia, Finland and central Canada.

Large-scale range shifts will have a major effect on biodiversity if species are unable to move to find suitable conditions. For example, Mexico has the highest diversity of reptiles in the world because of its ancient, isolated desert habitats. However, several species, including the threatened desert tortoise, may not be able to keep pace with the warming climate. In Africa, the nyala is vulnerable to expected habitat change in Malawi's Lengwe National Park, and scientists have predicted that South Africa's red lark could lose its entire remaining habitat. Most climate models suggest large-scale habitat losses in the prairie pothole region of North America, which produces 50–80% of the continent's ducks. Other studies predict almost complete loss of high altitude whitebark pine in Yellowstone National Park and of the unique Fraser fir-red spruce forest of the southern Appalachians and Great Smoky Mountains National Park.

The American Bird Conservancy has analyzed the likely changes in warbler ranges in the Great Lakes region of the US. Several migratory wood warblers, including the Cape May warbler, bay-breasted warbler and Tennessee warbler are expected to eventually be forced from the southern parts of their ranges and driven hundreds of kilometers northwards. Their former habitat of southern boreal forest may be transformed into grassland or shrubby habitat depending on the frequency of fires in a warmer, drier climate. These birds are major predators of the eastern spruce budworm which can devastate tens of millions of hectares of balsam fir and spruce forest in outbreak years. Without the birds to control the insects, outbreaks are likely to be far more common.

"Global warming represents a rapidly worsening threat to the world's wildlife and natural habitat."

Reports of ecosystem changes due to recent global warming are already coming in from many parts of the world. Costa Rica's golden toad may be extinct because of its inability to adapt to climate changes; birds such as the great tit in Scotland and the Mexican jay in Arizona are beginning to breed earlier in the year; butterflies are shifting their ranges northwards throughout Europe; alpine plants are moving to higher altitudes in Austria; and mammals in many parts of the Arctic—including polar bears, walrus and caribou—are beginning to feel the impacts of reduced sea ice and warming tundra habitat.

A doubling of carbon dioxide (CO_2) in the atmosphere has the potential to eventually destroy at least a third of the world's existing terrestrial habitats, with no certainty that they will be replaced by equally diverse or productive ecosystems, or that similar ecosystems will establish elsewhere. Unfortunately, some projections for global greenhouse gas emissions suggest that CO_2 will not only double from pre-industrial levels during the 21st Century but may in fact triple if action is not taken to rein in the inefficient use of fossil fuels such as coal and oil for energy production.

Amongst the countries likely to lose 45% or more of current habitat are Russia, Canada, Kyrgyzstan, Norway, Sweden, Finland, Latvia, Uruguay, Bhutan and Mongolia. Bhutan and Mongolia in particular are havens for extraordinary wildlife riches to which climate change represents an alarming new threat. In Canada, collared lemmings which are important prey for snowy owls, may lose as much as 60% of their habitat. Loss of tundra habitat could radically reduce the availability of vital breeding habitat for millions of geese and shorebirds. The red knot population of Russia's Taimyr Peninsula and the spoon-billed sandpipers that nest only in the Russian far east may be under particular threat as well as the rare red-breasted goose, emperor goose and tundra bean goose.

Local species loss may be as high as 20% in the most vulnerable arctic and mountain ecosystems. Fragmented habitats in highly sensitive regions including northern Canada, parts of eastern Siberia, Russia's Taimyr Peninsula, northern Alaska, northern Scandinavia, the Tibetan plateau, and southeastern Australia may be most at risk.

Individual mountain species that may be under threat from global warming in isolated mountain habitats include the rare Gelada baboon of Ethiopia, the Andean spectacled bear, central America's resplendent quetzal, the mountain pygmy possum of Australia and the monarch butterfly at its Mexican wintering grounds. Many coastal and island species will be at risk from the combined threat of warming oceans, sea-level rise and range shifts, all of which can add significantly to existing human pressures. The Galapagos penguin and marine iguana as well as several rare and endemic species of the Florida Keys—including Key deer, Big Pine Key ring neck snake and Blodgett's wild mercury—are likely to be among those threatened.

As can be seen from these examples, and the growing body of science, an alarm is sounding. The rate of global warming may be a critical determinant in the future of global biodiversity and we cannot afford to wait to reduce greenhouse gases. Urgent action is necessary to prevent the rate of change reaching a level that will be catastrophic for nature and which may bring about irreversible losses of our world's natural treasures.

The Threat of Global Climate Change to Biodiversity Is Exaggerated

by the Heartland Institute

About the author: *The Heartland Institute is a nonprofit public policy research organization.*

Much of what is reported about global warming in newspapers and on television is wrong. Unfortunately, few reporters have the training or background needed to distinguish real science and economic facts from political and ideological "spin."

Here are [some] facts you should know about global warming.

Most scientists do not believe human activities threaten to disrupt the Earth's climate.

Over 17,000 scientists have signed a petition saying, in part, "there is no convincing scientific evidence that human release of carbon dioxide, methane, or other greenhouse gases is causing or will, in the foreseeable future, cause catastrophic heating of the Earth's atmosphere and disruption of the Earth's climate."

The petition is being circulated by the Oregon Institute of Science and Medicine, an independent research organization that receives no funding from industry. Among the signers of the petition are over 2,100 physicists, geophysicists, climatologists, meteorologists, and environmental scientists who are especially well-qualified to evaluate the effects of carbon dioxide on the Earth's atmosphere. Another 4,400 signers are scientists qualified to comment on carbon dioxide's effects on plant and animal life. Nearly all of the signers have some sort of advanced technical training.

The qualifications of the signers of the Oregon Institute Petition are dramatically better than the 2,600 "scientists" who have signed a competing petition calling for immediate action to counter global warming. More than 90 percent of that petition's signers lacked credentials to speak with authority on the issue.

Excerpted from *Instant Expert's Guide to Global Warming*, an online publication of the Heartland Institute at www.heartland.org/studies/ieguide.htm. Reprinted with permission.

The entire list included just *one* climatologist.

Over one hundred climate scientists signed the 1996 Leipzig Declaration, which stated in part, "there does not exist today a general scientific consensus about the importance of greenhouse warming from rising levels of carbon dioxide. On the contrary, most scientists now accept the fact that actual observations from earth satellites show no climate warming whatsoever."

A survey of 36 state climatologists—scientists retained by state governments to monitor and research climate issues—conducted in 1997 found that 58 percent disagreed with the statement, "global warming is for real," while only 36 percent agreed. A remarkable 89 percent agreed that "current science is unable to isolate and measure variations in global temperatures caused only by man-made factors."

The most reliable temperature data show no global warming trend.

Global warming alarmists point to surface-based temperature measurements showing 1997 was the warmest year on record. But U.S. government satellites and weather balloons rank 1997 as the seventh *coolest* year since satellite measurements began in 1978. Which record is more reliable?

The Superiority of Satellite Data

Surface-based temperature records are too few in number and too unevenly spaced to generate accurate global temperature maps. Only 30 percent of the world's surface is land, so land-based temperature stations measure less than one-third of the Earth's climate. Urban stations, which are influenced by city heat anomalies, are over-represented; deserts, mountains, and forests are under-represented.

The global temperature record produced from satellite data has none of the problems faced by surface-based thermometers. Orbiting satellites cover 99 percent of the Earth's surface, not less than a third, and measure a layer of the troposphere that is above the effects of urban heat islands.

Satellite measurements are accurate to within 0.001 C. Because new satellites are launched into orbit by the National Aeronautics and Space Administration (NASA) before old ones are retired, overlapping data sets are created, ensuring that the new satellites are calibrated correctly.

Satellite data agree almost exactly with those recorded by weather balloons, even though the latter use an entirely different technology. While the satellite record extends back only to 1979, weather balloon data go back 38 years to 1960. Neither set of data shows a warming trend since 1979.

"Most scientists do not believe human activities threaten to disrupt the Earth's climate."

According to Dr. Roy Spencer, meteorologist and team leader of the NASA/Marshall Space Flight Center, "The temperatures we measure from space are actually on a very slight downward trend since 1979 . . . the trend is about 0.05 C per decade cooling."

Global computer models are too crude to predict future climate changes.

Predictions of global climate change are based on general circulation models (GCMs), complex computer programs that attempt to simulate the Earth's atmosphere. GCMs help scientists learn more about atmospheric physics, but they cannot predict future climates.

Problems with General Circulation Models

• GCMs can't explain past climate trends. While global temperatures have risen between 0.3 and 0.6 C over the past one hundred years, computer models predict that global temperatures should have gone up between 0.7 and 1.4 C by 1990. The two ranges do not even overlap.

• GCMs use "fudge factors" that are larger than the variables they are supposed to be measuring. In order to get their models to produce predictions that are close to their designers' expectations, modelers resort to "flux adjustments" that can be 25 times larger than the effect of doubling carbon dioxide concentrations. Richard A. Kerr, a writer for *Science*, says "climate modelers have been 'cheating' for so long it's almost become respectable."

• GCMs inaccurately model the effects of clouds. Most climate models assume that clouds absorb roughly 3 percent of the sun's radiation, but more recent estimates, published in *Science* in 1995, indicate that the absorption rate may be closer to 19 percent. This means past predictions were based on data that were off by more than 600 percent.

> *"A warmer world would probably be . . . beneficial to most plant and animal life."*

• GCMs are only as good as the data fed into them. The GCMs are programmed to assume an increase in greenhouse gas concentrations of 1 percent per year, even though the historical data show an annual increase of only 0.3 to 0.4 percent. Population growth and coal production figures were similarly exaggerated.

After correcting for these and other errors, Dr. Vincent Gray concludes "we can expect the *maximum* temperature rise between 1990 and 2100 to be 1C." Other scientists report similar results when the GCMs are run with accurate data. Most scientists agree that a 1C increase in global average temperatures over the span of 100 years would be too small to notice.

The IPCC did not prove that human activities are causing global warming.

The Intergovernmental Panel on Climate Change (IPCC) was created by the United Nations to act as a source of scientific advice on global warming. Its latest assessment, *Climate Change 1995,* contains this statement: "The balance of evidence suggests a discernible human influence on the global climate."

Upon this slender reed is hung the claim of a "scientific consensus" on the need to "stop global warming." Yet, how meaningful is this sentence?

"Balance of evidence" is a phrase used by scientists when evidence of a cause-and-effect relationship is unavailable. It is an admission that genuine proof has not been found. The word "suggests" means different people looking at the same data can disagree on its meaning. And "discernible" means detectible but by no means large or significant. It certainly does *not* mean "major," "troubling," or even "bad."

Dr. Frederick Seitz, president emeritus of Rockefeller University and past president of the National Academy of Sciences, has publicly denounced the IPCC report, writing "I have never witnessed a more disturbing corruption of the peer-review process than the events that led to this IPCC report."

Dr. Benjamin Santer, the lead author of the science chapter of the IPCC report, coauthored an article on the same subject at the same time saying until general circulation models are able to explain the past climate record, "it will be hard to say, with confidence, that an anthropogenic climate signal has or has not been detected."

Dr. Santer has also said, "It's unfortunate that many people read the media hype before they read the chapter. . . . I think the caveats are there. We say quite clearly that few scientists would say the attribution issue was a done deal." In a June 2, 1997 debate, IPCC chairman Dr. Bert Bolin said, "the climate issue is not 'settled'; it is both uncertain and incomplete."

The IPCC report, in short, has not ended scientific debate over global warming. According to its authors, more research is needed before we will know with confidence that human activities are affecting global temperatures.

A modest amount of global warming, should it occur, would be beneficial to the natural world and to human civilization.

Would some degree of warming be bad for most societies and natural environments? Probably not.

"During the 20th century," writes Dr. Patrick Michaels, "we have already proceeded more than half way to doubling the natural carbon dioxide greenhouse effect. Here is what resulted: Life expectancy doubled in the free and developed world. The developing world is catching up as their emissions rise. Corn production per acre increased five-fold. The growing season in the coldest latitudes increased slightly, but enough to increase greenness by 10 percent."

The small amount of warming that occurred during the past century consisted primarily of increased minimum temperatures at night and during winters. This means higher *average* temperatures, should they occur, would not result in more daytime evaporation, which some claim would lead to droughts and desertification.

Warmer Winters

Warmer winters would mean longer growing seasons and less stress on most plants and wildlife, producing a substantial benefit for the global ecosystem. Finally, past warming has been accompanied by increased cloudiness, a phenomenon also predicted by most global climate models. This means a warmer world would probably be a wetter world, which once again would be beneficial to most plant and animal life.

Vice President Al Gore claims that "hundreds of millions of people may well become even more susceptible to the spread of diseases when populations of pests, germs, and viruses migrate with the changing climate patterns." Gore has also claimed that global warming will cause floods, droughts, heavy rainfall, forest fires, retreating glaciers, and heavier snowfall.

In addition to often being at odds with each other, Gore's claims are at odds with most scientific research. The two historical epidemics described by Gore to validate his prediction were unrelated to climate change. The Black Death, for example, was transmitted by rats, which flourish in cool as well as warm climates. Cholera has been a threat in warm as well as cold climates, and is readily brought under control by treating water supplies with chlorine.

The latest research suggests that sea levels would decline, not rise, if temperatures rise, due to increased evaporation from the oceans and subsequent precipitation over land. Increasing polar temperatures by a few degrees would not cause ice or snow to melt because the original temperatures are so low that an increase of a few degrees would leave them well below freezing.

The "torrential" rainfalls Gore fears turn out to be any rainfall of 2 inches or more in a 24-hour period, something every farmer knows would likely be a blessing rather than a curse. The number and intensity of hurricanes occurring over the Atlantic Ocean (the ocean basin with the highest quality data) has steadily fallen since aircraft reconnaissance began in 1944.

The IPCC itself found "inadequate data to determine whether consistent global changes in climate variability or weather extremes have occurred over the 20th century," with some regions exhibiting greater variability and others less.

In short, a slightly warmer world would probably be greener and a little cloudier than our world today, but otherwise not much different.

Urban Sprawl Threatens Biodiversity

by Michael L. McKinney

About the author: *Michael L. McKinney is a geology professor at the University of Tennessee, Knoxville.*

Population growth, wasteful patterns of consumption, and diminishing natural resources are rapidly pushing many species to the brink of extinction. Even biologists have difficulty assessing the complexity and speed of human impacts on the biological world.

In the United States, many native species were initially threatened mainly by overhunting: the killing of large game species beyond their capacity to reproduce. The buffalo disappeared from the eastern United States in the early 1800s, and elk, panthers, wolves, and a few other large species disappeared by the middle part of that century. Though some species, such as wolves, are recovering, others, like the passenger pigeon, are gone forever.

The second stage of human impact in the United States, as in most nations, was the rapid transformation of the natural landscape by human settlements, especially the clearing of land for timber and agriculture. This led to extinction from habitat loss. Especially hard hit were species adapted to ancient, old-growth forests, prairies, river valleys, and other areas favored by farmers for growing foods.

The United States is now entering a third, and potentially much more devastating, stage of impact on native species. This is the transformation of the landscape by the geographic expansion of suburban areas into surrounding ecosystems, which is occurring at an alarming pace. This urban expansion has many names, including urban sprawl, development, suburbanization, and counter-urbanization. Whatever the name, it is driven by the migration of people from very dense concentrations in cities to outlying areas where people are much more widely dispersed across the landscape. Urban sprawl therefore greatly magnifies human impacts per person on the environment because the

Reprinted, with permission, from Michael L. McKinney, "There Goes the Neighborhood," *Forum for Applied Research and Public Policy*, Fall 2000.

dispersed inhabitants require a vast infrastructure of roads, parking lots, housing subdivisions, and many other physical transformations. It is not widely appreciated how much more harmful to natural ecosystems these urban transformations are than traditional farming and other rural land uses that allowed many native species to persist and even flourish.

Urban sprawl produces the local equivalent of a mass extinction. It eradicates over 90 percent of native species in the area, replacing them

"Urban sprawl produces the local equivalent of a mass extinction."

with a few non-native species that often become abundant pests because they lack natural enemies. Even worse, the impacts of urban expansion are so dramatic and persistent that it will take many decades and probably centuries for natural systems to recover, assuming they ever get the chance. In brief, the current model for the expansion of cities is the terminal—in both senses of the word—stage of human impact on natural ecosystems.

Ironically, urban sprawl is driven in large part by the desire of urban inhabitants to experience more natural surroundings. Indeed, there is a strong positive statistical correlation between household income and the number of native species still surviving in a housing development. People clearly prefer natural surroundings when they can afford them. Implicit in this irony, however, is an important source of optimism: if suburbanites can become more educated, they are likely to take steps to reduce the harm done to native ecosystems. In fact, many of these steps are painless, even money-saving activities, such as resisting the urge to destroy small wetlands—which reduce storm flooding—and planting native species, which saves considerable lawn maintenance.

There is a growing realization that federal laws such as the Endangered Species Act, intended to protect species, have failed to fulfill their promise. Therefore, promoting biodiversity at local levels may be the strongest weapon against extinctions, since the policy decisions causing most extinctions in the United States are made at the local level by developers, individual landowners, conservation alliances, and local and state governments.

Asphalt Deserts

To natural ecosystems, the most devastating aspect of sprawl is so deceptively simple: pavement. Largely a result of the automobile's need for roads and parking space, pavement covers an increasingly large amount of surface area during urban expansion. While about 2 percent of the total U.S. surface area is now covered by roads, over 50 percent of many metropolitan areas is covered with pavement.

The main impact of pavement on aquatic species is a vast increase, from several hundred to a thousandfold, in the amount of water discharge, sediment, toxic chemicals, sewage, and other major water pollutants. When just 10 percent of the land is covered with pavement, local creek and lake ecosystems suffer profound species losses. The initial stages of development, for example, typically eliminate over half the fish, snail, and clam species in nearby streams.

The number of terrestrial species also declines as the amount of pavement increases. The most obvious reason for this is that plants generally cannot penetrate pavement to reach the soil. In widely paved areas such as parking lots, the landscape becomes a biological wasteland with a species diversity below that found even in the most barren deserts, and no habitat for most mammals and songbirds, which need trees, shrubs, and grasses for food and shelter.

Notable exceptions include the few species preadapted through evolutionary accident to inhabit highly urbanized habitats, such as pigeons, starlings, house mice, and black and brown rats. Such species, often called human commensals, or synanthropes, abound because humans have eliminated their natural competitors and enemies and supply them with large quantities of food.

Most of these species were originally from Europe or Asia and have become globally distributed via human transport. Their evolutionary preadaptations include an ability to reproduce in human edifices; urban pigeons, for example originally nested on rock cliffs. And they consume available foods; most suburban and urban birds are seed eaters that thrive on bird feed, or scavengers that subsist on food scraps. As global commerce increases, the rate at which such non-native species are introduced into local ecosystems is increasing exponentially. If current trends persist, this replacement of native species with the

> *"To natural ecosystems, the most devastating aspect of sprawl is . . . pavement."*

same few commensals will result in a monotonous, globally homogenized biosphere, a "planet of weeds."

Before we can mitigate impacts of sprawl, we must realize that these urban biological wastelands are endpoints of a long process by which native species are removed from an area over a period of many years, usually decades. This process is obvious in the suburbs and the advancing fringes of cities where natural ecosystems are swallowed and transformed into concrete deserts.

The first step is fragmentation of habitat. Roads and other forms of development will fragment a formerly continuous wetland, forest, or other natural habitat into progressively smaller islands. Such fragmentation greatly accelerates the loss of habitat. The most direct and obvious effect is road-kill mortality, which accounts for the deaths of millions of small mammals and birds each year in the United States alone.

Another fragmentation effect is the isolation of populations so that individuals have a difficult time finding mates for breeding. This is seen in many endangered species, such as the Florida panther, where inbreeding is common and birth rates have dropped dramatically.

Finally, the rapid diffusion of housecats, people, and other sources of disruption infringes on fragments and produces "edge effects" in the remaining habitat caused by greater access to the interior of the fragment. Domestic cats, for example, have an instinctive fear of larger predators such as coyotes, which often include housecats as a main part of their diet. Therefore, cats will rarely prey on songbird nests that are more than a few hundred feet from the edge of a forested area. The smaller the forest fragment, the greater is this threat.

The fossil record shows that even mass extinctions had a few winners, species that benefited from catastrophic environmental changes. Such species move into the areas vacated by the extinct species and transform the composition of the ecosystem. The rise of mammals, for example, could never have occurred without the extinction of dinosaurs, by a huge meteorite.

So it is with urban sprawl. As fragmentation proceeds, the creation of more open space attracts species adapted to such areas—robins and mockingbirds that forage for insects on the ground, for example—or those that forage for seeds, like cardinals and mourning doves. Such species are also able to nest in available shrubs.

Common mammals in fragmented suburban areas include rabbits, which prefer short grasses, deer that browse on shrubs, and a variety of middle-sized omnivorous species such as raccoons, opossums, coyotes, and skunks. These omnivores can reach population densities much higher than in natural areas because they have learned to take advantage of garbage, vegetable gardens, and other resources provided by humans. Indeed, studies show that there are now 10 times more deer, raccoon, and skunks in the United States than existed before European settlement began. Because humans provide food and remove natural predators and competitors, these suburban dwellers become superabundant pests.

Among plants, the winners of fragmentation include grasses, shrubs, and other species that colonize open areas after a disturbance. As with suburban animals, some of these winners become so abundant that they are pests in the form of weeds. Because development is accompanied by the widespread importation of non-native ornamental plants used in landscaping, many of these become weedy pests. Examples include kudzu, dandelions, and honeysuckle, which overgrow and kill native plants.

What does this mean for preserving habitat? A key place to start is at the fringes, where urban sprawl is expanding. In most cases, the initial stages of urban expansion into surrounding regions actually increase the number of species in the area. While this may seem counterintuitive, it is a well-established fact of ecological theory: intermediate levels of disturbance tend to maximize biodiversity. In this case, the initial stages of fragmentation create a mosaic of habitats that allow a wide variety of species to coexist in the area, often more than before modern human intrusion. Examples are land at the fringe of suburban expansion, especially farmland sought by real estate developers.

This high species diversity outside urban peripheries is a crucial and largely ignored opportunity for planners and developers who wish to enhance the quality of life in the suburbs and simultaneously promote the conservation of biodiversity. Public opinion polls in the United States consistently show that a large majority of residents of suburban areas have a strong interest in preserving natural features of their area as well as a strong concern for the extinction of other species.

Fortunately, there is a growing awareness of this among planners. So the main question, as usual, is whether local governments will implement recommendations made by them or ignore them for short-term political or economic reasons.

"Individual homeowners can . . . make substantial contributions to native species preservation."

On a regional scale, suburban development should therefore seek to preserve the high native species diversity that occurs in the initial stages of habitat fragmentation. This would require preserving some of the habitat fragments, such as wetland and forest habitat, that sustain populations of native species. Current regulations and environmental-impact assessments do not require this unless a threatened species is involved, and such species are so rare that they are generally not a factor in urban growth issues.

From an ecological standpoint, such wilderness set-asides need not be particularly large, especially if the preservation of birds, plants, fish, and invertebrates such as insects are the goal. Even a few acres can sustain adequate populations of many species of these groups. In addition, efforts should be made to connect the fragments with corridors of naturalized vegetation to reduce isolation.

In many areas, the best candidates for connecting corridors are riverbank, or riparian, ecosystems such as land adjacent to streams that serve as natural pathways for many species. Naturalized riparian zones greatly reduce water pollution by absorbing toxic runoff, serve as habitat for aquatic birds and other species found nowhere else, buffer the area from flooding by absorbing storm waters, and can serve as popular pathways for hikers and bikers.

What Homeowners Can Do

Individual homeowners can also make substantial contributions to native species preservation. The rapidly growing literature on backyard biodiversity testifies to the importance of biological variety to the quality of life, as well as the biological and economic absurdity of traditional lawn ecosystems.

Few homeowners realize that the suburban lawn landscape is historically rooted in a century-old attempt to emulate wealthy European estates. This emulation is so extensive that lawn grass is now the most widespread cultivated plant in the United States, covering an area greater than the state of Pennsylvania. What many homeowners don't understand is that the lawn of an estate was only a small part of a larger picture. European estates also included large forests and farmland that provided game, crops, and livestock for the owners, as well as good habitat for a variety of wildlife.

Chapter 2

Biologically, a suburban lawn is an attempt to arrest the natural process of ecological succession. In succession, open spaces created by forest fires and other disturbances become colonized by grasses, which are soon replaced by shrubs and then trees. Similarly, birds adapted to open spaces, such as robins, gradually become replaced by birds adapted to shrubs and trees, such as warblers. The typical American lawn is an enormously expensive attempt to use lawnmowers, weed whackers, pesticides, and herbicides to prevent ecological succession and maintain the yard in a highly disturbed condition that is grossly out of equilibrium with its natural state.

Aside from expense, these lawn ecosystems are bad for native biodiversity. Lawn ecosystems are spatially monotonous, with very few plant species to create spatial diversity of habitat, while later successional stages attract more species because the addition of many shrubs and diverse tree species produces a greater diversity of habitat than is found in lawns. The most common plants in suburban yards are non-native grasses, shrubs, and trees. Such plants as honeysuckle and English ivy can become invasive and displace native species. These non-native plants support a lower number of native bird and other native animal species because natives are not adapted to them.

"Short-sighted policies that promote sprawl have huge economic and ecological costs."

With increasing awareness of these problems with lawn ecosystems, more surburbanites are finding alternative means of landscaping their yards. Homeowners can provide spatial variation in the vegetation by planting a variety of native shrubs and trees and by reducing or eliminating the area devoted to manicured grasses.

While individual homeowners can make a difference in their own neighborhoods, there is strength in numbers. Perhaps the most-effective organization in the United States for promoting conservation in the face of rampant development has been the Nature Conservancy. This group has become adept at working with local officials and businesses, educating the public, and, most important, raising money to buy rare habitats in immediate danger of development. As yet, however, the total acreage being developed remains vastly greater than the increase in acreage protected by such private groups or government agencies.

There are also a few cases where enlightened developers have managed to combine development with conservation of native species. A good example is Spring Island, South Carolina, a 3,000-acre island located off the Atlantic coastline that was targeted for massive commercial development in the mid-1990s. Fortunately, the developers, the Spring Island Company, realized that the relatively pristine nature of the island—including its bobcats, rare songbirds, gray foxes, and rare native plants—might be used to enhance overall value of the development. Careful biological surveys were used to identify key habitats to be preserved in an undeveloped state. As a result, about a third of the island is now set aside as wildlife habitat. Construction of new houses and other commercial developments was generally restricted to previously disturbed areas on the island, such as old farms and homesites.

Perhaps most important, the Spring Island Trust was created from a 1.5 percent fee on all homesites. The fee provides the money needed to maintain the integrity of the wildlife preserves. Rather than leaving maintenance of preserves to homeowners or a hodgepodge of poorly enforced regulations, the trust has established a professional organization that assumes responsibility for preserving habitat on the island.

The developers of Spring Island Trust have been able to charge premium prices for homes and building sites on the island. For example, homesites range in cost from $250,000 to over a million dollars. While few homeowners can afford such prime real estate, other developers can learn to adopt the basic principles of conservation to more-affordable developments.

Despite the perennially contentious and vehement debate over federal laws on endangered species, the current mass extinction of native species in the United States is actually being driven by the sum of many policy decisions being made at local levels of city, county, and state government. There has been a clear and undeniable tendency for local policy in most areas to encourage urban sprawl and other forms of land use that are invariably catastrophic to the local native ecosystems. The cumulative results of this policy are not visible to the policymakers, who focus only on local desires for growth and operate on the assumption that locally extinguished native species will survive elsewhere. If, however, all local policymakers adopt that attitude, such species will eventually become extinct throughout their range.

Short-sighted policies that promote sprawl have huge economic and ecological costs. Many cities now spend millions of dollars practicing restoration ecology, which seeks to rebuild ecology parks, artificial wetlands, and other reconstruction efforts in areas where ecosystems have been destroyed for decades by intensive human activities. It costs much more to restore ecosystems than to preserve them; it would therefore make more economic sense to invest in preserving wildlife habitat that has not yet been destroyed.

Local policymakers need to shake off this tunnel vision. They need to make serious efforts to regulate urban sprawl. Specifically, developers should be required to set aside key habitats, such as wetlands, forests, and prairies in parcels large enough—at least several acres but usually much more—to support a viable population of native species. Public support for such efforts is generally very high, so the major obstacle will be the financial interests of real-estate developers and a few others who profit from ecologically disastrous land-use decisions.

Homeowners can also be educated to promote native biodiversity in their own yards. Experience shows that most homeowners will readily do so because a diversity of native species improves the quality of life for the human inhabitants.

Urban Sprawl May Not Threaten Biodiversity

by James R. Dunn

About the author: *James R. Dunn is the retired founder and president of Dunn Corporation, an environmental consulting firm. He is co-author of* Conservative Environmentalism.

Many environmentalists worry that suburban growth is reducing the diversity of wildlife. The Sierra Club's Carl Pope recently wrote that urban sprawl "fragments landscapes—and fragmented landscapes are the biggest threat to America's wildlife heritage."

This claim may be true in California, but it is not supported in New York State. I live on abandoned farmland in a suburban area outside Albany that looks like a wildlife refuge.

When our agricultural lands are abandoned because they are no longer competitive, they usually reforest naturally. Subsequently, when these lands near cities become residential areas, people typically plant trees and shrubs, often in places where there have been none before. Deer habitat improves, as does habitat for robins, woodpeckers, chickadees, grouse, finches, hawks, crows, and nuthatches, as well as squirrels, chipmunks, opossums, raccoons, foxes, and rabbits. My backyard has more than fifty bird species.

Today, even once-extirpated species like turkey and coyote are abundant enough to be hunted near where I live. Bear, mountain lion, and moose are occasionally spotted. Wildlife in New York State overall is more abundant now than in 1492.

Using Deer to Measure Habitat

Measuring the quality of wildlife habitats is not easy, but one statistic, the annual harvest of buck deer by hunters, is a good reflection of how well the habitat nurtures deer and also an indicator of the quality of habitat for many birds and other animals. To determine the quality of this habitat, I tabulated buck deer

Reprinted, with permission, from "Wildlife in the Suburbs," by James R. Dunn, *PERC Reports*, September 1999. Available online at www.perc.org/wildlife.htm.

harvests for counties containing or adjacent to major cities across New York State. These are the "suburbanized" counties. I then compared those statistics to average state records.

Since 1970, the deer population multiplied 7.1 times (a 610 percent increase) in suburban areas and only 3.4 times (a 240 percent increase) in the state overall. And for the entire 68-year period from 1930 to 1998, the deer herd increased 44.1 times in suburban areas versus 12.6 times for the state as a whole. Clearly, areas of maximum suburbanization produce a better habitat for deer than do other areas of the state.

The improvement in deer habitat began with the loss of farmland during the twentieth century, as modern agricultural technology led to greater food production from less land and the prime farming areas shifted westward. It continued as people in the cities became wealthier and began

> *"The best areas for most wildlife are the . . . fragmented landscapes of suburbia."*

moving out into land that had been previously farmed. The best areas for most wildlife are the places with abundant wood edges—the fragmented landscapes of suburbia. One researcher found this to be the case in California and even in Finland.

Abandoned Farms

Nonsuburban New York State is typical of the eastern states in which most of the 209 million acres of America's abandoned farmlands are located. When farming was abandoned, the land typically reverted to natural cover. In New York State, forest cover increased from 25 percent in 1900 to 61 percent in the 1990s, according to the latest New York State Department of Environmental Conservation statistics.

At first, as farms returned to forest, the fragmented landscape, as in suburbia today, was good for wildlife, and deer proliferated. However, as the forests matured, the food available for deer began to drop off. In many areas, once the present-day almost continuous forest was achieved, as in the Adirondacks, wildlife did not fare so well. In the Adirondack wilderness, where much of the forest is over one hundred years old, the deer count is down. In the Adirondacks' Hamilton County, for example, deer harvests were high in the period 1930–1965, but have dropped by 50 percent since then.

Conditions in the Adirondacks are similar to those of the entire Appalachian chain from Maine through Alabama and Georgia. The almost unbroken forest is beautiful to see and experience, but it is not prime wildlife habitat. Similarly, deer harvests in the heavily forested states of Maine, New Hampshire, and Vermont have been dropping in recent years, due in part to the diminution of prime habitat.

During my years as a geologist in this area, I discovered that many roads on old topographic maps are no longer used. These roads serviced a checkerboard of farms, orchards, and grazing lands during the 1800s and until about 1920. The roads were abandoned when agricultural lands were no longer needed. Thus the trend in this forest area has been toward greater continuity, not toward less, in spite of what critics say about "suburbanization."

Great Conservationists

The causes of the great changes I have described have much to do with economics and little to do with conservationists. *Audubon* recently published a list of the greatest conservationists of the twentieth century. The list was what you might expect. No producers of wealth; mostly writers, crusaders, politicians, and bureaucrats—individuals such as Rachel Carson, Paul Ehrlich, Lester Brown; several presidents; and historical figures like John Muir and Gifford Pinchot.

Yet when I look around at my little suburban forest, I realize that none of the people on Audubon's list contributed in any significant way to the conservation miracle that surrounds me. So I want to prepare an alternate list. The great conservationists on my list would include the entrepreneurs and innovators behind Dow Chemical, International Harvester, Monsanto, Caterpillar Tractor, and John Deere. These are the people directly responsible for the almost unbroken forest that extends from Maine's Canadian border down the Appalachians almost to the Gulf of Mexico and, indirectly, for my small forest with its frequent wood edges. By revolutionizing agriculture, they have changed our landscape, giving some of us a chance to walk for hours on end without the interference of civilization and others a chance to mingle with wild animals.

My wife and I enjoy our little forest in what was once an apple orchard. We are grateful for the conditions that have prolonged our lives and made them more comfortable while simultaneously multiplying the trees and the wildlife that surround us.

Damming Rivers Threatens Freshwater Biodiversity

by Elaine Robbins

About the author: *Elaine Robbins is a writer for* E Magazine, *an environmental issues publication.*

An inevitable part of many 1950s science documentaries was an awestruck tribute to our ability to "tame nature"—by building huge dams and controlling the flow of mighty rivers. There are an estimated 800,000 dams on the planet and 40,000 large dams—an incredible 20,000 in China alone.

The really big dams are the largest structures ever built by man, engineering marvels as awe-inspiring as the great pyramids of Egypt. And they rival the pyramids for the sheer magnitude of construction: It took 5,000 workers on 24-hour shifts for five years to build the colossal Hoover Dam.

A growing coalition is trying to remove the Glen Canyon Dam in Arizona and restore the Colorado River's original flow.

Dams have also brought great benefits to society. In the 1930s, the great era of dam building in the United States, they brought electricity to rural areas. They helped control flooding and brought irrigation to the arid West. Says Marc Reisner, author of *Cadillac Desert*, the classic account of dam-building in the American West, the Hoover Dam's "turbines would power the aircraft industry that helped defeat Hitler, would light up downtown Los Angeles and 100 other cities. . . . Hoover Dam proved it could be done."

Dismantling Dams

But 50 years later, there are signs that these monuments to the industrial age may not be as permanent as their builders planned. In a proposal that would have been unthinkable 10 years ago [1989], a range of groups are calling for the dismantling of Arizona's Glen Canyon Dam, to restore the Colorado River's original flow. Even Daniel Beard, former commissioner of the Federal Bureau of Reclamation and once a staunch dam defender, has called for Glen Canyon to be dismantled.

From Elaine Robbins, "Damming Dams: Is One of the Greatest Engineering Marvels of the Industrial Age Becoming Obsolete?" *E/The Environmental Magazine*, January/February 1999. Reprinted with permission from *E/The Environmental Magazine*. Subscriptions are $20/year. Subscription Dept.: PO Box 2047, Marion, OH 43306; Phone: 815-734-1242.

Glen Canyon isn't the only target of the new dam deconstructionists. Last December [1998], the Quaker Neck Dam in North Carolina became the first big dam to come down. The Edwards Dam in Maine will be removed next summer [1999], and a dam on the Elwha River in Washington will likely be next. As many as a dozen dams are now slated to be dismantled in the U.S., American Rivers [a conservation group] reports.

Why the seemingly sudden shift? In many cases, the benefits don't justify the damage to fisheries and river ecoystems. Studies in Cambodia, Canada, Laos, Thailand, Brazil and many other countries concluded that dams have a significant effect on fisheries—disrupting migratory fish patterns and spawning habits. On the Columbia River in the American west, for example, the estimated cost of losses to salmon fisheries between 1960 and 1980 was $6.5 billion, according to the National Marine Fisheries Service. The World Bank, the largest single international financier of large dam projects, admits that the results of these studies could mean that the bank's "assumptions about the environmental impact of dams are wrong."

Steve Glazer, chair of the Sierra Club's Colorado River task force, sees the effects on western river basins. "Dams have a tremendous impact on natural function in ecosystems," he says. "Because of the changes in temperature and in water quality, the native fish in the Colorado River are all threatened by the construction of dams."

> *"Large dams threaten some of the world's greatest remaining stores of biodiversity."*

New dam construction fragments river habitat the same way a six-lane freeway breaks up land habitat. Juvenile fish are often stranded trying to make the journey to the sea. As reservoirs are filled, severe and immediate flooding leaves river ecosystems significantly altered, and sometimes devastated. But it's not just the species directly affected that are in danger. Dams prevent the seasonal flooding that create species-rich flood plains. And native species downstream often can't survive the colder waters released beneath a dam. Estuaries at the mouth of rivers, deprived of freshwater flow, are often devastated as well.

Dams Threaten Biodiversity

As dam builders move into developing nations, large dams threaten some of the world's greatest remaining stores of biodiversity. According to Philip Williams, president of the California-based International Rivers Network (IRN), existing plans for six major hydroelectric dams threaten the Mekong, "whose biodiversity is second only to the Amazon and whose fishery and floodplains support much of the population of Cambodia." The $1.5 billion San Roque Dam in the Philippines, partially financed by the Export-Import Bank of Japan, is the largest private hydroelectric project in Asia, and is expected to cause considerable erosion and damage local fisheries.

And dams are part of a plan to build a 2,000-mile shipping channel into the Pantanal region of Brazil, one of the world's largest tropical wetlands. In Sarawak, on the island of Borneo in Malaysia, preparations were made for "Operation Noah"—an attempt to relocate some of the 220 mammal and bird species, 104 fish species, and 1,230 plant species, many unique to Borneo—that were threatened by the planned $5.4 billion Bakun Dam. Fortunately, the project was indefinitely postponed in September 1997.

Human Costs

Dams also have incalculable human costs, as people are displaced and archaeological treasures inundated. (Since human civilizations often rise along rivers, riparian areas harbor a disproportionate share of the world's archaeological sites.) When China finishes its Three Gorges Dam on the Yangtze in 2009, for example, the project will flood an area with 1,208 known historic sites, and displace nearly two million people.

In *Silenced Rivers: The Ecology and Politics of Large Dams*, IRN's Patrick McCully estimates that 30 to 60 million people have been displaced by large dams. "The available evidence suggests very few of these people ever recover from the ordeal, either economically or psychologically," he writes.

"We're beginning to understand that we need to put ecosystems back into the equation," says Sandra Postel, director of the Global Water Policy Project. "Even if dams aren't decommissioned or breached, I think there will be more of an effort to manage them in a way that restores some of the ecological functions that have been lost."

Even in poor regions like the African Sahel, hard-hit by drought and famine, there is evidence that the benefits dams bring may not outweigh the environmental and human costs. According to a World Resources Institute analysis of a major regional dam project on the Senegal River, many hoped-for economic benefits still hadn't materialized more than 10 years later. But valley fisheries were devastated, forcing people to truck in fish from the coast. Incidents of bilharzia, diarrheal diseases and malaria increased and surprisingly, nutrition has not improved as expected.

As the true costs of large dams are better understood, governments may learn the value of small-scale solutions. Environmentalists and river advocacy groups urge a better planning process for large dams. They argue that more efficient energy use and water distribution can go a long way toward making new dam projects unnecessary.

Our mighty dams might have been built to last through the ages, but there's nothing that says we can't shorten their lifespans.

Reckless Exploitation of Ocean Resources Threatens Marine Biodiversity

by Elliott Norse

About the author: *Elliott Norse, a marine biologist who has worked with the Environmental Protection Agency, the Ecological Society of America, and the Center for Marine Conservation, founded the Marine Conservation Biology Institute in 1996 to promote research in marine conservation biology.*

The sea is so vast that it seems invulnerable, a boundless cornucopia of resources for our appetites and a convenient toilet for our wastes. But humankind is more powerful than we realize, and the living sea is in real trouble. By applying scientific understanding about marine biodiversity and how humans affect it, we can make better decisions. Knowledge does not guarantee that we will do the right thing, but we will make better decisions with it than without it.

There is just one ocean, the world ocean system. The Black Sea flows into the Mediterranean, which flows into the Atlantic, which is connected to the Arctic Ocean, and through that to the Pacific and the Indian Oceans. They are all connected to one another through aquatic pathways. The herbicide sprayed onto a golf course in Chicago's suburbs is washed into streams, then the Illinois River, then the Mississippi River, which carries it into the Gulf of Mexico, then into the Atlantic Ocean, and from there into all the world's oceans.

Artificial Divisions

Not recognizing this unity, we draw political lines on maps that have nothing to do with marine ecosystems. We divide Georges Bank between Canada and the United States; Canada manages its part one way and the United States manages it another way, so we screw up things for the Canadians, and they screw up things for us. We fail to protect, restore, and sustainably use the bounty of the living sea in Georges Bank and elsewhere in part because of political divisions

Excerpted from Elliott Norse, "Marine Biodiversity," in *Life Stories: World-Renowned Scientists Reflect on Their Lives and the Future of Life on Earth*, edited by Heather Newbold (Berkeley & Los Angeles: University of California Press, 2000). Copyright © 2000 Heather Newbold. Reprinted with permission.

that have no relationship to ocean circulation, submarine topography, and biological processes such as dispersal and migration.

Generally, a marine area is imperiled to the extent that it is influenced by what happens on land. The flow of materials, including sediments, nutrients, and toxic materials, is usually downhill from land to sea, so the sea is the collecting basin for much of what people do on land. Consequently, the marine places in the worst trouble are those adjacent to and thus most affected by activities on land. The Black Sea, for example, is surrounded by six nations—Turkey, Georgia, Russia, Ukraine, Romania, and Bulgaria—which have a long tradition of enmity and noncooperation. They do, however, have a strong incentive to work together to protect the Black Sea's living resources, which provide them with seafood important to their people; but there is one further complication. In addition to effluent from these six countries, rivers flowing into the Black Sea, such as the Danube, carry wastes from many more, including Switzerland, Austria, and Yugoslavia. These nations pay no penalty for destroying the Black Sea, whereas the Russians, Turks, and Bulgars, who also mess it up, pay for it when the Black Sea does not yield them the benefits that it used to. The six Black Sea coastal nations have no way to prevent the nations lining influent rivers from polluting them. We need an international agreement that recognizes that every place in the sea is downstream from every other place.

"Aside from depleting targeted fish populations, commercial fishing reduces biological diversity in other ways."

Like our political constructs, our economic systems work against us. One pernicious effect of a free-market economy was originally pointed out by Colin Clark, a mathematician at the University of British Columbia. He explained how our economic system ensures the destruction of natural resources, including long-lived species such as whales, sea turtles, and fishes. If you manage them for maximum sustainable yield, and they yield, say, 3 percent per year, that is a lower return on investment than the 5 percent you might get in a bank account. Thus, it is more profitable to liquidate them and invest the capital in something that pays a higher yield. The game becomes "take the money and run." Further, people who use natural resources have a strong incentive to maximize their returns by passing the costs of doing business (the harm they do to fish habitat, for example) to the rest of us while pocketing all the profits.

World Fisheries in Peril

That reasoning helps explain why the world's fisheries are collapsing. Economic forces motivate fishermen to eliminate what could be a sustainable resource, and political forces prevent regulatory agencies from regulating them. We are liquidating our marine capital: most fish stocks are depleted, overfished by three and a half million fishing vessels around the world. National governments spend $125 billion dollars every year to catch $70 billion worth of rapidly declining fish. Subsidies for fleet expansion lead to more and bigger boats chasing fewer and smaller fish. As Daniel Pauly and coauthors noted in a landmark paper in *Science* last year, we are fishing farther down food webs. That is, increasingly we are eating what we formerly used for bait. This is eliminating the bigger fishes at higher trophic levels, such as shark, swordfish, tuna, grouper, and cod.

"We are destroying the living sea and the biosphere it supports."

Once people used the power of their arms or the winds to take small wooden boats with gear made of natural materials into the trackless opaqueness of the sea. Now we use huge steel fossil-fuel-powered boats with durable, nondegradable gear that is all but invisible to fish. We have turned the sea transparent with precision fish finders, global positioning systems, and daily Internet downloads precisely locating temperature conditions in which certain species feed. Hotspots can be fished until they are emptied. The sea is still dangerous for fishermen, but it is far more dangerous for fish; technology has stacked the deck in favor of the eaters against the eaten.

Fishing is the last major commercial hunt for wildlife. Aside from depleting targeted fish populations, commercial fishing reduces biological diversity in other ways. It catches huge numbers of unwanted organisms in towed nets, in gill nets, and on longlines, then throws them overboard after they die on deck. Shrimping is even worse than other kinds of fishing. I have been on shrimpers where only 5 percent of the catch consists of shrimp. The other 95 percent of marine life—sponges, starfish, crabs, and a wide variety of fishes—become bykill. Recently two Canadian biologists reported that a large, long-lived fish that is not targeted in any fishery, the barndoor skate, is nearing extinction because so many have been caught incidental to commercial fishing operations.

The Marine Conservation Biology Institute's (MCBI's) first scientific workshop on emerging issues examined the worldwide effects on marine ecosystems of trawling and similar fishing methods that tow heavy gear across sands, muds, gravel, boulders, and other bottom types. With my workshop cohost, Les Watling of the University of Maine, a marine benthic ecologist, we compared trawling, scallop dredging, and similar kinds of towed fishing techniques with a more familiar kind of disturbance on land—clearcutting. It put my years of work on forest conservation biology to good use.

Clearcutting and trawling are remarkably similar kinds of disturbances. Of course, there are differences—after all, the gear varies, and loggers clearcut to get the trees, not the birds and mammals living among them. But they both disturb most of the structure-forming organisms that provide habitat for many other species. And both of them cause a substantial nutrient loss from the affected site. Yet the difference in area is astounding: whereas the forest loss due to clearcutting each year is about one hundred thousand square kilometers (the size of Indiana), the area trawled each year is vastly larger.

We calculated nearly fifteen million square kilometers (twice the area of the contiguous United States). Even if we overestimated, trawling is still the greatest disturbance in the sea worldwide.

Other Threats

Fishing is only one of the major threats to marine biodiversity. The sea is filled with signs that things are getting worse, quickly. A century ago, Chesapeake Bay oysters cleaned the bay by filtering its water and supported a fishery one hundred times larger than today's; now oysters have been laid low by a lethal combination of overfishing, nutrient pollution, and diseases. The northern right whales that Captain Ahab and his real-life counterparts pursued to the ends of the earth have almost disappeared; the few that remain have failed to recover in number more than sixty years after whaling for them ostensibly stopped. Some are struck by ships; some are drowned in fishing gear—that we know. But is noise pollution preventing them from hearing the sounds of potential mates, are potent chemical pollutants inhibiting their reproductive and immune systems, or have we so changed food webs in the sea that they no longer have enough to eat? Coral reefs above a depth of 50 meters (165 feet) in the Indian Ocean have been devastated in the past year by increases in temperature. It has just been reported that there are no live corals left in the Maldive Islands: they are gone, which does not bode well for the thousands of other species that lived in them. These are all indicators that the sea is in trouble.

We are destroying the living sea and the biosphere it supports. I believe we have it in us to be wise, compassionate, and loving of our home, just as we can be stupid, greedy, and destructive. Which we choose will determine whether we survive or eliminate ourselves (and take countless other species with us). It is definitely happening, as evidenced by all the signs that our ignorance and lack of concern about the environment are coming back to haunt us.

As one of my heroes, David Ehrenfeld of Rutgers University, points out, we humans think we are all that counts. But we are just one among millions of species on this planet. Every bite of food we eat, every drop of water we drink, every breath of air we breathe comes to us courtesy of biological diversity. Living things are our essential resources and life-support systems, and our existence depends entirely upon their existence, functioning, and well-being. Even if we are not touched with wonder by the beauty of other living things, it is in our own interest to save them because without them we cannot exist.

Chapter 3

Are Commercial Farming Practices Harming Agricultural Biodiversity?

Chapter Preface

The loss of biological diversity does not only affect wildlife and natural ecoystems, but global agriculture and food production as well. Agricultural production relies on a relatively narrow selection of domesticated varieties of plants and animals, such as wheat, rice, and cattle. (Of the five thousand plant species humans have historically consumed, twenty presently make up around 90 percent of the world's food supply.) In addition, farmers depend on numerous other species of life, including soil microbes and insect pollinators, to grow crops.

Concerns have been voiced regarding both the loss of species diversity and the loss of genetic diversity within species in the agricultural sphere. The United Nations Food and Agriculture Organization (FAO) has estimated that since the beginning of the twentieth century, about 75 percent of the genetic diversity of agricultural crops worldwide has been lost. In 1900, for example, seventy-five hundred different varieties of apples existed in North America; more than six thousand varieties have since become extinct. Genetic diversity in agricultural animals has also declined as rare breeds of cows, pigs, and sheep die out at a rate of one per week, according to biodiversity activist Jy Chiperzak. Chiperzak and others view the decline in genetic diversity as a serious problem for food security because a reliance on just a few species of plants or animals increases the risk of massive crop failure due to diseases or pests.

Some observers have blamed modern trends in agriculture in America and other parts of the world for declining biodiversity. Since World War II especially, American farms have been characterized by the intense cultivation of hybrid crop varieties whose high yields are reliant on heavy applications of chemical fertilizers, herbicides, and pesticides. The "green revolution" of the 1960s brought similar farming techniques (commercially bred seeds, irrigation, use of pesticides and fertilizers) to Asia and other regions of the world. Advocates of modern intensive agriculture argue that not only does it increase crop yields and produce enough food to prevent famines, but that it directly preserves biodiversity by enabling farmers to grow more food on less land, thus saving wildlife habitat that would otherwise have to be converted to cropland. But critics argue that the spread of commercial farming throughout the world, at the expense of traditional farmers who often cultivate many localized varieties of plants and animals, results in declines in genetic and species biodiversity that may jeopardize agriculture's continuing productivity. Differing opinions on the relationship between biodiversity and agriculture are examined in the following articles.

Commercial Agriculture Is Detrimental to Biodiversity

by John Tuxill

About the author: *John Tuxill is a research fellow with the Worldwatch Institute, an environmental research organization.*

Snaking along the border of Minnesota and the Dakotas, the Red River Valley has long been one of North America's leading grain-producing regions. Blessed with fertile prairie soils deep enough "to bury a man standing," Red River farmers have intensified their production in recent decades, and planted more and more of their land to just two crops, wheat and barley.

Such specialization is supposed to be the key to success in the brave new world of multinational agribusiness. Yet the last few years have been anything but bountiful for most Red River farmers. In the early 1990s, following several years of abnormally cool, wet weather, their fields were hit with unprecedented outbreaks of a fungal disease called "wheat scab."

But according to Brian DeVore of the Minnesota-based Land Stewardship Project, the fungus is benefiting from more than just the weather. Many of the region's farmers have recently adopted a "no till" cultivation system that is designed to conserve soil. Standard cultivation prepares the soil for planting by plowing, but as the soil is broken up it becomes vulnerable to erosion. "No till" reduces erosion by leaving the previous year's broken stalks in place and planting through them. Unfortunately, however, those crop residues are a perfect home for the fungus in between growing seasons. A few decades ago, one solution would have been to let cattle graze down the residue, but there are few cattle in the region any more. Cattle production has grown increasingly specialized too; few of the valley's farmers can compete with the enormous livestock operations elsewhere. So the fungus has its way with these vast, monotonous expanses of wheat, one field after another, year in and year out: that must be the wheat scab version of heaven.

The bottom line is that disease and record low grain prices have cost Red

Excerpted from John Tuxill, "The Biodiversity That People Made," *Worldwatch*, May/June 2000.
Reprinted by permission of the Worldwatch Institute via the Copyright Clearance Center.

River farmers over $4.2 billion since 1992. Nearly half of that loss is directly attributable to the scab. On the Minnesota side of the river, wheat and barley plantings in 1999 were down some 35 percent compared to their levels at the start of the decade. One-fifth of the region's farmers went out of business in 1997 alone.

Biodiversity in Agriculture

Such problems are usually debated in economic terms, but they are related just as fundamentally to the loss of biological diversity in agriculture. Biodiversity refers to the variety inherent in life—both the genetic variety within single species and the "species variety" within ecosystems. For most people, the term probably evokes Nature with a capital "N"—tropical rain forests, coral reefs, mountain wildernesses, and other untrammeled corners of our planet. Not surprisingly, most of our efforts to protect biodiversity have focused on such places.

Yet there is another side to biodiversity, one that is very much a part of human history. As agriculture developed over the past eight millennia, farmers domesticated several hundred different crop species, and developed hundreds of thousands of different varieties within those crops. In the hands of early European farmers, for instance, an inconspicuous herb of coastal Mediterranean hillsides gradually became cabbage, kale, cauliflower, broccoli, and somewhat more recently, kohlrabi and brussels sprouts. Native American farmers took five shrub species with small, bright fruit originally adapted to attract birds, and diversified them into hundreds of eye-catching and tongue-searing varieties of chile pepper. This ancient form of "cooperation" between people and plants has produced a vast wealth of *genetic diversity* within crop species.

Traditional agriculture fosters diversity in another dimension too, particularly on land used, not for commercial production, but primarily for "subsistence production"—that is, land that farmers cultivate for their own households. In just about any part of the world, subsistence production results in a highly diverse agricultural landscape. You'll find intensively cropped fields for staples such as wheat, corn, rice, or potatoes; fallow fields covered in more unkempt vegetation, where the soil is "resting" to regenerate its fertility; an orchard or garden plot for fruits, vegetables, and herbs; a woodlot for fuelwood and other forest products. This kind of land use, replicated on farm after farm, creates substantial *ecological diversity.*

Today, both forms of agricultural biodiversity are receding in the face of commercial production, which usually demands a high degree of uniformity. The economic and political pressure on farms to grow for the mass market is a pervasive effect of the globalization of agriculture, and in many places, farmers are forsaking the practices that

> *"Biodiversity refers to the variety inherent in life—both the genetic variety within a single species and the 'species variety' within ecosystems."*

have long fostered biodiversity—practices that have sustained farming for millennia. But it's becoming increasingly obvious that the current agricultural paradigm will be far less sustainable. Intensive monoculture farming is exacting a heavy ecological toll in the form of pesticide and fertilizer pollution, erosion, freshwater depletion, and the destruction of wildlife habitat. And as farmers in such places as the Red River Valley have found, the social costs can be very steep as well. The message from such places is now very plain: we've no hope of achieving a sustainable agricultural system unless we can find ways to restore what scientists now call "agrodiversity."

Hotspot Agriculture

During the 1920s, a brilliant young Russian scientist named Nikolai I. Vavilov undertook to answer a question that must at the time have seemed vast in its implications if rather bizarre: what was the origin and significance of genetic variation among crop plants? Vavilov was a firm adherent to the emerging disciplines of evolutionary theory and genetics, and he approached his studies with enormous intellectual energy. From a home base in St. Petersburg at the All-Union Institute of Applied Botany and New Crops (which he headed after 1925), Vavilov organized expeditions not only to the fields and gardens of remote corners of the Soviet Union, but also to Iran, Ethiopia, Mexico, Japan, and some 50 other countries. Tens of thousands of different crop specimens made their way into his collections.

> *"Agricultural biodiversity . . . [is] receding in the face of commercial production, which usually demands a high degree of uniformity."*

Vavilov's career was tragically cut short in 1939 when he was deported to a Siberian labor camp, where he died the following year. But he had lived long enough to produce the first comprehensive picture of agrodiversity. He realized, in the first place, that the world's crop diversity was not distributed randomly; it was instead concentrated in particular regions. In Afghanistan and northern Pakistan, for instance, Vavilov found farmers growing nearly a hundred varieties of "soft" wheat (the kind best suited for making bread)—several times more than had been documented in all of Europe. He argued that the region where a crop showed the greatest number of unique and unusual forms was likely also to be where it was first domesticated. These are also regions where the wild plants from which crops descended—their wild relatives—can often be found growing in nearby natural habitats.

Most of these regions remain "hotspots" of crop diversity today. In the Andes of Peru, for instance, peasant farmers continue to grow thousands of traditional varieties—or "landraces"—of potatoes, corn, and peppers, as well as lesser-known crops such as *quinoa* (a grain), *ulluco* (a multihued tuber that thrives at altitudes over 4000 meters), and *tarwi* (a bean related to the lupine flower).

Vavilov was also one of the first researchers to draw attention to the tremendous environmental and cultural diversity present in traditional small-scale farming. He astutely noted, for instance, that crop genetic diversity was often particularly rich where farmers had to cope with a great deal of variability in local climate, soil conditions, and other environmental factors, as in mountainous regions like the Caucasus and the Andes.

> *"Genetic diversity has long been important in pest control."*

Such regions also contain some of the best examples of agrodiversity on an ecological level. They are ever-changing mosaics of cultivated and fallow fields, hedgerows, orchards, irrigation ponds, windbreaks, woodlots—along with patches and corridors of native vegetation. That, for example, is what anthropologists Christine Padoch and Wil de Jong found when they studied several *Ribereño* communities on the edge of the Amazon River floodplain in eastern Peru. *Ribereños* are a people of mixed indigenous and European ancestry, long established in western Amazonia. In just one village, Padoch and de Jong found a dozen distinct kinds of agriculture. Some farmers cut small fields from mature upland rain forest, then burned and planted them with mixtures of up to 60 different crops, following a classic "slash-and-burn" or "swidden" regime. (Such crops are grown intensively for a year or two, then gradually abandoned as the forest regenerates.) Other farmers were planting rice along riverbanks inundated annually by the Amazon floodwaters. Later in the year, these same farmers might clear and plant young regenerating forest for a quick crop of cassava (a starchy tuber). Still other farmers were clearing competing vegetation away from fruit trees within older swidden plots, with the aim of gradually transforming them into native fruit orchards. And nearly every house had a kitchen garden beside it, for a ready source of fruits and vegetables, spices, medicines, and other useful items.

The ecological diversity of traditional farming landscapes can benefit many other species besides people and crops. It can provide important wildlife habitat, as long as hunting pressure is not too extreme. In Europe, for example, over half of all bird species depend on agricultural land for either winter or summer habitat. Tree sparrows and bullfinches sing along English hedgerows; black wheatears and great bustards haunt upland grainfields in Spain after harvests have been gathered in. But as traditional farming has declined across the continent in recent decades, so have populations of scores of bird species.

Traditional Farming and Biodiversity

The biodiversity associated with traditional agriculture is no coincidence—it has arisen precisely because people have actively fostered it. Although, of course, they wouldn't generally put it in these terms, traditional farmers all over the world have long favored biodiversity as a way to maintain longterm productivity. For instance, many indigenous cultures in Mexico and northern Central America have traditionally planted their staple crops of corn, beans, and squash all together rather than in separate fields. Agroecologists Steven Gliessman and M.F. Amador investigated this "polycropping" approach and found that it confers multiple advantages. The beans "fix" organic nitrogen, thereby enhancing soil fertility and improving corn growth. The corn in turn provides a trellis for the bean vines, and the squash plants, with their wide, shady leaves, help keep the weeds down. Overall, the scientists were able to show that total yields of the three crops grown together could be significantly higher than if the same area were sown in monocultures.

Polyculture is also an ancient form of pest control. Planting different crops together tends to create more ecological niches for beneficial organisms, such as parasitic wasps or predatory beetles, which attack pests. Of course, more diverse plantings may also offer more niches for pests and diseases too, but the likelihood of any one organism breaking out in epidemic levels is greatly reduced, since none are likely to affect all crops equally.

Within any particular crop species, genetic diversity has long been important in pest control too. In a genetically diverse planting, some individual plants will likely fare better during an infestation than others, and of course farmers will be quick to notice the best performers. The late Jack Harlan, an economic botanist from the United States, turned up an extreme example of this phenomenon on a visit to Turkey in 1948. He was there to study wheat, and he collected a particularly inauspicious looking specimen in one field: "tall, thin-stemmed, lodges badly [that is, it won't stay upright] . . . lacks winter hardiness . . . and has poor baking qualities." Yet when Harlan's seed collection was later evaluated, plant breeders discovered that this variety was "resistant to four races of stripe rust, 35 races of common bunt, ten races of dwarf bunt and [had] good tolerance to flag smut and snow mold." Over the centuries, in years when major outbreaks struck the Turkish fields, that variety might have saved many people from starvation.

Planting multiple varieties of a single crop can provide a kind of "insurance policy" for farmers in other ways as well. In eastern India the staple crop is rice, and in some villages, each farmer sows up to 10 different rice varieties, which vary in the amount of time and moisture they need to mature. That greatly increases the odds of reaping an adequate harvest whether the annual monsoons arrive early, late, sporadically, or in excess. The different maturation times also spread out the labor of planting, weeding, harvesting, and threshing—thereby making life much easier than it would otherwise be.

"Even the most tradition-conscious farmers now face a host of pressures to abandon their agrodiversity."

Diversity also has substantial culinary and esthetic value—another major benefit, as is apparent from the near-universal drive to exploit it in one way or another. Hungarians, for instance, took a particular fancy to chile peppers not long after they were introduced into Europe from the New World at the start of the 1500s. Today Hungarian peppers, known generally as *paprika,* are an indispensable element of the national cuisine and come in a host of varieties with different flavors, colors, and shapes—all of them developed by farmers and plant breeders over the centuries.

Just about everywhere, you can find farmers who are willing to experiment with new growing practices. But given half a chance, they will usually hedge their bets and reserve some of their land for traditional crops. For several decades, for instance, peasant farmers in the Tulumayo valley of Peru's central Andes have grown potatoes commercially, for the markets of Lima and other cities. Anthropologists Enrique Mayer and Stephen Brush found that the Tulumayo farmers were planting almost 90 percent of their fields to a handful of commercial varieties, but in the remaining 10 percent they mostly grew potatoes for their own cooking pot—and these latter spuds were invariably a diverse collection of traditional landraces. Their refusal to abandon these varieties reflects the central social and ceremonial role that potatoes and other indigenous crops play in native Andean cultures. Yet even the most tradition-conscious farmers now face a host of pressures to abandon their agrodiversity. And many of these pressures have been gathering force for the better part of a century.

Impoverished by Success

At the same time that Vavilov was scouring fields for clues to the origins of crop diversity, another agricultural visionary, the American plant breeder (and later U.S. Secretary of Agriculture) Henry A. Wallace was promoting a new approach to his craft—a technique for creating corn varieties of unprecedented productivity. By Wallace's time, plant breeding as a profession had existed for decades in the United States and many other countries, but professional breeders rarely produced varieties that out-performed the selections that skilled farmers made as a matter of routine.

The emerging science of genetics, however, brought a powerful focus to plant breeding. The new approach favored by Wallace involved making complicated crosses between highly inbred strains of corn, to take advantage of a genetic phenomenon known as "hybrid vigor," in which the first generation of a cross between those inbred strains tended to perform far better than its parents. Wallace also recognized that the high-yield traits were not stable. Planting the seeds of these high-performance hybrids would yield disappointing results, so farmers who wanted to use the hybrid system would have to return year after year to their suppliers for new seed. Hybridization was incompatible with the ancient practice of saving and replanting a part of last year's harvest.

A shrewd entrepreneur as well as a scientist, Wallace knew a good business opportunity when he saw it. His fledgling enterprise, the Hi-Bred Corn Company, was at the forefront of a revolution that would, in a matter of decades, transform U.S. agriculture from a family-based craft to an increasingly central-ized commercial industry. (Wallace's company, now a DuPont subsidiary known as Pioneer Hi-Bred, has become the world's largest seed producer.) Jack Kloppenburg, a rural sociologist at the University of Wisconsin, has written that Wallace "understood, perhaps better than any American of his generation, the process by which agricultural production was being in-tegrated into modern industrial capi-

> *"In the United States, varietal diversity in most crops plummeted over the course of the 20th century."*

talism." In 1930, virtually the entire corn crop (and all other crops as well) con-sisted of traditional "open-pollinated" varieties, whose seeds could be readily saved and replanted. By 1965, nearly 95 percent of all U.S. corn acreage was in hybrid varieties.

Many other aspects of the corn crop changed between 1930 and 1965 too. Muscle power—both human and animal—was replaced by the internal combus-tion engine. Breeders standardized corn ripening times and stalk height to ac-commodate an increasingly mechanized harvest. To boost yields further, hybrid varieties were bred to consume as much fertilizer as possible; over that 35-year time-span, U.S. fertilizer use increased 17-fold. Corn yields per unit area quadrupled, allowing the total harvest to rise dramatically even as the annual area planted to corn declined. The farm population declined as well—in the northern corn belt, for instance, the number of farms shrank by 35 percent be-tween 1935 and 1960. And one of the most revealing changes of all involved crop diversity. In 1930 there would have been hundreds if not thousands of lo-cal corn varieties in the country's fields. By 1969, a mere six hybrids accounted for 71 percent of all U.S. corn area.

What happened to corn has happened to many other crops as well. In the United States, varietal diversity in most crops plummeted over the course of the 20th century; on average, over 90 percent of the varieties grown in the country a century ago are no longer in commercial production or present in a major seed storage facility. Among lettuce varieties, for example, the losses total 92 percent. Out of 408 pea varieties shown in the seed catalogs of 1903, only 25 have been relocated—a 94 percent reduction. By 1970, just two varieties of peas accounted for 96 percent of the U.S. commercial crop. Nor is this problem peculiar to the United States; although the data can be hard to come by, most of the industrialized world seems to have suffered similar losses.

The genetic diversity of livestock has also been in decline. Jules Pretty, a rural development expert who directs the Centre for Environment and Society at the University of Essex in the U.K., notes that "In Europe, some 750 breeds of horses, cattle, sheep, goats, pigs, and poultry have gone extinct since the begin-ning of the 20th century; and a third of the remaining 770 breeds are in danger of disappearing by 2010."

The Green Revolution

During the 1950s and 1960s, the agricultural "Green Revolution" brought extremely uniform, "high input" varieties to the developing world. (In contrast to landraces, these crops don't generally perform well without substantial doses of artificial fertilizer, pesticides, and water—hence "high input.") In many areas, grain production increased sharply—but at a substantial cost. The old polycultural landscape yielded to monoculture: the new regime usually produced only one commodity, instead of a range of foods, medicines, and so on. And in the staple crops of Asia, Latin America, and Africa, the disease of genetic erosion emerged swiftly. One single variety of wheat blanketed 67 percent of Bangladesh's wheat fields in 1983, and some 30 percent of India's a year later. In 1982, a single high-input rice variety known as "IR-36" was grown on more than 11 million hectares in Asia—an area the size of Guatemala.

In industrialized countries, a great many crop varieties had vanished from field and orchard without any apparent public concern. But by the late 1960s, plant breeders like Erna Bennett and Sir Otto Frankel were raising the alarm over the potential impact of the Green Revolution in developing countries. The rapid response reflects the importance that breeders attached to the world's centers of crop diversity, nearly all of which are in developing countries.

That concern has nothing to do with the picturesque appeal of traditional farming—it's based on the "real world" recognition that agriculture is a form of biological warfare. Under the demanding conditions of high-input commercial farming, even the most rigorously bred varieties do not remain viable for long. Faced with rapidly evolving insects and diseases, with accumulating salt residues from irrigation, and with an assortment of other stresses, the typical commercial variety has a useful life of only about 5 to 10 years. This rapid turnover of varieties has been termed "diversity in time" by plant breeder Don Duvick, in contrast with the "diversity in space" seen in traditional farming. Keeping a constant stream of new varieties in the pipeline requires an extensive breeding infrastructure, involving both the public and private sectors. Professional breeders are now engaged in an enormous high-stakes relay race to develop ever more robust varieties before those already in commercial fields succumb to current stresses.

Even now, in the era of biotechnology and after over a century of professional plant breeding, commercial agriculture is still entangled in a kind

> *"The industrialization of agriculture has also dramatically reduced ecological diversity in farm landscapes."*

of breeder's paradox: the commercial crops remain dependent on regular genetic infusions from the landraces they are displacing. Timothy Swanson, an economist at University College in London, estimates that plant breeders still return each year to landraces and their wild relatives for about 6 percent of the germplasm lines used in their breeding. (The remainder are advanced breeding lines and established commercial varieties.) Six percent per year is a pretty substantial dependence, and there is little prospect of lessening it anytime soon. It is true, of course, that biotechnology has effectively broadened the gene pool available for creating new varieties, but most of the really useful traits, such as increased yield and drought tolerance, involve complex combinations of genes, and cannot be transferred from unrelated or even distantly related organisms. For these traits, breeders must continue to draw on landraces and their close wild kin.

Reduced Ecological Diversity

The industrialization of agriculture has also dramatically reduced ecological diversity in farm landscapes. The commercial regime demands an economy of scale, so as production intensifies, the tendency is to bring as much of the farmscape as possible into the monoculture and to reduce or eliminate fallow periods. Under such pressure, the old patchwork of wildlife habitat generally vanishes—witness the population crashes of farmland birds in Europe, or the declines in ducks that breed in the "prairie pothole" wetlands of the U.S. upper midwest. Crop resources lose out in this simplification process as well. For example, according to Gary Paul Nabhan, an ecologist at the Arizona-Sonora Desert Museum, the wild chiles and gourd plants that used to

"Ultimately, the fate of agrodiversity will be decided by the degree of importance we attach to farming as a social activity."

grow abundantly along the margins of bottomland fields in northwest Mexico have declined markedly, now that those fields have been converted into intensive monocultures.

Nor is this simplification just a matter of losing species. It also entails an impoverishment of ecological *function:* the "services" provided by the old ecological diversity go into decline as well. That's why, in simplified commercial farmscapes, farmers have to apply large amounts of artificial fertilizer to compensate for the loss of processes like fallowing, which restore fertility naturally. They have to apply chemical pesticides to compensate for the loss of natural pest controls like polycropping and complex crop rotations. And if they're growing crops that aren't wind pollinated, they may have to rent hives of insect pollinators (usually the European honeybee), to compensate for the loss of native insects.

The side effects of these substitute services are considerable. Every year, for instance, an estimated 3 million people are poisoned by pesticides. Some of these chemicals are highly persistent, and contamination of groundwater is a growing concern in many heavily farmed regions. Such problems can reach far beyond the fields themselves. For example, fertilizer-laced run-off from farms in the U.S. midwest is borne by the Mississippi River into the Gulf of Mexico, where it is apparently helping to trigger massive algal blooms. The blooms deplete the water of oxygen, creating a "dead zone" in which nearly all marine life is asphyxiated—including much of the rich fishery for which the Louisiana coast is famous. Last year, the annual dead zone was the largest ever, covering nearly 20,000 square kilometers, an area the size of the state of New Jersey.

In addition to the damage they're inflicting, these substitute services tend to be much less stable than their traditional analogs because they lack natural complexity. They have little "built-in redundancy" and that makes them, in a sense, accidents waiting to happen. Take pollination, for example. Gary Paul Nabhan and entomologist Stephen Buchmann have documented widespread declines in efficient native pollinators of many crops in North America, from blueberry bees in Maine to alkali bees that have a fondness for alfalfa in the Great Basin. As a result, North American vegetable and fruit production has become highly dependent upon the introduced European honeybee.

Though not particularly efficient pollinators, honeybees are consummate generalists, readily visiting a wide variety of crops, and they are easily managed by people. Over the past several decades, however, millions of North American honeybee colonies have been lost due to a host of problems, the most recent of which is a widespread infestation of two types of introduced parasitic mite. According to the U.S. Department of Agriculture, the country's bee industry is in an "unprecedented crisis," and Nabhan and Buchmann warn that nationwide honeybee declines could reach 80 percent, causing crop losses that may exceed $5 billion annually.

Yet amid the many problems created by what we now consider to be "conventional" agriculture, there are many signs of hope. Scattered about the farming landscapes of developing and industrialized countries alike are farmers who seek alternative approaches to their craft. Some are doggedly maintaining their traditions, like the rice farmers in Java who continue to plant their local, long-stemmed rices in the face of intense government pressure to convert to monocultures of high-input varieties. Others, like many small-scale organic producers in Europe and the United States, are experimenting with various forms of polyculture. Such efforts represent the future of agrodiversity. . . .

Government Subsidies

The current momentum of agro-industrial development would be considerably reduced were it not directly fostered by a slew of policies and subsidies in nearly every country. In both the United States and the European Union, for example, most government crop supports target just a handful of major crops, rather than the more diverse crop combinations favored by smaller farms. It's hardly surprising, then, that most beneficiaries are large commercial farms, not small-scale farmers. In many developing countries, such as those in southern Africa, farmers cannot qualify for government agricultural credit programs unless they agree to plant high-input varieties.

Governments commonly cite laudable objectives for these policies, such as increasing national self-sufficiency in staple foods. But monoculture farming does not make ecological sense, and increasingly its economic justification is coming under question too. A growing body of evidence suggests that large operations are actually far less productive and efficient than areas of equivalent size and quality worked by smaller producers. And big operations generate far more waste and pollution per unit area.

Ultimately, the fate of agrodiversity will be decided by the degree of importance we attach to farming as a social activity. Diversity will not persist without thriving rural communities to support it. Conversely, the preservation of diversity can yield major social benefits. That principle is reappearing even in the Red River Valley, in the activities of people like Jaime DeRosier, a farmer who is not content with the standard wheat and barley regimen. DeRosier also grows organic sunflowers, corn, and soybeans in complex rotations, deploying up to six different cover crops to keep pests and weeds under control. He plants nitrogen-fixing legumes to boost soil fertility, and allows for occasional summer fallow periods. He is even thinking of adding specialty crops like green beans and sugar beets. As one of the few financially stable farmers in the region these days, his advice is constantly sought by other growers looking to make a change for the diverse.

In farmers like Jaime DeRosier . . . we have the makings of another and very different kind of Green Revolution—one that could put global agriculture on a sustainable footing. But this is not a transition that farmers can make on their own. The question is: are the rest of us—as consumers, voters, and policy makers—willing to back them up?

Commercial Farming Practices Threaten the Genetic Diversity of Farm Animals

by Lawrence Alderman

About the author: *Lawrence Alderman is a consultant specializing in animal breeding and the founder and president of Rare Breeds International, an organization that coordinates international genetic conservation efforts.*

The loss of plant genetic material—from the destruction of the rainforest, disappearance of valuable medicinal plants, and the decline of old domesticated varieties of vegetables and other plants—is well publicized, and most people are aware of the inexorable advance of overwhelming monoculture. Less well known is the loss of animal genetic diversity, which has equally serious implications for efficient and sustainable systems of food production.

Many breeds have become extinct not because they lacked genetic merit, but because they were unfashionable or evolved in remote areas. It is precisely because they were not in the mainstream of the livestock industry, however, that they would have made a valuable contribution to genetic diversity. Galloway horses from southwestern Scotland, for example, were a famous trotting breed; and Suffolk Dun cattle in eastern England were the superior dairy breed of their time. Both are now extinct. Their valuable and distinctive characteristics could not save them from the ultimate fate of peripheral breeds in a world where their destiny was dictated by transitory whims rather than intrinsic merit.

Invisible Death

The crushing finality of extinction of a species or breed can obscure our understanding of the threat of the erosion of genetic diversity, which occurs in other ways. Extinction of a breed is obvious and dramatic. But the cumulative

Reprinted, with permission, from "Genetic Diversity Blueprint," by Lawrence Alderman, *Forum for Applied Research and Public Policy*, Fall 2000.

loss of the paired alleles that determine a particular characteristic such as hair color or milk production is equally damaging.

Genetic variability in any static, closed population is continually augmented by mutation, but it is simultaneously depleted at a much greater rate by changing frequencies of individual alleles. As a result, some disappear. Traditional Hereford cattle, for instance, have declined from a globally popular breed with a rich genetic diversity in the 1960s to a small nucleus group in the 1990s, and the genes of a few dominant animals have exerted a disproportionate influence on the breed. The combined effect of these two factors has reduced the number of alleles at nine loci from 57 in the 1960s to 48 in the 1990s—a loss of 16 percent of the original genetic material in five or six generations. Thus, the Hereford still has the distinctive markings of the breed,

> *"The loss of animal genetic diversity . . . has . . . serious implications for efficient and sustainable systems of food production."*

with a reddish coat and white head, but it has lost much genetic variability that previously made it resilient in the face of environmental challenges.

The last few decades of the 20th century saw shrinking populations of most breeds, while advanced reproductive technologies in increasingly intensive systems of production have led to the emergence of a few dominant breeds. The race to achieve more-rapid change underlies the development of techniques such as cloning and sexing of semen. These techniques allow breeders to replicate favorite animals or eliminate births of unwanted bulls, for example, in a dairy herd.

The search for higher production from individual animals has also led to the use of antibiotics as growth promoters, hormones such as bovine somatatrophin (BST) to stimulate milk production, slurry lagoons to treat large amounts of animal waste from large commercial operations, and battery cages that restrict laying hens to extremely small cages. These techniques represent the unethical and inhumane face of livestock farming, and they have encouraged the expansion of the few breeds that are able to tolerate such unnatural conditions.

Some sectors of the livestock industry have implemented monoculture systems of production like those that prevail in arable farming. In the dairy industry, for instance, the process of Holsteinization has seen a wave of black-and-white cattle sweep over many parts of the world. In the case of poultry, the three industrial breeding companies that control global turkey production rely on a standard type of bird and have created even greater uniformity. When these ubiquitous breeds become genetically derelict, as they inevitably will in a constantly changing environment, viable alternatives may no longer be available. Other breeds, particularly of dairy cattle and turkeys, are being marginalized to such a degree that their ability to contribute variety to the livestock industry—an essential element of adaptation—is significantly jeopardized.

Problems of Uniformity

The debate on such subjects as genetic diversity can become quite emotional, but these issues deserve critical and clinical scrutiny. It is understandable that major retailers want access to standard products, and a uniform population of animals allows more precise standardized management and more predictable results. Similarly, the development of genetically modified plant organisms gives large companies greater control over all stages of crop production.

Uniformity certainly has short-term financial advantages, but it is a cul-de-sac of danger. It makes a whole population vulnerable to the same diseases. Indeed, uniform performance means uniform susceptibility. It places the future of food production in the hands of those whose motivation is profit and wrests control from small producers who provide variety and quality. This state of affairs sits uneasily on those who are increasingly aware of other, more altruistic, considerations such as animal welfare, variety in the food supply, protection of the environment, and food security based on a local supply of products not subject to the vagaries of agribusiness.

Currently, supporters of animal welfare not only condemn intensive production methods, they also disapprove of expectations that cows yield more than 15 gallons of milk per day or that hens lay every day throughout the year. Beef bulls and turkey stags, distorted by muscular hypertrophy so that they are unable to mate naturally, excite equal dismay and censure. Overcrowding in feedlots also threatens human health through proliferation of *E coli*, salmonella, bovine spongiform encephalopathy [Mad Cow Disease], and similar disease organisms. The linked triumvirate of intensive farming, dominance of big business, and loss of biodiversity has exerted a powerful influence that consumer interests and the general public only now are beginning to resist.

Marketing Rare Breeds

The change in attitude that has occurred in the last few years has probably been triggered by health scares more than by awareness of the loss of genetic diversity. Renewed awareness and evaluation by consumers of the food presented to them has led to a resurgence of traditional values and traditional breeds. It is this sequence of events that offers the greatest hope for maintaining the diversity of animal genetic resources.

In Britain, the rejection of beef from mainstream production during the bovine spongiform encephalopathy crisis of the early 1990s demonstrated the determination of consumers not to accept food that might be unsafe or lethal. This period saw the growth of niche markets and the purveying of food by small producers direct to the consumer. Integral to this process was the role of old-fashioned native breeds.

In 1994, the United Kingdom affiliate of Rare Breeds International, an organisation working to conserve endangered breeds of animals, launched the Traditional Breeds Meat Marketing scheme, which was intended to publicize the quality of native breeds and expand a market for their distinctive products. The success of this scheme depended on the high quality of meat from breeds that had flirted with extinction, such as White Park cattle, which produced beef preferred by consumers. It was a joint of beef from this breed that so impressed [King] James I in 1617 that he knighted it "Sir Loin." Yet the White Park had been reduced to only 65 breeding cows in 1970. In the sheep category, it is found that the best quality mutton comes from Balwen sheep, a breed that survived in only one flock at the head of the Tywi valley in Wales at the end of the great storms of 1947.

The meat from primitive breeds such as these is high in healthy polyunsaturated fatty acids and has superior taste and texture. The public is now beginning to understand that good-tasting meat can be healthy for you, as well as good for the environment and the local farmer.

The final turn to complete the revolution to preserve genetic diversity in livestock is the realization that the interests of the consumer are served by variety rather than uniformity. There are large differences among breeds, and these must be encouraged. The adaptation of traditional breeds to

> *"The conservation of animal genetic resources epitomizes the need for responsible long-term planning to replace the current focus on maximizing production and profit."*

natural systems gives them an ecological advantage, and the combined result of genetic merit and environmental effect is the key to products that are both healthy and of high quality.

Rare pig and poultry breeds in Britain are suited to outdoor systems and thus enjoy a better quality of life than those raised in intensive agricultural operations. White Park cattle roam throughout the year on the top of Salisbury Plain, while Portland and Norfolk Horn sheep continue to graze the sweet sward of their native heath. Tasting panels and guests at prestigious banquets and other gourmet gatherings generally favor meat from these breeds. What better vindication could there be of the need for biodiversity?

But good quality meat is only one food product that benefits from local production and less intensive farming. Genuine Parmesan cheese manufactured from the milk of local Reggiana cattle in Italy is superior in both texture and taste to its ersatz cousin sold in many grocery stores. And connoisseurs of color will appreciate the hues of naturally colored wool produced by primitive breeds of sheep that have survived in isolated areas in many parts of the world. In addition, genetic conservation can also be justified based on health reasons. An anti-carcinogenic factor has been discovered in the milk of rare Shetland cattle, for instance.

Back to the Future

Despite the huge loss of genetic material that has occurred already and the continuing damage being inflicted as a result of short-term profit motivation, the opportunity exists to save and conserve the genetic variability of remaining domestic breeds. But time is a critical factor. The awareness that we are curators of a vital legacy for future generations must be expressed in a philosophy of responsibility for the environment and its genetic diversity. Are the necessary resources for this task available? Breeders, educators, policymakers, and the general public urgently need to develop active programs of conservation. These programs must acknowledge that breeds adapted to native climates and cultures are a fundamental element of sustainable production. The necessary expertise for guiding appropriate programs exists in organizations such as Rare Breeds International.

Further research needs to be applied in evaluating the benefit of locally adapted breeds in the sustainable development of agriculture. In Britain, a blueprint for nonintensive beef production has been demonstrated by a herd of White Park cattle that remains outdoors throughout the year in an upland area without any supplementary feed. This experimental herd, raised entirely on pasture, has proven that these cattle are less expensive to maintain and produce a higher quality product than more popular breeds that need shelter in bad weather and supplemental feed. But more important, their management is compatible with animal welfare and enhancement of the environment. Similar systems need to be developed in other areas.

Intensive production of livestock is not sustainable. Indeed, intensively bred livestock compete with humankind for food. Consider, for instance, that feed-lot animals require 3 kilograms (6.6 pounds) of grain to produce 0.5 kg (1.1 pounds) of beef. As world population increases, grain will be diverted from animal feed. Meanwhile, native-adapted breeds that produce beef from grass will become increasingly critical for future food security, especially since much of the rangeland worldwide used for cattle raising is unsuitable for intensive cropping.

The essential contribution of native breeds needs to be protected against damage from ongoing genetic erosion caused by exotic livestock breeds. National governments should be encouraged to require the preparation of genetic impact studies before importation of exotic genetics is permitted.

The conservation of animal genetic resources epitomizes the need for responsible long-term planning to replace the current focus on maximizing production and profit. The fallacy of unrestricted intensification of agricultural systems as a secure basis for food production is being gradually exposed. The alternative policy places greater emphasis on efficiency of production and seeks to exploit the adaptation of native breeds and the insurance of biodiversity as the measures best calculated to maintain quality of life into the third millennium.

Capitalism Threatens Agricultural Biodiversity

by Linda Featheringill

About the author: *Linda Featheringill writes for* The People, *a publication of the Socialist Labor Party of America.*

It's said that variety is the spice of life, but capitalism—particularly as applied to agriculture—is doing much to destroy the variety of life on earth. Non-human life forms that occupy the land—plants, animals, insects and microorganisms—do not, as far as we know, hold opinions on economic philosophies. Yet, economic activities shape many aspects of their existence, and they in turn have many effects on humanity.

No More Family Farms

Agriculture, essential to human survival, becomes increasingly perverted by the capitalist profit motive as agricapitalism pushes out family and middle-sized farms. Strictly speaking, of course, the family farm, on which the farmer and his family members performed all the labor, is a thing of the past, at least in this country. The few that remain cut no figure in the agriculture industry. They were pushed out by the growth of the middle-sized farmer, who first brought hired labor, advanced machinery and industrial methods of production to the industry. Now, of course, even the middle-sized farmer is being pushed out by the huge agricapitalist concerns that increasingly dominate the countryside.

This is not news, of course, because the process of concentration in agriculture has been going on for generations. Socialists are not among those who would say that this is wholly a bad thing. The development and application of science and technology in agriculture have, so to speak, plowed the way for greater productivity and efficiency. They have opened the door to the production of an agricultural abundance that can be produced with a minimum of arduous toil. That potential will be realized under a sane socialist system of industrial democracy and production to meet human requirements. Not so under

Reprinted, with permission, from Linda Featheringill, "Agribusiness Thins Genetic Diversity in Food Supply," *The People*, May 1997.

capitalism, however, where science and technology in farming have been perverted to profit demands, have aided in reducing the agricultural and rural populations to a fraction of the national population, and have increased the burden and exploitation of a dwindling number of agricultural workers. These, however, are not the only baneful effects capitalist concentration has on agriculture.

All businesses have to operate with profit as their goal. To achieve profits, farm capitalists look for ways to cut production costs and improve yields. The advances in labor-displacing mechanization mentioned have played the primary role by reducing the amount of human labor power needed to farm. Another way is to design or discover a plant having characteristics that make it easy to harvest, and then to concentrate on the cultivation of that plant.

Such plants may have consistent growth patterns, so that an entire field of the plant would stand at the same height at maturity, which would make it easier to harvest by machines. If a given variety of a plant had a uniform maturation rate, the field would be ripe and ready to harvest at the same time. This would reduce both labor costs and product loss. Other desirable characteristics might be the ease with which the plant turns loose of its fruit, the toughness of the skin on the fruit and the particular shape of the ripe plant, which might facilitate packing and shipping. It is also more "efficient" to grow many acres of a single plant than it is to cultivate a variety of crops.

Biodiversity Loss

Historically, of course, cotton and tobacco were the "cash crops" in the South, while wheat and corn filled the same role in the prairie states. Agricapitalism today applies the same principle of concentration on a much wider scale. One result of choosing varieties of plants that meet the assembly-line criteria is that many varieties of vegetation have ceased to exist. Keay Davidson, whom *The Plain Dealer* of Cleveland describes as "chief science writer for the *San Francisco Chronicle,*" recently summed up how far this has gone.

An article by Davidson, "Cloning a Threat to Agriculture," and apparently reprinted from the San Francisco newspaper, appeared in *The Plain Dealer* of March 10, 1997. Alluding to the Irish potato famine of the 19th century, Davidson wrote:

"If farmers continued growing a diversity of genetic types, they would have alternate breeds to fall back on during a potato famine-type crisis.

"Agricapitalists are not in business to 'enrich their genetic harvest,' but their profit harvest."

But diversity has waned over the past century in the United States: 91 percent of the different breeds of corn have disappeared, along with 95 percent of the varieties of cabbage, 94 percent of peas, 86 percent of apples and 81 percent of tomatoes, according to plant pathologist Jane Rissler of the Union of Concerned Scientists in Washington."

Food plants such as those mentioned are not the only agricultural products affected.

"Many livestock also have suffered a loss of diversity," Davidson added. "For example, most modern U.S. dairy cows belong to a single breed, the familiar black-and-white Holsteins. In the 1930s, 'there were 30 breeds of pigs listed as commercial breeds,' said Don Bixby, director of the 4,000-member American Livestock Breeds Conservancy."

Consequences of Biodiversity Decline

What happens when only a few varieties of food crops remain in the fields? Remember that the size of the population of any living creature largely depends on the food available. Faced with the presence of many acres of a single variety of a plant, the microbes living in the soil (bacteria, yeast and mold) that can use that plant do well, while other microorganisms may fail to reproduce and may die off because of a lack of food. The remaining species thrive and may spread vigorously. This has happened in the past, as when potato blight went through Ireland more than once and Dutch elm disease traversed the entire eastern half of the United States. Microbial populations in a given area are greatly affected by the economic decisions of the farmers.

Insects react in a like manner. Those that can live off the produce of monoculture become great in number, while the number of other plant-eating insects shrinks. The populations of those animals that eat insects also change because of the altered food supply. The numbers and species of

"Capitalism, by destroying the diversity of life, threatens every living thing."

birds, frogs, toads, lizards, fish and other animals near capitalist megafarms become distinctly different as their food supplies change. The economic decisions of farmers alter the local populations of both insects and insect eaters.

Thus we can see that capitalist cultivation practices affect not only the humans who consume agricultural products, but also plant, insect, microbial and animal populations.

Cloning Not a Factor

Incidentally, the recent advances in cloning that prompted Davidson's article obviously are not responsible for the enormous loss of agricultural diversity over the last 100 years, and may not become a significant factor in reducing that diversity even further for years to come.

"For now, because of its great cost, and complexity, agriculture experts don't see cloning as a near-term threat to the genetic integrity of U.S. agriculture," Davidson wrote. "Trouble could arise, though, if agriculturists find ways to mass-clone livestock and crops as cheaply as Silicon Valley makes microchips.

"The threat is not cloning but 'economic pressures for uniformity of product,'

[Caird] Rexroad [of the U.S. Department of Agriculture] said."
What those economic pressures are we have already seen.
Davidson asked, "What's the solution?" His answer was that, "The White House should at least declare a 'moral commitment' to genetic diversity in agriculture. Working with Congress, it could come up with financial incentives to encourage farmers to enrich their genetic harvest. . . ."
Davidson apparently forgot, overlooked or just plain ignored that agricapitalists are not in business to "enrich their genetic harvest," but their profit harvest. Without pausing here to evaluate his proposed "solution" (except to say that more than half a century of federal farm subsidies have done nothing to slow either the concentration of capital in agriculture or its effects), we say there is a better solution.

The Socialist Solution

In a socialist economic system, food production would be organized for consumption and not for profit. The economic obstacle to preserving, protecting and enhancing variety would be removed. The industry would then have every incentive to cultivate the widest possible variety of fruits and vegetables, etc., to enhance the lives of all. Those working in agriculture under socialism would also be sensitive to the relationship of farms to the rest of the natural world, and they could concentrate their knowledge and abilities on growing food in ways that are in harmony with other forms of life, while still producing an abundance. In a socialist society, food producers would not have to disturb or destroy the complex balance of ecological systems to provide society with the indispensable products of their labor.

It is still true that there is more to life than economics. As this limited example shows, however, decisions made in response to economic factors mold and shape our entire world.

Variety is not only the spice of life, it is essential to life. Capitalism, by destroying the diversity of life, threatens every living thing. We had best destroy it before it destroys us.

Corporate Control over Genetic Resources Threatens Biodiversity

by Vandana Shiva

About the author: *Vandana Shiva, a physicist and ecologist, is the founder of Navdanya, an India-based movement for biodiversity conservation and farmers' rights. She is the author of several books including* Biopiracy: The Plunder of Nature and Knowledge *and* Stolen Harvest: The Hijacking of the Global Food Supply.

More than 3.5 million people starved to death in the Bengal famine of 1943. Twenty million were directly affected. Export of food grains continued in spite of the fact that people were going hungry. At the time, India was being used as a supply base for the British military. More than one-fifth of India's national output was appropriated for war supplies. The starving Bengal peasants gave up over two-thirds of the food they produced. Dispossessed peasants moved to Calcutta. Thousands of female destitutes were turned into prostitutes. Parents started to sell their children.

As the crisis began, thousands of women organized in Bengal in defense of their food rights. "Open more ration shops" and "Bring down the price of food" were the calls of women's groups throughout Bengal.

After the famine, the peasants also started to organize. At its peak the Tebhaga movement, as it was called, covered 19 districts and involved 6 million people. Everywhere, peasants declared, "We will give up our lives, but we will not give up our rice." In the village of Thumniya, police arrested some peasants who resisted the theft of their harvest. They were charged with "stealing paddy."

A half-century after the Bengal famine, a new and clever system has been put in place that is once again making the theft of the harvest a right and the keeping of the harvest a crime. Hidden behind complex free-trade treaties are innovative ways to steal nature's harvest of seed and nutrition.

Reprinted from Vandana Shiva, "Stuff of Life," *Yes!* Summer 2000, which was adapted from the author's book *Stolen Harvest: The Hijacking of the Global Food Supply* (Cambridge, MA: South End Press, 2000). Copyright © 2000 by Vandana Shiva. Reprinted with permission.

I focus on India both because I am an Indian and because Indian agriculture is being especially targeted by global corporations. However, this phenomenon of the stolen harvest is not unique to India. It is being experienced in every society, as small farms and small farmers are pushed to extinction, as monocultures replace biodiverse crops, and as farming is transformed from the production of nourishing and diverse foods into the creation of markets for genetically engineered seeds, herbicides, and pesticides.

How Farmers View Seed

For centuries, Third World farmers have evolved crops and given us the diversity of plants that provide us nutrition. Indian farmers evolved 200,000 varieties of rice. They bred rice varieties such as Basmati. They bred red rice and brown rice and black rice. They bred rice that grew 18 feet tall in the Gangetic floodwaters and saline-resistant rice that could thrive in coastal water.

The seed, for the farmer, is not merely the source of future plants and food; it is the storage place of culture and history. Free exchange of seed among farmers has been the basis of maintaining biodiversity as well as food security; it involves exchanges of ideas and knowledge, of culture and heritage. It is an accumulation of tradition and of knowledge of how to work the seed. Farmers learn about the plants they want to grow in the future by watching them grow in other farmers' fields.

Paddy, or rice, has religious significance in most parts of India and is an essential component of most religious festivals. The *Akti Festival* in Chattisgarh, where a diversity of indica rices are grown, reinforces the many principles of biodiversity conservation. In Southern India, rice grain is considered auspicious; it is mixed with *kumkum* and turmeric and given as a blessing. New seeds are first worshipped, and only then are they planted. Festivals held before sowing seeds, as well as harvest festivals celebrated in the fields, symbolize people's intimacy with nature.

For the farmer, the field is the mother; worshipping the field is a sign of gratitude toward the Earth, which, as mother, feeds the millions of life forms that are her children.

Claiming Seed as Property

The new intellectual-property-rights regimes, which are being universalized through the Trade Related Intellectual Property Rights Agreement of the World Trade Organization (WTO), allow corporations to usurp the knowledge of the seed and monopolize it by claiming it as their private property. Over time, this results in corporate monopolies over the seed itself. Corporations like RiceTec of the United States are claiming patents on Basmati rice. The soybean, which evolved in East Asia, has been patented by Calgene, which is now owned by Monsanto. Calgene also owns patents on mustard, a crop of Indian origin. Centuries of collective innovation by farmers and peasants are being hijacked by corporations claiming intellectual property rights over plants.

Today, 10 corporations control 32 percent of the commercial seed market, valued at $23 billion, and 100 percent of the market for genetically engineered, or transgenic, seeds. These corporations also control the global agrochemical and pesticide market. Just five corporations control the global trade in grain. In late 1998, Cargill, the largest of these five companies, bought Continental, the second largest, making it the single biggest factor in the grain trade. Monoliths such as Cargill and Monsanto were both actively involved in shaping international trade agreements, in particular the Uruguay Round of the General Agreement on Trade and Tariffs, which led to the establishment of the WTO.

This monopolistic control over agricultural production, along with structural adjustment policies that favor exports, results in floods of exports of foods from the US and Europe to the Third World. As a result of the North American Free Trade Agreement (NAFTA), the proportion of Mexico's food supply that is imported has increased from 20 percent in 1992 to 43 percent in 1996. After 18 months of NAFTA, 2.2 million Mexicans have lost their jobs, and 40 million have fallen into extreme poverty. One out of two peasants is not getting enough to eat. As Victor Suares has stated, "Eating more cheaply on imports is not eating at all for the poor in Mexico."

Engineering Life

Global corporations are not just stealing the harvest of farmers. They are stealing nature's harvest through genetic engineering and patents on life forms. Crops such as Monsanto's Roundup Ready soybeans, designed to be resistant to herbicides, lead to the destruction of biodiversity and increased use of agrochemicals. They can also create highly invasive "superweeds" by transferring the genes for herbicide resistance to weeds.

Crops designed to be pesticide factories, genetically engineered to produce toxins and venom with genes from bacteria, scorpions, snakes, and wasps, can threaten non-pest species and can contribute to the emergence of resistance in pests and hence the creation of "superpests."

To secure patents on life forms and living resources, corporations must claim seeds and plants to be their "inventions" and hence their property. Corporations like Cargill and Monsanto see nature's web of life and cycles of renewal as "theft" of their property. During the debate about the entry of Cargill into India in 1992, the Cargill

"Hidden behind complex free-trade treaties are innovative ways to steal nature's harvest of seed and nutrition."

chief executive stated, "We bring Indian farmers smart technologies, which prevent bees from usurping the pollen." During the United Nations Biosafety Negotiations, Monsanto circulated literature that claimed that "weeds steal the sunshine."

A worldview that defines pollination as "theft by bees" and claims that diverse plants "steal" sunshine is one aimed at stealing nature's harvest. This is a worldview based on scarcity.

A worldview of abundance is the worldview of women in India who leave food for ants on their doorsteps, even as they create the most beautiful art in kolams, mandalas, and rangoli with rice flour. Abundance is the worldview of peasant women who weave beautiful designs of paddy to hang up for birds when the birds do not find grain in the fields. This view of abundance recognizes that, in giving food to other beings and species, we maintain conditions for our own food security. It is the recognition in the Isho Upanishad that the universe is the creation of the Supreme Power meant for the benefits of (all) creation. Each individual life form must learn to enjoy its benefits by farming a part of the system in close relation with other species.

> *"Free exchange of seed among farmers has been the basis of maintaining biodiversity as well as food security."*

In the ecological worldview, when we consume more than we need or exploit nature on principles of greed, we are engaging in theft. In the anti-life view of agribusiness corporations, nature, renewing and maintaining herself, is a thief. Such a worldview replaces abundance with scarcity, fertility with sterility.

What we are seeing is the emergence of food totalitarianism, in which a handful of corporations control the entire food chain and destroy alternatives. The notion of rights has been turned on its head under globalization and free trade. The right to food, the right to safety, the right to culture are all being treated as trade barriers that need to be dismantled.

Save the Seed

In 1987, the Dag Hammarskjold Foundation organized a meeting on biotechnology called "Laws of Life." This watershed event made it clear that the giant chemical companies were repositioning themselves as "life sciences" companies, whose goal was to control agriculture through patents, genetic engineering, and mergers. At that meeting, I decided I would dedicate the next decade of my life to finding ways to prevent monopolies on life and living resources, both through resistance and through building creative alternatives.

The first step I took was to start *Navdanya,* a movement for saving seed, protecting biodiversity, and keeping seed and agriculture free of monopoly control. The Navdanya family has started 16 community seed banks in six states in India. Navdanya today has thousands of members who conserve biodiversity, practice chemical-free agriculture, and have taken a pledge to continue to save and share the seeds and biodiversity they have received as gifts from nature and their ancestors.

On March 5, 1998, on the anniversary of Mohandas Gandhi's call for the salt *satyagraha,* a coalition of more than 2,000 groups started the *bija satyagraha,* a non-cooperation movement opposing patents on seeds and plants. Literally, *satyagraha* means the struggle for truth. Gandhi said, "As long as the superstition that people should obey unjust laws exists, so long will slavery exist. And a nonviolent resister alone can remove such a superstition."

In 1999, news of Monsanto's genetic-engineering trials in India leaked to the press. These trials were being carried out in 40 locations in nine states. State agricultural ministers objected that they had not been consulted on the trials, and they released the locations of the trial sites. Immediately, farmers in Karnataka and Andhra Pradesh uprooted and burned the genetically engineered crops. In Andhra Pradesh, the farmers also got a resolution passed through the regional parliament and put pressure on the government to ban the trials. After the first uprooting by farmers, the government itself uprooted the Bt-crops in other locations.

Food Democracy

In India, the poorest peasants have been organic farmers because they could never afford chemicals. Today, they are joined by a growing international organic movement that consciously avoids chemicals and genetic engineering.

- In Britain, the Genetix Snowball movement, was launched in 1998 when five women uprooted Monsanto's crops in Oxfordshire.
- In February 1999, an alliance of UK farm, consumer, development, and environmental groups launched a campaign for a "Five-Year Freeze" on genetic engineering.
- In 1993 in Switzerland, a grassroots group, the Swiss Working Group on Genetic Engineering, collected 111,000 names favoring a referendum to ban genetic engineering. The biotech industry hired a public relations company for $24 million to defeat the referendum in 1998. But the debate is far from over. A similar referendum was organized by Greenpeace and Global 2000 in Austria.
- In Ireland, the Gaelic Earth Liberation Front dug up a field of Roundup Ready sugar beet at Ireland's Teagase Research Centre at Oakport.
- In France, farmers of *Confederation Paysanne* destroyed Novartis's genetically engineered seeds. France later imposed a moratorium on transgenic crops.

Throughout Europe, bans and moratoriums on genetic engineering, in response to growing citizen pressure, are increasing.

A survey released in November 1998 by the agribusiness-affiliated International Foods Safety Council found that 89 percent of US consumers think food safety is a "very important" issue—more important than crime prevention. Seventy-seven percent were changing their eating habits due to food-safety concerns. A *Time* magazine poll published in its January 13, 1999, issue found that 81 percent of US consumers believe genetically engineered food should be labeled; 58 percent said they would not eat genetically engineered foods if they were labeled. In 1998, over $5 billion worth of organic food was consumed in the US, where the organic market is growing 25 percent annually.

A Democracy of Life

Ecological and organic agriculture is referred to in India as ahimsic krishi, or "nonviolent agriculture," because it is based on compassion for all species and hence the protection of biodiversity in agriculture.

Our movements advocate the recovery of the biodiversity and intellectual commons. By refusing to recognize life's diversity as a corporate invention and hence as corporate property, we are acknowledging the intrinsic value of all species and their self-organizing capacity. By refusing to allow privatization of living resources, we are defending the right to survival of the two-thirds majority that depends on nature's capital and is excluded from markets because of its poverty. The movement is also a defense of cultural diversity, since the majority of diverse cultures do not see other species and plants as "property" but as kin.

This larger democracy of life is the real force of resistance against the brute power of the "life sciences industry," which is pushing millions of species and millions of people to the edge of survival.

These are exciting times. It is not inevitable that corporations will control our lives and rule the world. We have a real possibility to shape our own future. We have an ecological and social duty to ensure that the food that nourishes us is not a stolen harvest. In this duty, we each have the opportunity to work for the freedom and liberation of all species and all people—no matter who we are, no matter where we are.

Commercial High-Yield Farming Practices Preserve Biodiversity

by Dennis T. Avery

About the author: *Dennis T. Avery directs the Center for Global Food Issues at the Hudson Institute, a nonprofit organization that advocates practical approaches to public policy issues.*

The obvious environmental problems and solutions are not necessarily obvious at all. Organic farming and the time-proven techniques of traditional agriculture hold great emotional attraction. Pure foods without chemical fertilizers and pesticides seem clearly preferable to the methods of large agribusiness. Could they be the cure for the unrelenting destruction of earth's forests and its diverse flora and fauna?

Ironically, developed world demands for these "obvious" solutions may push the world into famine and destroy the planet's biodiversity far faster than chemicals and overpopulation. Only the judicious application of the "evils" of high-yield farming may give us the time to prevent such calamities. Contrary to common wisdom, saving the environment and reducing population growth are likely to come about only if governments significantly increase their support for high-yielding crops and advanced farming methods, including the use of fertilizers and pesticides.

The biggest danger facing the world's wildlife is neither pesticides nor population but the potential loss of its habitat. Conversion of natural areas into farmland is the major impact of humans on the natural environment and poses a great threat to biodiversity. About 90 percent of the known species extinctions have occurred because of habitat loss.

Whereas many industrialized countries see their farms occupying less and less of their land, worldwide the opposite is true. The World Bank reports that cities take only 1.5 percent of earth's land, but farms occupy 36 percent. As

Reprinted, with permission, from "Saving Nature's Legacy Through Better Farming," by Dennis T. Avery, *Issues in Science and Technology*, pp. 59–64, Fall 1997 Copyright 1991 by the National Academy of Sciences.

world population climbs toward 8.5 billion in 2040, it will become even more clear how much food needs govern the world's land use. Unless we bolster our efforts to produce high-yielding crops, we face a plow-down of much of the world's remaining forests for low-yield crops and livestock.

For decades and certainly since the 1968 publication of Paul Ehrlich's *The Population Bomb*, overpopulation has riven the world's conscience. Each regional famine catalyzed by crop failures or weather brings it further to the fore. Yet we seem unaware of how crucial the green revolution has been in forestalling famine and simultaneously saving the environment.

By maximizing land use, the green revolution's high-yield crops and farming techniques have been vital in preserving wildlife. By effectively tripling world crop yields since 1960, they have saved an additional 10 to 12 million square miles of wild lands, according to an analysis that I conducted and which was published in early 1997 in *Choices*, the magazine of the American Agricultural Economics Association. Without the green revolution, the world would have lost wild land equal to the combined land area of the United States, Europe, and Brazil. Instead, with hybrid seeds and chemical fertilizers and pesticides, today we crop the same 6 million square miles of land that we did in 1960 and feed 80 percent more people a diet that requires more than twice as many grain-equivalent calories.

The green revolution, however, has had its detractors. Since the publication of Rachel Carson's *Silent Spring* in 1962, developed-world residents have been bombarded with claims that modern farming kills wildlife, endangers children's health, and poisons the topsoil. Understandably, we love the natural ways of life. For many centuries, humans seemed to grow their crops quite well without deadly chemicals that poison soil, plants, insects, and animals. The organic gardening and farming movements look fondly on that ideal. Unfortunately, those techniques are ill suited to the modern world for two strong reasons.

First, they worked in a much less populous world. Such techniques and the plants they favor require large amounts of relatively fertile land supporting small numbers of people. In modern Europe, Asia, and the developing world, such low-yield farming is impractical. Second, many of those techniques are incredibly destructive to soil and forests, degrading biodiversity quickly and irrevocably. Slash-and-burn agriculture, the time-honored primitive farming method, is perhaps the most harmful to the environment.

Ironically, in a world facing the biggest surge in food demand it will

> *"Conversion of natural areas into farmland . . . poses a great threat to biodiversity."*

ever see, many environmentalists who want to preserve natural areas are recommending organic and traditional farming systems that have sharply lower yields than mainstream farms. A recent organic farming "success" at the Rodale Institute achieved grain-equivalent yields from organic farming that were 21 percent lower and required 42 percent more labor. Such yields may be theoretically kinder to the environment, but in practice they would lead us to destroy millions of square miles of additional natural areas.

Meanwhile, Greenpeace and the World Wildlife Fund have gathered millions of European signatures on petitions to ban biotechnology in food production. They do not protest the use of biotechnology in human medicine, but only where it could help preserve nature by increasing farm productivity.

Humans might be able to meet their nutritional needs with less strain on farming resources by eating nuts and tofu instead of meat and milk. So far, however, no society has been willing to do so. For example, a *Vegetarian Times* poll reported that 7 percent of Americans call themselves vegetarians. Two-thirds of these, however, eat meat regularly; 40 percent eat red meat regularly; and virtually all of them eat dairy products and eggs. Fewer than 500,000 Americans are vegan, foregoing all resource-costly livestock and poultry calories. The vegetarian/vegan percentages are similar in other affluent countries.

The reality is that as the world becomes more affluent, the average person will be eating more meat and consuming more agricultural products. If population growth stopped this hour, we would have to double the world's farm output to provide the meat, fruit, and cotton today's 5.9 billion people will demand in 2030 when virtually all will be affluent. There are no plans, nor any funding, for a huge global vegan recruiting campaign. Nor does history offer much hope of one's success.

> *"By maximizing land use, the green revolution's high-yield crops and farming techniques have been vital in preserving wildlife."*

Meanwhile, in what used to be the poor countries, the demand for meat, milk, and eggs is already soaring. Chinese meat consumption has risen 10 percent annually in the past six years. India has doubled its milk consumption since 1980, and two-thirds of its Hindus indicate that they will eat meat (though not beef) when they can afford it.

According to the United Nation's Food and Agricultural Organization (FAO), Asian countries provide about 17 grams of animal protein per capita per day for 3.3 billion people. Europeans and North Americans eat 65 to 70 grams. The Japanese not long ago ate less than 20 grams, but are now nearing 60 grams. By 2030, the world will need to be able to provide 55 grams of animal protein per person for four billion Asians, or they will destroy their own tropical forests to produce it themselves. It will not be possible to stave off disaster for biologically rich areas unless we continue to raise farm yields.

To make room for low-yield farming, we burn and plow tropical forests and drive wild species from their ecological niches. Indonesia is clearing millions of acres of tropical forest for low-quality cattle pastures and to grow low-yielding corn and soybeans on highly erodable soils to feed chickens. Similarly, a World Bank study reports that forests throughout the tropics are losing up to one-half of their species because bush-fallow periods (when farm lands are allowed to return to natural states) are shortened to feed higher populations.

Pessimists have said since the late 1960s that we won't be able to continue increasing yields. However, world grain yields have risen by nearly 50 percent in the meantime. If we'd taken the pessimists' advice to scrap agricultural research when they first offered it, the world would already have lost millions of square miles of wildlife habitat that we still have.

Nor is there any objective indication that the world is running out of

> *"Unfortunately, the world is not gearing up its science and technology resources to meet the agricultural and conservation challenge."*

ways of increasing crop yields and improving farming techniques. For example, world corn yields are continuing to rise as they have since 1960, at about 2.8 percent annually, in what's rapidly becoming the world's key crop. The yield trend has become more erratic, mainly because droughts decrease yield more in an eight-ton field than they do in a one-ton field. U.S. corn breeders are now shooting for populations of 50,000 plants per acre, which is three times the current Corn Belt planting density, and for 300-bushel yields.

Also, the International Rice Research Institute in the Philippines is redesigning the rice plant to get 30 percent more yield. Researchers are putting another 10 percent of the plant's energy into the seed head (supported by fewer but larger stalk shoots). They're using biotechnology techniques to increase resistance to pests and diseases. The new rice has been genetically engineered to resist the tungro virus—humanity's first success against a major virus. The U.S. Food and Drug Administration is close to approving pork growth hormone, which will produce hogs with half as much body fat and 20 percent more lean meat, using 25 percent less feed grain per hog. Globally, that would be equal to another 20 to 30 millions tons of corn production per year.

The world has achieved strong productivity gains from virtually all of its investments in agricultural research. The problem is mainly that we haven't been investing enough. One reason for underinvesting is pessimism about how much can be gained through research. But if humanity succeeds only in doubling instead of tripling farm output per acre, the effort will still save millions of square miles of land. Besides, the more pessimistic we feel about agricultural research, the more eager we should be to raise research investments, because there is no doubt that we will need more food.

Throughout history, soil erosion has been by far the biggest problem affecting farming sustainability. Modern high-yield farming is changing that situation dramatically. Simple arithmetic tells us that tripling the yields on the best cropland automatically cuts soil erosion per ton of food produced by about two-thirds. It also avoids pushing crops onto steep or fragile acres.

Relatively new methods such as conservation tillage and no-till farming are also making a big difference. Conservation tillage discs crop residues into the top few inches of soil, creating millions of tiny dams against wind and water erosion. In addition to saving topsoil, conservation tillage produces far more earthworms and subsoil bacteria than any plow-based system. No-till farming involves no plowing at all. The soil is never exposed to the elements. The seeds are planted through a cover crop that has been killed by herbicides. The Soil and Water Conservation Society says that use of these systems can cut soil erosion per acre by 65 to 95 percent.

Organic farmers reject both these systems because they depend on chemical weed killers, not plowing and hoeing, to control weeds. However, these powerful conservation farming systems are already being used on hundreds of millions of acres in the United States, Canada, Australia, Brazil, and Argentina. They have been used successfully in Asia and even tested successfully in Africa.

The model farm of the future will use still more powerful seeds, conservation tillage, and integrated pest management along with still better veterinary medications. It will use global positioning satellites, computers, and intensive soil sampling ("precision farming") to apply exactly the seeds and chemicals for optimum yields, with no leaching of chemicals into streams. Even then, high-yield farming will not offer zero risk to either the environment or to humans. But it will offer near-zero and declining risk, which will be more than offset by huge increases in food security and wild lands saved. . . .

Unfortunately, the world is not gearing up its science and technology resources to meet the agricultural and conservation challenge. U.S. funding for agricultural research has declined for decades in real terms, though the cost and complexity of the research projects continue to rise with the size of the challenge. The federal and state governments increased their spending on agricultural research from $1.02 billion in 1970 to $1.65 billion in 1990, a one-third decline in constant dollars. Public funding rose to $1.8 billion in 1996. Likewise, private sector agricultural research spending rose from $1.5 billion in 1970 to $3.15 billion in 1990, a 15 percent real decline.

Overseas, the research funding picture is worse. Europe has never spent heavily on agricultural research. Only a few of the developing world countries, including Brazil, China, and Zimbabwe, have even sporadically spent the few millions of dollars needed to adapt research to their own situations. All told, the entire world's agricultural research investment is probably less than $15 billion a year.

A telling example of the world's cavalier attitude toward agricultural research occurred in 1994, when the United States and other donor nations failed to come up with a large part of the budget for the Consultative Group on International Agricultural Research (CGIAR). CGIAR is the key international vehicle for creating high-yielding crops, supporting a network of 16 agricultural research centers in developing countries. Thus, global agricultural research almost literally went bankrupt at the very moment when the world was pledging another $17 billion for condoms and contraceptive pills at the UN meeting on population in Cairo. The World Bank subsequently stepped in on a conditional basis to keep the CGIAR research network running.

Historically, the U.S. Agency for International Development (AID) provided about 25 percent of CGIAR research funding, or about $60 million per year. Currently [1997], this has fallen to about $30 million per year in much cheaper dollars, or about 10 percent of AID's budget. Indeed, despite the centers' success in raising world crop yields, AID has since shifted its priorities sharply from agricultural research to family planning. Given the sharp downward trends in birthrates in developing countries, additional family planning funds are likely to make only a modest difference in the world's population. However, Western intellectuals and journalists highly approve of population management.

In sum, world spending on agricultural research is tiny, especially if you consider that in 1996, the U.S. food industry alone produced $782 billion in goods and services and that the federal government subsidizes farmers to the tune of nearly $100 billion a year. (The European Union spends another $150 billion a year on farm subsidies.) Meanwhile, agricultural research has saved perhaps one billion lives from famine, increased food calories by one-third for four billion people in the developing world, and prevented millions of square miles of often biologically rich land from being plowed down. . . .

> *"Agricultural research has . . . prevented millions of square miles of often biologically rich land from being plowed down."*

Feeding the world's people while preserving biologically rich land will require two key things: more agricultural research and freer world trade in farm products. Expanded agricultural research should be the top priority.

Congress should double the federal government's $1.4 billion annual investment [as of 1997] in agricultural research and adopt substantially higher farm yields as one of the nation's top research priorities. No other nation has the capacity to step into the U.S. research role in time to save the wild lands. . . .

In addition, in order to use the world's best farmland for maximum output, farm trade must be liberalized. Farm subsidies and farm trade barriers, although they are beginning to be reduced, have not only drained hundreds of billions of dollars in scarce capital away from economic growth and job creation, they now represent one of the biggest dangers to preservation of biologically diverse lands. The key dynamic in the farm-trade arena is Asia's present and growing population density. Without an easy flow of farm products and services, densely populated Asian countries will be tempted to try to rely too much on domestic food production. But it will be extremely difficult to do. By 2030, Asia will have about eight times as many people per acre of cropland as will the Western Hemisphere. It already has the world's most intensive land use. In reality, countries reduce their food security with self-sufficiency. Droughts and plagues that cut crop yields are regional, not global.

The United States must convince the world that free trade in farm products would benefit all, particularly those in developing countries. . . .

Finally, a renewed emphasis on high-yield farming aimed at preserving biodiversity will require a change in mind-set on the part of key actors: environmentalists, farmers, and government regulators in particular. The environmental movement must postpone its long-cherished goal of an agriculture free from man-made chemicals and give up its lingering hope that constraining food production can somehow limit population growth. Until we understand biological processes well enough to get ultrahigh yields from organic farming, environmentalists must join with farmers in seeking a research agenda keyed primarily to rapid gains in farm yields whether they are organic or not.

> *"High-yield farming feeds people, saves land, and fosters biodiversity."*

Farmers must accept that environmental goals are valid and urgent in a world that produces enough food to prevent famine. They must collaborate constructively and helpfully in efforts such as protecting endangered species and improving water quality. Without such reasonable efforts, farmers will not get public support for high-yield farming systems and liberalized farm trade.

Government regulators at all levels must realize that chemical fertilizers, pesticides, and biotechnology techniques are powerful conservation tools. For example, the Environmental Protection Agency (EPA) must stop regarding a pesticide banned as a victory for the environment. Having dropped the economic rationale protecting some high-yield pesticide uses, EPA should now take into consideration the potential for new pest-control technologies to save wild lands and wild species through higher yields, both nationally and globally.

Education can play a big role in changing the mind-sets of the various actors. For example, the U.S. Department of State, which has already announced an environmental focus for U.S. foreign policy, could work to ensure that the concept of high-yield conservation is appropriately encouraged in international forums. The U.S. Department of Education could collaborate with USDA to help the nation's students understand the environmental benefits of high farm yields.

On all fronts, this is a time for pragmatism. We know that high-yield farming feeds people, saves land, and fosters biodiversity. We know that agricultural research is the surest path to those same goals. The narrower goals should be subsumed into the larger ones for the short- to mid-term future. A combination of agricultural science and policy can combine for the welfare of the planet, its people, its animals, and its plants. Achieving those crucial aims will mean rethinking population, farming methods, fertilizers, and many related controversial aspects of agriculture.

Genetic Engineering May Be a Boon to Biodiversity

by Alvin L. Young

About the author: *Alvin L. Young is director of the Center for Risk Excellence at the U.S. Department of Energy's Argonne National Laboratory in Illinois.*

What should we do with genetically modified foods in the twenty-first century? A more appropriate question perhaps would be what will the twenty-first century be without genetically modified foods? Before we consider either question, let us examine a future scenario. By its very nature, agriculture disrupts the natural ecosystem. Combine this very significant disruption of the land, water, and air with the unceasing march of mankind via urban sprawl and population growth and the future may indeed be bleak.

Increasingly, the media are focusing on individuals who tell us that the future should be one of vast green spaces interlaced with a sustainable agriculture. With minimal use of pesticides, fertilizers, and energy, an incredible variety of bountiful and healthful foods will be produced. Under their scenario, the future will be free of food irradiation, agribusiness conglomerates, and genetically modified organisms. Don't misunderstand me, I would love a world free of pollution, as green as Ireland and with a balanced global ecosystem abounding with species diversity. But I am a realist. The answer to mankind's unchecked population growth and need for habitable land and water is science and technology, not pretty words and empty phrases.

In an era of great regulatory uncertainty and government oversight, farmers are in a very risky business. Vocal environmentalists frequently demand food that is grown with organic fertilizers rather than pesticides or hormones, "free-ranging," and nurtured with the purity of bottled water. Yet, they demand all this at a price that allows them to commit less than 15 percent of their income for food. Having spent so little to support the real cost to the farmer, they then sponsor "Farm Aid" concerts and sing of the loss of the family farm. But do they really recognize the challenges facing the agricultural producing community?

From Alvin L. Young, "U.S.: Develop and Deploy." This article appeared in the December 1999 issue of, and is reprinted with permission from, *The World & I*, a publication of The Washington Times Corporation, © 1999.

Farmers know that to stay in business, feed their families, and plan for their future, they must maximize their profits. That means keeping the cost of inputs such as fertilizers, pesticides, and tillage low to produce the largest yields that meet the highest standards of food quality for marketing. Farmers also know that to compete successfully, they need every opportunity and advantage that science and technology can offer. It's a historical fact that the first farmer to adopt a technology profits most from its adoption. Increasingly, farmers are being forced to raise crops on marginal lands. They must compete for water rights with large cities and find more efficient ways to harvest, process, and transport produce and livestock to global markets. This is the setting in which we now find the first "fruits" of molecular biology.

Discovering how DNA stores and transmits the genetic information (genome) from one generation of an organism to the next, and how the genome defines a species or regulates an ecosystem, has been the great scientific quest of the past 40 years. We are now sequencing the genomes of hundreds of species of plants, animals, and microorganisms. . . . Within the next few years, the gene maps for most of our domesticated plants and animals will be available in powerful electronic databases.

In addition to sequencing the genome, we are on the path that extends from understanding fundamental genetic information to understanding how the whole physiological system of an organism works. How do plants withstand the attack of pests, or how do they regulate temperatures, maintain salt balance, and efficiently use the available water? And how can we manipulate them so they use light more effectively in ways that enhance the level of nutrients or storage products? Our current goal is to use the diversity of genes that nature provides to develop new combinations of genomes that favor greater efficiency of production under human and environmental stresses while also increasing the healthfulness and usefulness of the products. In the twenty-first century, even greater benefits of this technology can be realized.

A New Scenario

A revolution in agriculture is under way. Large areas of genetically modified crops of soybeans, corn, cotton, and canola have already been grown successfully in the Western Hemisphere. In 1999, in the United States, 15 million hectares (37 million acres) were planted with transgenic crops for which the weeds, insects, and viruses were easily controlled. Compared to their non-transgenic cousins, these crops required less pesticide and tillage and minimized soil erosion.

Worldwide about 28 million hectares (69.1 million acres) of transgenic plants are being grown in 1999. This area is predicted to triple in the next five years, assuming that producers and consumers are shown the benefits of this new technology. It is anticipated that the molecular revolution will occur in three generations. The first generation, which is represented by the current transgenic crops, is intended to profit the producer. The second generation will benefit the consumer, while the third generation will benefit mankind and the global ecosystem.

Exciting ongoing research shows that transgenic plants can produce healthier food and be used as chemical factories. We know that there's more to good nutrition than protein, carbohydrates, oil, vitamins, and minerals. Many other food components contribute to health, as demonstrated by recent research showing that phytochemicals and nutriceuticals enhance wellness. Many phytochemicals appear to be associated with lower morbidity in adult life. The goal of increasing their content in agronomic crops will become compelling. Meanwhile, an effort is under way to change the types of lipids (fats) that occur in our crops, fruits, and vegetables, making products healthier for the consumer. An exciting aspect of this research is that the most efficient way to obtain the results is through the seed. These seeds can be made available to every farmer, rich or poor, worldwide.

Vast regions of the earth are much too salty to support agriculture. Freshwater will be the most crucial and limiting natural resource in the twenty-first century. Unless agriculture can develop new solutions, wars will be fought over this resource. But thanks to molecular (genetic) engineering, plants are being modified to flourish even when watered with concentrated salt solutions. Research is progressing on drought tolerance, and identification of genes providing that tolerance will soon be available to plant breeders. The

> *"The charge that biotechnology is eliminating species is without fact."*

beauty of the technology is that only the genes of interest need be inserted, whereas traditional breeding requires the movement of thousands of genes, as well as years of effort to backcross to obtain those key genes. More important, the insertions of genes involve local breeds, those varieties that the plant breeder has spent years developing for a particular climate and population. The charge that biotechnology is eliminating species is without fact. Thanks to the new technology, we are in an incredible position to save and preserve the world's germ plasm.

Disease and pest resistance is another crucial area for the breeder and molecular biologist. We are seeing significant increases in mass mortalities due to disease outbreaks, and a tidal wave of exotic species is transforming ecosystems worldwide. Increased human mobility, the shipping and entry of infected cargo, and the impact of climate variability all promote these outbreaks and invasions. Clearly, using biocides and introducing natural predators cannot be the only answers.

Understanding the molecular basis for infection, invasion, and predation will allow ecologists to use the genes that nature provides to reestablish the balance. Far-fetched? I don't think so. In a hundred years, we will look back over the twenty-first century and marvel at the impact biotechnology had.

The Free Market Can Enhance Agricultural Biodiversity

by David Schap and Andrew T. Young

About the authors: *David Schap is an economics professor at the College of the Holy Cross in Worcester, Massachusetts. Andrew T. Young is a graduate of that institution and a doctoral student at Emory University in Atlanta, Georgia.*

From the early 1900s, American farmers were becoming well able to "read" maize and recognize which physical characteristics translated into varying yields, quality, insect and disease resistance, and even aesthetic value. By 1925, the University of Illinois Department of Agronomy compiled a list of distinct corn strains totaling 19 (7 white strains and 12 yellow strains). By 1990, a market for privately produced hybrid maize seed in the United States had developed in excess of $2 billion a year. Along with this market, and other hybrid seed markets, came the establishment of legally enforceable private property rights in the form of trade secret laws and the patentability of privately bred and engineered strains.

The existence of this market has brought sharp criticism from some individuals and organizations concerned with the effect of the market on biodiversity. K. Dawkins, M. Thom, and C. Carr conclude:

> The emphasis on finding and isolating plants with the most marketable traits leads to the decline of other plant species, as only those required to create new techno-varieties are cultivated. . . . In addition, the privatization of genetic resources that have been engineered and patented accelerates the trend toward monocultural cropping.

According to such a view, the private maize seed market is detrimental to biodiversity. In contrast, others highlight the benefits associated with the private maize seed market. Stephen Smith, a research fellow at Pioneer Hi-Bred International Inc., one of the largest producers of hybrid maize seed worldwide,

Excerpted from David Schap and Andrew T. Young, "Enterprise and Biodiversity: Do Market Forces Yield Diversity of Life?" *Cato Journal*, vol. 19, no. 1 (Spring/Summer 1999). Copyright © Cato Institute. All rights reserved. Reprinted with permission.

noted: "If U.S. maize agriculture was today still using [nonprivate] varieties, U.S. maize production would be down annually by about 40–52 percent from its current level." According to this view, the market for hybrid maize seed has made the production of maize, a staple food source, more efficient and abundant, benefiting humans fundamentally through enhanced nourishment.

At the root there appears to be a conflict between the efficiency of the market and the preservation of biodiversity. The conflict is real, however, only if the market is at odds with biodiversity. Does the market destroy biodiversity? We contend that it does not. Rather the market often can, and indeed does, *provide* biodiversity—both deliberately and as an unintended consequence of market forces. . . .

Biodiversity and the Market

Consider the question of whether biodiversity can be a good provided by the market. Roger Sedjo observes: "It is well recognized that wild genetic resources—the genetic constitutions of plants and animals—have substantial social and economic value as repositories of genetic information." The value of such genetic information can be realized within, but not exclusively within, the development of drugs and pharmaceuticals, the commercial markets for hybrid seed, the selective breeding of cattle, and the enjoyment many of us find intrinsic in the many shapes and forms of nature. But can these biological resources be preserved and provided under a system of private property rights that are exchanged via markets? Many individuals and organizations feel that the market mechanism of resource allocation is incompatible with, and a threat to, biodiversity. For instance, the Institute for Agriculture and Trade Policy has expressed deep concern that "the privatization of [biological] knowledge threatens biodiversity." Even popular economic textbooks speak of "market failure" in the case of various environmental issues, including biodiversity. . . . Two economists [P.I. Olson and J.A. Swaney] who have focused their attention on biodiversity have gone so far as to write: "Pollution, population, and the market—these are the three principal pressures threatening biodiversity."

Is the market system at odds with biodiversity? The market is the mechanism by which private property rights to utilize resources are exchanged between individuals, or groups of individuals, at prices that

> *"The market often can . . . provide biodiversity—both deliberately and as an unintended consequence of market forces."*

render the exchanges beneficial to the parties involved. . . . Well-defined property rights include the right to use, the right to receive revenues from use, and the right to transfer.

Before one can explore the compatibility of the market system with biodiversity, one must ponder not only whether the property rights to biodiversity itself can be privately held, but also whether property rights to biological traits, knowledge, species, tissues, cells, and genes can be privately held. These issues affect the direct provision of biodiversity in the market, as well as the indirect provision of biodiversity as a natural byproduct of market interaction.

To begin with some basics, a dictionary definition for biodiversity is: "Biological diversity in an environment as indicated by numbers of different species of plants and animals" [Merriam-Webster's Collegiate Dictionary, 10th ed., 1993]. This is simplistic in that it does not reveal the vast amount of biodiversity recognized *within* a given species; nevertheless the definition is useful in that it points out that biodiversity is found in different frameworks—the dictionary terms these frameworks "environment[s]." This is important because biodiversity is not solely interpreted in a global sense; biodiversity exists as well within smaller frameworks, such as a farmer's fields, an individual's backyard, genetic make-ups within one unique species, and the greenhouse of a flower shop.

Depending on the context, biodiversity need not necessarily be a good thing. Consider the horticulturist who diligently pulls weeds and sprays his or her prize-winning flower garden with pesticides, or the tropical fish hobbyist who regularly cleans the aquarium so that specific fish are the only thriving life forms. In flower and vegetable gardens, aquariums, pet stores, hospitals, and even our own bodies (consider what we use penicillin for), increasing biodiversity can certainly

> *"Game ranches are quite biodiverse in their livestock."*

foster disutility. Nevertheless, for convenience sake, biodiversity will be thought of as a good throughout the remaining discussion.

In many cases, biodiversity itself is indeed a good and falls under well-defined property rights. In situations characterized by low transaction costs, voluntary exchanges of individuals and groups of individuals assure that the good is provided to the mutual benefit of the concerned parties.

Game Ranching

Consider now a specific case in which biodiversity is a good with well-defined property rights that are exchanged in a fluid market, namely game ranching:

> Game ranching is a truly private enterprise. It is the private ownership of wildlife carried out on private property, typically for profit. In the U.S., the ownership of domestic wildlife is divided between state and federal governments. Most game ranchers raise "exotics," that is, non-native animals not traditionally farmed or ranched. Those species can be privately owned under U.S. law [quoted from Ike Sugg, *Wall Street Journal*, August 31, 1992].

These game ranches are quite biodiverse in their livestock. Ike Sugg also reports, for example, that the Exotic Wildlife Association, an international game ranching organization, estimated its ownership in 1992 at 200,000 head of approximately 125 species. Interestingly, Sugg further notes that over 19,000 of those head belonged to species which are considered threatened or endangered in their natural environments; and some species, such as the Scimitar-horned oryx, owe their present existence to game ranchers. In the case of game ranching, profit motivates ranchers to cultivate a product— biodiversity of game—as an investment, the cost of which is less than hunters value the chance at exotic sport, pelts, and meat. The result: biodiversity is provided by the exchange of property rights from ranchers to hunters.

Fish, Tea, and Horses

Consider next the commonplace case of tropical fish collectors. Collectors gain utility from maintaining populations of tropical fish in aquariums and, as one would suspect, their demand is answered by other parties who are willing to supply the fish. Mbuna Coast Aquatics, located in Austin, Texas, was established in 1994 and has since specialized in providing tropical fish collectors with different types of African cichlids (rockfish), native to Africa's Great Rift Lakes. The company ships these fish to customers, the fish having been "selectively raised or carefully imported either from [their] hatchery or from other dedicated hobbyists." Once more, a profit-motivated supplier invests in the cultivation of a certain frame of biodiversity at a cost less than what it would cost those who demand that frame of biodiversity, and the result is mutually beneficial exchange on the market.

Situations in which individuals value biodiversity itself constitute but one way in which the market can provide biodiversity. Biodiversity can also be produced as a byproduct of the market. Consider the demand for tea. Many consumers have a favorite brand, or a narrow range of favorite teas. The consumer who enjoys Earl Grey may not care at all about the diversity of tea plants on the planet; the same would be true of the consumer who fancies only green tea. However, the Ten Ren Tea and Ginseng Company of New York, New York, provides teas to a wide range of these tea consumers. Owned and operated by fourth generation tea farmers, Ten Ren Tea and Ginseng Company explains that it grows and processes more than 30 varieties of tea from different leaves native to different regions of the world. Even though tea consumers need not care about a biodiverse supply of tea leaves for brewing, the market, catering to the numerous desires of individuals, provides such a biodiverse supply. Furthermore, Ten Ren Tea

> *"As the market furnishes private goods to private demanders, biodiversity can arise spontaneously."*

and Ginseng Company need not be concerned with tea leaf biodiversity in any moral or ethical sense, but need only have a commercial interest in tea leaf biodiversity for such biodiversity to be brought forth as an unintended consequence of market processes.

Also consider Select Breeders Service, Inc., a company specializing in stallion semen "cryopreservation." For horse breeders who are either looking to profit through the virility of their stallions, or looking to inseminate their mares with sperm from a stallion with desirable traits, Select Breeders Service will freeze stallion semen and ship it nationwide. The frozen product remains viable in cryogenic freeze for over eight years (a figure based on the longest term supported by the success of Select Breeders Service in achieving the pregnancies of mares). Once again, no horse breeder need care about biodiversity for its own sake. Stallion owners need only concern themselves with the profits attainable through the sale of their stallions' semen. Mare owners need only care about impregnating their horses with what will someday be a beautiful, fast horse. And once again, Select Breeders Service, Inc. need only be concerned with the profit to be gained with their cryogenic and transportation services, including a $150 handling fee for shipment of the good. Still, the result is genetic (bio)diversity being shipped nationwide to be combined with other sources of genetic diversity. Because purchasing customers have diverse individual preferences of equine traits, biodiversity of horses obtains.

> *"Biodiversity . . . is a good that can be provided by self-interested participants in the market."*

Market Forces

Our examples point to the fact that market provision of biodiversity occurs in two essentially different contexts: first, as a direct product, when biodiversity itself is sought by demanders and furnished directly by suppliers (such as with game ranching or tropical fish); and second, more subtly, as a naturally occurring byproduct, as when particular private goods are sought by idiosyncratic demanders and are furnished by suppliers who unintentionally provide biodiversity (such as with tea). In the latter context, the resultant biodiversity can be considered unintentional in multiple ways. First of all, it is the prospect of gains from trade that motivates the market behavior of suppliers and demanders, not especially or necessarily a concern for biodiversity. Also, when a profit-motivated, individual supplier furnishes a biodiverse product line it may merely be because that supplier happens to deal with a variety of demanders, none of whom individually need care about product (bio)diversity. In addition, even in situations in which specialized suppliers provide only a singular product to specific demanders, suppliers nonetheless individually contribute to an aggregate biodiversity that was no part of their intention. Like many other salubrious consequences of market forces, no one has to plan for biodiversity in these contexts, but it happens nonetheless.

As the market furnishes private goods to private demanders, biodiversity can arise spontaneously. Even more remarkable is that market-induced biodiversity can emerge in contexts in which biodiversity is itself a public good, meaning a good that has the characteristics of being nonrival (many can consume it jointly without interference) and nonexclusive (if it is provided to any one consumer, it is provided to many, perhaps all consumers). By way of example, . . . consider biodiversity of maize seed as being a public good: all of us simultaneously may consume the existence/preservation of multiple strains of maize seed (though, of course, not the seed itself); and if multiple strains exist in the world for any one of us, they exist for all of us. . . . Here again, as previously noted, the provision of biodiversity need be no one's intention or conscious plan. Biodiversity arises as a natural byproduct of commerce. . . .

In addressing the concerns surrounding the issue of preserving and enhancing biodiversity, we hope to have reconciled knowledge of market forces and environmental awareness. We have argued that biodiversity, to the extent that it is desirable, is a good that can be provided by self-interested participants in the market. Concrete examples document both the direct market provision of biodiversity and its indirect occurrence as a natural byproduct of commerce. . . .

Since the time of Adam Smith, it has been recognized that self-interested actors are often led by an invisible hand to undertake private actions that yield desirable social outcomes which are no part of any individual's intention. Concerning the portion of our analysis highlighting the indirect market provision of biodiversity, we have in essence proposed and defended a Smithian corollary: biodiversity is frequently an unintended yet desirable consequence of market forces.

Chapter 4

How Can the World's Biological Diversity Best Be Preserved?

The Search for Biodiversity Solutions: An Overview

by Fred Powledge

About the author: *Fred Powledge is an agricultural research consultant and a writer specializing in environmental and agricultural issues.*

More than 11 years ago [in 1986], a group of prominent scientists gathered in Washington, DC, to report on a new way of looking at the planet and the people who use it. The staff of the National Research Council, which cosponsored the conference with the Smithsonian Institution, came up with a new term to describe the subject of the inquiry: biodiversity.

The word (spelled Bio Diversity and sometimes BioDiversity in documents at the time), was short for "biological diversity," nine syllables that refer, in the words of Harvard entomologist E.O. Wilson, to the "variation in the entirety of life on the planet."

The conferees at the 1986 National Forum on BioDiversity approached their subject from many angles, reflecting disciplines that are not known for their eagerness to communicate with one another: land and marine biology, geology, entomology, environmentalism, zoo management, government forestry, grassland ecology, and agricultural economics. On one matter they agreed, as stated by Wilson in a 1988 book based on the forum (*Bio Diversity.* National Academy Press, Washington, DC): Biological diversity was in a state of "unprecedented urgency" brought on by rapid population growth, extinction of species caused by habitat elimination, and discoveries of new, beneficial uses for many previously neglected organisms.

Assessing the State of Biodiversity

In October 1997, many of the original forum participants, along with a number of newcomers, gathered again at the National Academy of Sciences to assess the state of biodiversity. They were able to cite some progress in addressing the "unprecedented urgency." One frequently mentioned example was the

Reprinted, with permission, from Fred Powledge, "Biodiversity at the Crossroads," *BioScience*, May 1998; © 1998 American Institute of Biological Sciences.

world's accelerated attention to climate change, precipitated by the then-imminent 1997 Kyoto global warming conference, which began in early December. Another was New York City's decision to put money into continued protection of its vast upstate watersheds, which deliver high-quality drinking water to the city, rather than to invest in costly treatment plants to make polluted Hudson River water potable. But those who attended the forum also delivered dire warnings about the deteriorating state of the world's biodiversity.

Judging from the comments of most of the four dozen speakers, there is ample reason to be pessimistic about biodiversity's future. The world seems to have moved only sluggishly to face such threats to diversity as rapid population growth (with accompanying demand for food and habitat), deforestation, global climate change, and degradation of Earth's soil and water, all of which destroy or alter biological diversity at a previously unheard-of rate. Peter Raven, the Academy's home secretary and head of the Missouri Botanical Garden, set the tone at the outset when he declared: "We have every reason to be pessimistic about the future. . . . The world has moved downhill a great way since the first forum, and we haven't done anything" in the way of solving the problems of biodiversity that is "consistent with the threats."

After more than three days of intense discussion, it was clear that the people who study biodiversity's destiny don't completely agree on what that destiny is. Furthermore, they are still lamenting the fact, as did Wilson and others in 1986, that science has identified scarcely more than a tiny fraction of the organisms that are out there. And for those plants and animals that have been found and identified, science still doesn't know how to measure their importance. An indication of our uncertainty about what is there comes from Sir Robert M. May of the University of Oxford, who places the total number of species in the world at somewhere between 2 million and 100 million. "I think a plausible range could be 5 to 15 million, and if I had to guess, I'd guess around 7 million," he said. Researchers are identifying about 10,000 new species each year, May added.

But although knowledge may be scant, that doesn't mean that a lot of people aren't committed to solving the problems of biodiversity. From the halls of the National Academy of Sciences to the laboratories and field books of researchers in the world's poorest countries, a loose and diverse fellowship of scientists, policymakers, non-governmental agency staffers, and environmentalists is devoting its energies to heading off what it sees as Earth's sixth great extinction. As was evident at the 11-year reunion of the forum in 1997, this time known as the Forum on Nature and Human Society, the crusade to identify and save biodiversity is taking on a new degree of seriousness.

What's in a Name?

One of the problems related to biodiversity that was discussed at the forum was the need to identify, count, and classify the world's species. Many speakers complained that science is still taking baby steps when it comes to knowing what organisms are in the forests and in the oceans—let alone how their significance should be measured. May spoke of science's "differential attention" to species that results in abundant knowledge about birds but "little affection for nematodes."

May's countryman, David Hawksworth, deplored society's lack of knowledge about soil in particular. Hawksworth is director of the United Kingdom's International Mycological Institute and president of the International Union of Biological Sciences. Science, he said, knows "something . . . of the functional interconnections of different groups of organisms—you see straightaway that fungi are very important there at the base—but the ignorance is absolutely huge when we start to look at numbers of species of bacteria, fungi, nematodes, and so on, which are clearly crucial in how systems operate. When we start to look at what happens in soil, we even lack the techniques for examining biodiversity in a standardized way and relating what the organisms do to functions of ecological relevance."

If science is still in the dark about what goes on in soil, it is abysmally unenlightened about the oceans. Jerry Schubel, president of the New England Aquarium in Boston, said that "our knowledge of the world ocean and the biodiversity it supports is very fragmented," despite (or because) the ocean covers 71 percent of Earth's surface and is "the planet's greatest repository of biological diversity." As on land, the immense storehouse of genetic diversity in the oceans—particularly the near-shore areas—is being destroyed by human developments faster than it can be catalogued.

> *"The people who study biodiversity's destiny don't completely agree on what that destiny is."*

Why is it so important to find, count, name, and classify millions of species that previously were ignored or simply not seen? BioNET-International, an organization of systematists, puts it succinctly: "The name is the key to knowledge. No name—no information. Wrong name— wrong information." Science has always reveled in discovering and cataloguing the most minute components of life, but the search has been given new impetus by several recent trends. The most frequently mentioned of these was unprecedented habitat destruction, much of it in the tropical areas, which house the majority of the world's diversity.

In addition, enormous strides in science's ability to look at organisms at the molecular level have opened up new worlds of possibilities for using genetic material from diverse species in medicine, agriculture, and industry. In a world that is acutely aware of intellectual property rights and patents, genes are money. Moreover, the shrinking of the world by global trade has increased chances that non-indigenous species can invade new territories and wreak genetic havoc there. Finally, as our list of potential new uses of biological diversity expands, our ignorance of what is out there becomes ever more apparent.

Hawksworth is a major player in an effort to assemble the correct names and correct information. At the forum he promoted an effort called Systematics Agenda 2000, an international coalition of individuals and organizations with a lofty goal: "To discover, describe, and classify the world's species." Once global species diversity is inventoried, Systematics Agenda 2000 wants to synthesize the data into "a predictive classification system" and put the information into retrievable form.

> *"The crusade to identify and save biodiversity is taking on a new degree of seriousness."*

The benefits of such an inventory would be significant, according to the coalition. Society's storehouse of useful resources would be expanded, conservationists and policymakers would have higher quality data on which to base their decisions, newfound knowledge of species diversity would help researchers discover new products and produce better food crops and medicines, and baseline data would be useful in monitoring climate and ecosystem change.

Alien Invaders

The systematics community has begun a serious response to the challenge of biodiversity ignorance, but the worlds of research and policy are less advanced when it comes to another threat: alien species, which disrupt and in some cases wipe out naturally occurring biological diversity.

Daniel Simberloff, of the University of Tennessee, called the problem of non-indigenous species a "colossal" one. It is also a growing one, thanks to increased air traffic and changes in global trade. Alien species, Simberloff said, easily disrupt entire ecosystems and the services those ecosystems provide. They replace native species, change existing water- or nitrogen-cycling regimes, deprive indigenous animals of their normal diets, introduce new pathogens against which native species have no defenses, and change the genetic makeup of native species by mating with them.

Solving the problem of non-indigenous species, Simberloff said at the Washington forum, will not be easy. Keeping the non-natives out is well-nigh impossible; furthermore, he said, "risk assessment procedures for introduced species are in their infancy. They basically rely on the guesses of teams of experts. . . . In addition, they're enormously expensive." Simberloff rejects a "black list" system, which bans known troublemaker species, in favor of a "white list" approach, in which "any species proposed for introduction should have been subjected to some sort of review and approved" as harmless to native biodiversity before being allowed to enter a new environment. But many special interest groups, ranging from importers of exotic pets and ornamental plants to hunters and fishers, strongly oppose such action.

Running through many conversations about biodiversity these days, and omnipresent during the three days of the Washington forum, was the specter of a frightening word: extinction. It was explicit or implicit in virtually every presentation at the meeting: Many researchers are convinced that the world, which has been through at least five major extinctions in its history, is entering another. Thomas E. Lovejoy, counselor for biodiversity and environmental affairs at the Smithsonian Institution, told his colleagues that although biodiversity loss "proceeds in increments which often seem inconsequential, there is virtual unanimity among professional scientists that, given present trends, the planet is likely to be ravaged biologically with the loss of one-quarter to one-half of all species within a century."

Stuart L. Pimm, of the University of Tennessee spoke on the chilling topic, "The Sixth Extinction: How Large, How Soon, and Where?" Concentrating on bird life, for which comprehensive global statistics are available, Pimm and graduate student Thomas M. Brooks reckoned the rate of bird extinctions in Earth's previous history, and accepted the calculations of BirdLife International of Cambridge, UK, that 1100 species of birds worldwide are "on the verge of extinction."

It is well known that bird species are adversely affected by loss of habitat. Pimm and Brooks used that knowledge together with remote sensing data on the scope and speed of habitat fragmentation through deforestation to predict the number of species that will eventually become extinct.

By applying what they called "mathematical witchcraft" on exponential decay and half-life in fragmented habitats, Pimm and Brooks calculated the half-life of species persistence to be approximately 50 years. Therefore, they argued, "if the current rates of habitat destruction of forest [continue], 50 percent of all the planet's species will be on the path to extinction, and the 50-year half-life, the ticking time bomb of destruction, will have been set on a much larger scale for many, many more species.

"In short, on the basis of what we are doing now, which has already inflated the rates of extinction to 1000 times what they should have been, a species now does not last a million years; it lasts a thousand years. What we're going to do in the future is going to make species last on average only a hundred years."

Climbing Down from the Ivory Tower

Warnings of imminent danger were commonplace at the Washington forum and in other conversations about biodiversity. Still, there was a noticeable tendency among many of the scientists at the forum (and virtually all of the nonscientists) to move the issue out of the comfortable towers and laboratories of academe and into the rough, unpredictable, and sometimes dangerous world of practicality—the world in which biological diversity lives and dies.

Gary K. Meffe, a conservation biologist from the University of Florida, complained at the Washington forum that the culture of the university system, especially in the United States, "does little to foster creativity and does a lot to promote conservatism and the status quo." With its "territorialities and high disciplinary walls," the campus rewards conformity and is obsessed with increased funding, rather than with solving problems. Consequently, Meffe says, much of the real action in biology conservation is taking place off campus— even in industries that make their livings through resource extraction. He offered "the metadiscipline of conservation biology," with its emphasis on communication across disciplines and its willingness to connect "ecological conditions to individual human health or social conditions," as a handy device for reinvigorating science's approach to genetic diversity.

For Norman Myers, author and consultant in environment and development from Oxford, UK, one partial and very practical solution lies in establishing priorities for what should be saved—a tacit acknowledgment that the world doesn't have the time, money, or perhaps inclination to save everything. Myers and many other scientists concerned about extinction advocate the special protection of "hot spots" of abundant diversity, which are situated largely in the tropics. Hot spots, said Myers (who popularized the term in 1988), "are areas with exceptional concentrations of species that are found nowhere else—that is, they are endemic—and also areas that are under exceptional threat of habitat destruction." Several years ago, Myers was able to identify 18 such places, most in tropical forests. Lately he has been working with Conservation International to update the list, and it now contains 25 areas.

> *"Running through many conversations about biodiversity . . . was the specter of a frightening word: extinction."*

Myers says his research shows that "if we could safeguard, let's say, 15 out of the 25 hot spots, we could knock an enormous dent in the entire mass extinction problem. I calculate that we could reduce it by at least a quarter, probably one-third, and possibly by a half." But, he adds, hot spots are not all that easy to protect. They are the very places that are under the greatest pressures from agriculture and development, both of which receive what he called "perverse subsidies" that promote unsustainable practices.

Biodiversity and Economics

One way that biodiversity can be protected, nurtured, and conserved—and perhaps the only possible and clearly obvious way, in the minds of many who study it—lies in identifying the monetary values of biological diversity clearly, in ways that politicians, other funding sources, and the general public can easily comprehend. This runs against the grain of many scientists who pursue the ideal of pure research: "It puts prices on ecology and biology," grumbles Schubel, of the New England Aquarium. But for many others, it is fast becoming the only hope.

Graciela Chichilnisky, a mathematician and economist who directs Columbia University's Program on Information and Resources, thinks of biodiversity as a form of knowledge that should be treated as capital. It is all part of what Chichilnisky calls "the knowledge revolution." Indeed, Norman Myers points out that society already is comfortable thinking in economic terms about several components of biodiversity—medicines from plants, ecotourism, and, increasingly, the value of carbon that resides in forests.

> *"Many . . . scientists concerned about extinction advocate the special protection of 'hot spots' of abundant diversity."*

Several participants in the Washington forum referred to the contribution recently made to the economic-value-of-environment discussion by Robert Costanza, the director of the University of Maryland's Center for Environmental and Estuarine Studies, in Solomons, Maryland. Costanza and a dozen colleagues published a widely discussed article in the 15 May 1997 issue of *Nature* that assigned values to the world's ecosystem services and natural capital.

In what they acknowledge is a "crude initial estimate," but which nevertheless copes seriously with a subject ecologists and economists have circled about for decades, the authors placed values on "ecosystem services" in 17 major categories. They defined such services as "flows of materials, energy, and information from natural capital stocks which combine with manufactured and human capital services to produce human welfare." The bottom line: For the entire biosphere, such services are in the range of US$16–$54 trillion per year, with an average of US$33 trillion per year. (David Pimentel of Cornell University, along with a team of graduate students, presented their own estimates in the December 1997 issue of *BioScience*. They calculated the global value of biodiversity's contributions at close to US$3 trillion a year, and the US contributions at US$319 billion. The "major contributions" of biodiversity on their list included organic waste disposal, soil formation, biological nitrogen fixation, crop and livestock genetics, biological pest control, plant pollination, and pharmaceuticals.)

Costanza and his coauthors anticipated the objections of colleagues and environmentalists who are uncomfortable with the notion of placing values on nature. "The issue of valuation is inseparable from the choices and decisions we have to make about ecological systems," they wrote. "So although ecosystem valuation is certainly difficult and fraught with uncertainties, one choice we do not have is whether or not to do it."

An Optimistic View

Gretchen C. Daily, of the Center for Conservation Biology at Stanford University, agreed with the need to place values on ecosystem services and pronounced herself "pretty optimistic" about the whole matter. In sharp contrast to the prevailing atmosphere of imminent doom, she presented a more upbeat outlook from a "purely anthropocentric, selfish self-interest, economic-prosperityin-general, well-being point of view. . . . that is about the importance of biodi-versity in supplying life support services, ecosystem services, to humanity." Daily's definition of such services was "all the conditions and processes that we take for granted here on Earth, but through which natural ecosystems, and the species that make them up, sustain and fulfill human life." It would be nice, she said, if humanity could continue taking these services for granted, "but we re-ally are disrupting them in a major way."

The solution? "Basically, we need to start looking at these systems that sup-ply our basic services as natural capital," Daily said, "and we need to start man-aging biodiversity like a capital asset, which it is. If it's properly safeguarded and managed, it will yield a flow of benefits over time." This concept shouldn't seem so foreign, she said. Society is comfortable with managing other forms of capital—for example, a city's physical infrastructure and the "human capital" of social statistical accounting such as the census and infant mortality. "But we don't do this at all, in any systematic way, for our natural capital," said Daily, "and it's just crazy."

Daily would first set up a basic ledger—an accounting scheme to identify ex-isting ecosystem goods and services, determine which goods are supplying which services and in what quantities, and what the quality of the services is. Second, she would determine how society should manage those goods and ser-vices, and how the ecosystem will react to human intervention.

"We need to know how these services depend on the condition and the extent of the ecosystems supplying them," Daily said. "How disturbed or heavily im-pacted can a system be and still supply us with these services? We need espe-cially to find out where the critical thresholds lie. At what point will water pu-rification services of a given watershed be overwhelmed by too much agricultural runoff? . . . We need to know how amenable, and over what time scale, ecosystems are to repair." Then society should explore the "possibilities for technological substitutions; what are the costs and what are the benefits of trying to substitute technology for these services that we've depended on throughout our history?"

After all this basic accounting, Daily says, consumers of biodiversity should start assigning values to it. "We need to determine the marginal value of ecosystems and their services. That means, what is the cost or benefit as-sociated with either destroying or saving habitat? We also need to take into consideration the 'context de-pendency valuation'—that is, people

"By no means does everyone concerned with biological diversity wax enthusiastic about turning nature over to economists."

in different parts of the world and different cultures and different times in the future are likely to value these things in different ways, and that has to be incor-porated into policies we design." After all, the value of most services performed by biodiversity lies in the future. "Finally," Daily says, "we need to find ways to safeguard this natural capital, to develop institutions and financial mechanisms for capturing and then distributing these values in a way that provides incentives for saving them."

Science and Politics

By no means does everyone concerned with biological diversity wax enthusiastic about turning nature over to economists who will place price stickers on it. But few deny that before any meaningful steps can be taken to save Earth's biodiversity from further deterioration, science must do a better job of determining what is there in the soil, in the forests, in the air, and in the oceans, and the roles it all plays in the life of the planet. And, they say, scientists must work harder at presenting their findings to the people who make decisions.

In addition to arguments such as those of Daily and Chichilnisky about the importance of priority setting and value setting on biological material, another prominent theme, although far less controversial, is one in which many scientists have been reluctant to become involved until now: the degree to which science should be openly politically active in protecting biodiversity.

The two disciplines are not very compatible. Science is concerned with long-range effects and thinks of itself as independent of special interests, whereas politics functions behind the blinders of frequent elections and instant results (or at least promises of them), and feels it must serve special interests or lose its power. But the meeting at the National Academy of Sciences and comments by individual researchers elsewhere reveal an increased acceptance of the fact that science must get more involved with politics. There is a not-too-hidden agenda of hoping to influence politicians with the power to allocate money for the classification, study, protection, and conservation of biodiversity.

"There is a need," Myers said wryly, "for certain biology professionals to understand not only about the flows of energy through ecosystems, but also the flows of influence through the corridors of power." Hawksworth added: "Special pleading, looking as though we're impoverished, not getting as much as the astronomers or whatever, doesn't work with funding agencies. This is especially true if we want to ask for the funds to do what we've always been doing." Funding sources, he said, want to support projects in which they can have part ownership.

"We have to become sales people as well as scientists," Hawksworth said. "We need to develop new skills and approaches. . . . Major funding is always linked to political agendas. . . . We need to learn how to talk to politicians. We scientists by our nature are cautious, tending to present tentative results which always seem to call for further research. The politicians want answers and answers as quickly as possible."

Conservation Efforts Should Focus on Biodiversity "Hotspots"

by Russell A. Mittermeier, Norman Myers, and Cristina G. Mittermeier

About the authors: *Russell A. Mittermeier is president of Conservation International, an environmentalist organization. Norman Myers is an Oxford University ecologist and the author of* The Sinking Ark *and other works. Cristina G. Mittermeier is a marine biologist and coauthor of* Megadiversity: Earth's Biologically Wealthiest Nations.

As we all know, our planet is suffering from a variety of environmental ills, with issues like global warming, ozone layer depletion, toxic chemical emissions, acid rain, erosion, land degradation, air, soil, and water pollution, and a variety of other issues making news on a daily basis. These so-called "brown" environmental issues are a focus of attention because they are immediately and directly evident to us and relatively easy to quantify. Add to these the pressures of population growth in the developing world and overconsumption in the developed world, and we are faced with a situation that looks very bleak indeed. However, as serious as these problems are, we believe that the most far-reaching environmental problem that we currently face is the grand scale loss of our planet's biological diversity. This biodiversity, simply defined, is the sum total of all life on Earth, that wealth of species, ecosystems, and ecological processes that makes our living planet what it is—after all is said and done, still the only place in the entire universe where we know with certainty that life exists. It is our living resource base, our biological capital in the global bank, and what distinguishes it perhaps more than anything else is the fact that its loss is an *irreversible process.* Although we already have or can develop technologies to combat other environmental ills—often lacking only the political will or the economic incentive to put them into place—biodiversity loss cannot be re-

Excerpted from the introduction to *Hotspots: Earth's Biologically Richest and Most Endangered Terrestrial Ecoregions,* by Russell A. Mittermeier, Norman Myers, and Cristina G. Mittermeier (Mexico City: CEMEX/Conservation International, 1999). Reprinted with permission.

solved through technological "fixes." Loss of biodiversity and the impending extinction crisis that we face cannot be reversed or rectified through biotechnology, virtual reality, or computer-generated images, and we are certainly never going to find another planet that has gone through Earth's unique and very special evolutionary history. Once a species of plant or animal goes extinct, it will never be seen again, and we now face not just the loss of individual species, but the loss of entire biotic communities, entire ecosystems, upon which we ourselves ultimately depend for our own survival. . . .

As we enter the next millennium, it is critical that we take stock of what has been accomplished to date, and determine how and where we must invest in the first couple of decades of the twenty-first century to have maximum impact on the future. In order to make this happen, we need to recognize three major challenges confronting us. The first of these is our appalling ignorance of the rest of life on Earth, the second is the establishment of clear priorities for conservation investment and action, and the third is the effective investment of financial and human resources that do become available. This [essay] is dedicated largely to the second and third of these challenges, and aims to identify a priority-setting approach—the hotspots—that results in maximum efficiency in biodiversity conservation. However, before entering into our discussion of the hotspots, we would be remiss not to mention briefly the first of these challenges, which relates to our lack of knowledge of biodiversity.

The simple fact is that our knowledge of biodiversity is embryonic at best, and in many ways our highly sophisticated twenty-first century "technological society" is still in the Dark Ages in terms of our understanding of the rest of life on Earth. Science has thus far described somewhere between 1.4 and 1.8 million species of living creatures, animals, plants and microorganisms, with 1.5 million being the preferred estimate. However, estimates and projections made over the past 10-15 years have ranged from 5 million to 10 million to 30 million to even 100 million or more. . . .

Much of this undescribed diversity is in the soils and the canopies of the world's tropical rain forests, in the large tropical rivers, and in the deep ocean trenches; however, some of it, amazingly, is still in our own backyards. Needless to say, if our basic ignorance of the simple number of other species is approximately one to two orders of magnitude, think about how little we know of the multitudes of ecological processes involving this vast number of species—a level of ignorance that must be in the range of at least two or three orders of magnitude beyond our shortcomings in basic alpha taxonomy. . . .

However, in spite of this ignorance, we have to proceed with what we *do* know, and use those species and ecosystems of whose existence we *are* aware and which are reasonably well-studied as surrogates for all those others that remain to be described. Available information does indicate that we have already lost some 57% of the Earth's primary tropical rain forests, that the coral reefs are being overfished, overcollected, dynamited and poisoned into oblivion, and that large portions of the best-studied groups of organisms are in danger of extinction. . . .

Indeed, all indications are that we are standing at the opening phase of a mass extinction event that will be comparable in scale to the five great extinction episodes that have taken place in the history of life on Earth, the most recent being the loss of the dinosaurs some 65 million years ago. Impending extinction rates *are at least four orders of magnitude faster than the background rates seen in the fossil record.* That means on the order of *10,000 times higher*, a frightening prospect to say the least. If allowed to continue, the current extinction episode, the first to be driven by the actions of a single species, could well eliminate between one third and two thirds of all species in the next century. . . .

Given the many problems that we face, this biodiversity crisis sometimes seems overwhelming, especially if viewed only from a global macro level. This has resulted in much "gloom and doom," as exemplified by recent publications like Quammen's "Planet of Weeds," in which the author expresses his belief that we will lose up to two thirds of Earth's species regardless of what we do. . . . We believe that such pessimism is both *dangerous* and *unjustified*; *dangerous* because it provides an excuse for vested interests to write off the need for biodiversity conservation, and *unjustified* because we firmly believe that there are viable solutions. Clearly, we don't mean to minimize the critical nature of the problem, but we are convinced that there are measures that can be taken to maintain global biodiversity and that, if designed and implemented properly, need not be all that expensive. We simply have to break down the crisis into manageable units, and this requires clear *priority-setting* at global, regional, and local levels.

> "*All indications are that we are standing at the opening phase of a mass extinction event.*"

Priority setting starts with the premise that biodiversity is by no means evenly distributed over the planet, and that certain areas are far richer than others in overall diversity and especially in endemic species (i.e., species that are found only in a particular place and nowhere else). Furthermore, priority setting must take into account the degree of threat, and it happens that some of the areas with the greatest concentrations of biodiversity are also under the most severe threat. By focusing on those areas that combine high diversity, high endemism, and high degree of threat, we can determine which are most likely to lose significant portions of their biodiversity over the next few decades. This may not always be politically appropriate or convenient, but it enables us to get maximum "conservation bang for each buck invested" and it is really essential if we are going to maintain the full range of life on Earth.

Several different priority-setting approaches have been used in recent years. . . .

The approach that we believe has by far the greatest merit is one that is based on the work of . . . Dr. Norman Myers. In two classic papers on *threatened biodiversity hotspots*, Myers was really the first to introduce the concept of global priority setting into the international biodiversity conservation arena. In his 1988 paper, he used vascular plants as indicators for biodiversity and identified 10 *threatened hotspots* in the tropical rain forests of the world, estimating that they contained 13% of all plant diversity in just 0.2% of the land area of the planet. In a subsequent analysis, he added four other rain forest areas and four Mediterranean-type ecosystems, and came up with a total of 18 areas that accounted for 20% of global plant diversity in just 0.2% of the land area of the planet. In a subse-

> *"Priority setting starts with the premise that biodiversity is by no means evenly distributed over the planet."*

quent analysis, he added four other rain forest areas and four Mediterranean-type ecosystems, and came up with a total of 18 areas that accounted for 20% of global plant diversity in just 0.5% of the land area of the planet.

Beginning in 1989, both Conservation International and the Chicago-based MacArthur Foundation adopted Myers' *threatened hotspots* as the guiding principle for their conservation investments. . . .

To summarize, the basic premises of our priority-setting approaches are as follows:

- *The biodiversity of each and every nation is critically important to that nation's survival and must be a fundamental component of any national or regional development strategy;*
- *Nonetheless, biodiversity is by no means evenly distributed over the surface of our planet, and some areas, especially in the tropics, harbor far greater concentrations of biodiversity than others;*
- *Some of these high-biodiversity areas (e.g., tropical rain forests, coral reefs, deep ocean trenches, Mediterranean-type ecosystems) are under the most severe threat;*
- *To achieve maximum impact with limited resources, we must concentrate heavily (but not exclusively) on those areas richest in diversity and most severely threatened;*
- *Investment in them should be roughly proportional to their overall contribution to global biodiversity; and*
- *Finally, analyses of biodiversity priorities must be based on actual data, first and foremost on species diversity and endemism, on phyletic diversity, and on ecosystem diversity, and subsequently on degree of threat, in order to be truly effective.*

Conservation International, the MacArthur Foundation, and others used the hotspots concept for a period of some eight years, based mainly on Myers' two original papers (1988, 1990) and the map-based update by Conservation International (1990). However, given the growing importance and acceptance of this concept in global biodiversity conservation planning and the fact that Conservation International intended to base a major fund-raising campaign on the hotspots, we felt that a reanalysis and reassessment of the hotspots was timely and appropriate. With this in mind, we organized a mini-workshop in the Washington, D.C. offices of Conservation International for a three-day period in March, 1996. The purpose of this exercise was to review the hotspots concept, reevaluate its validity, identify criteria for what constitutes a hotspot, add or subtract areas as appropriate, and begin a detailed data analysis to serve as an underpinning for future use of the concept. Some 20 experts were involved in this preliminary exercise, including the originator of the concept, Norman Myers. . . .

To summarize the results of our March, 1996 meeting and subsequent deliberations:

- *The hotspots concept is indeed a valid approach, especially for determining priorities among terrestrial ecosystems;*
- *As originally indicated by Myers, plants should be the baseline criterion for a hotspot, given the fact that most other forms of life depend on them;*
- *Endemism, and especially plant endemism, should be the primary criterion for hotspot status, with plant diversity, and vertebrate endemism and diversity also being taken into consideration;*
- *Invertebrate data should be included where available, but it was too inconsistent to serve as a principal criterion at this time; the same is true of freshwater fish data;*
- *Degree of threat should provide the second layer of analysis for hotspot status, once an area meets the endemism criterion;*
- *All regions originally identified by Myers were in fact valid hotspots, and should remain on the hotspots list;*
- *Based on the new criteria, several other regions qualify for the new, revised list;*
- *Although some key areas for freshwater biodiversity are obviously included within the terrestrial hotspots identified here, a separate analysis for freshwater hotspots is urgently needed as well; and*
- *Marine systems also require their own hotspots analysis.*

The results of the current hotspots reanalysis have involved some 100 experts. . . . The study took approximately two and a half years, and should be considered an ongoing research effort, rather than a completed project. Nonetheless, we feel that the work has now advanced to a stage at which we are ready to present our results. . . .

In all, we have identified 25 hotspots (Table 1). Sixteen of these are either the same as or incorporate the original 18 hotspots identified by Myers. One other, Mesoamerica, was added by Conservation International, and its validity is reaffirmed here. The remaining seven are new to the list, and result from the current analysis. . . .

Also included in this study as *honorable mentions* are the *Galápagos Islands* and the *Juan Fernández Islands*. Although neither of these small island groups makes the cutoff criteria as hotspots in their own right, we felt that their very special characteristics deserved recognition here. The Galápagos Islands have played a very important role in the history of evolutionary biology, have very high levels of endemism in certain groups of organisms and, given their small size, have very high per unit area diversity and endemism as well. The tiny Juan Fernández Islands, located in the Pacific Ocean off the coast of Chile, are very poor in vertebrates but have what may be the highest per unit area diversity and endemism of plants anywhere on Earth, including an endemic plant family in an area of only about 100 square kilometers (km^2). As a result, both of these "mini-hotspots" are included in our data analysis. . . .

In terms of the biomes represented in the hotspots, tropical rain forest formations predominate, with 15 of 25 (60%) hotspots partly or entirely consisting of this kind of vegetation (Table 1). This is not surprising given that Myers' original 10 hotspots were all tropical rain forest, and the fact remains that these forests overall are the richest and most diverse terrestrial habitats—in spite of rather feeble efforts over the past few years to downplay their importance. Nonetheless, we clearly recognize the great importance of other biomes as well, and a number of them are included on the hotspots list. Four (16%) of the hotspots are exclusively tropical rain forest, one (4%) includes both tropical and subtropical rain forest, five (20%) include both tropical rain forest and tropical dry forest; another five (20%) have tropical rain forest, tropical dry forest, and other non-forest elements (including desert, shrub-

> *"To achieve maximum impact with limited resources, we must concentrate heavily . . . on those areas richest in diversity and most severely threatened."*

land, or grassland formations); five (20%) are Mediterranean-type ecosystems; three (12%) consist of temperate forest and grasslands, one (4%) is a mix of tropical dry forest, woodland savannas, and open savannas; and one (4%) is exclusively an arid region (Table 1). Of particular note are the Mediterranean-type ecosystems, characterized by cool wet winters and warm dry summers. There are five of these in existence, and all of them qualify for the hotspots list on the strength of their high plant endemism.

The 25 hotspots range in original extent from New Caledonia at 18,576 km^2 to the Mediterranean Basin at 2,362,000 km^2, and cover 17,452,038 km^2 or 11.76% of the land surface of the planet, which is estimated at 148,429,000 km^2. The area remaining intact, in more or less pristine condition, ranges from the 2,000 km^2 of the Eastern Arc to the almost 357,000 km^2 of the Brazilian Cerrado. In terms of percentage, what remains varies from the 4.7% of the Mediterranean, the 4.9% of Indo-Burma, the 6.8% of the Western Ghats and Sri Lanka, and the 7.5% of the Atlantic Forest to the roughly 30% of Central Chile, meaning that all of these areas have lost at least 70–75% of their original natural vegetation and some as much as 95%. Cumulatively, these 25 areas plus the two mini-hotspots have lost almost 88%, and have only 12.28%, or 2,142,839

Chapter 4

Table 1. The 25 Hotspots With Principal Biome Types Represented, Original Extent of Natural Vegetation, Remaining Intact Natural Vegetation, and Area Currently Protected

Hotspot	Principal biome types represented	Original extent (km²)	Remaining intact (km²)	Area protected (km²)
Tropical Andes	Tropical rain forest Tropical dry forest High-altitude grassland (puna páramo)	1,258,000	314,500	79,687
Mesoamerica	Tropical rain forest Tropical dry forest	1,154,912	230,982	138,437
Caribbean	Tropical rain forest Tropical dry forest Xerophytic vegetation	263,535	29,840	41,000
Chocó-Darién-Western Ecuador	Tropical rain forest Tropical dry forest	260,595	63,000	16,471
Atlantic Forest Region	Tropical rain forest Subtropical rain forest	1,227,600	91,930	33,084
Brazilian Cerrado	Tropical dry forest Woodland savanna Open savanna	1,783,169	356,634	22,000
Central Chile	Mediterranean type	300,000	90,000	9,167
California Floristic Province	Mediterranean type	324,000	80,000	31,443
Madagascar and Indian Ocean Islands	Tropical rain forest Tropical dry forest Xerophytic vegetation	594,221	59,038	11,546
Eastern Arc Mountains & Coastal Forest of Tanzania & Kenia	Tropical rain forest	30,000	2,000	5,083
Cape Floristic Province	Mediterranean type	74,000	18,000	14,060
Succulent Karoo	Xerophytic vegetation	112,000	30,000	2,352
Guinean Forests of West Africa	Tropical rain forest	1,265,000	126,500	20,224
Mediterranean Basin	Mediterranean type	2,362,000	110,000	42,123
Caucasus	Temperate forest Grassland	500,000	50,000	14,050
Sundaland	Tropical rain forest Tropical dry forest	1,600,000	125,000	90,000
Wallacea	Tropical rain forest Tropical dry forest Xerophytic vegetation	346,782	52,017	20,415
Philippines	Tropical rain forest	300,780	24,062	3,910
Indo-Burma	Tropical rain forest Tropical dry forest	2,060,000	100,000	160,000
Mountains of South-Central China	Temperate forest Grassland	800,000	64,000	16,562
Western Ghats and Sri Lanka	Tropical rain forest	182,500	12,445	18,962
New Caledonia	Tropical rain forest Tropical dry forest Maquis shrubland	18,576	5,200	527
New Zealand	Temperate forest Grassland	270,534	59,400	52,068
Polynesia/Micronesia	Tropical rain forest Tropical dry forest	46,012	10,024	4,913
Southwest Australia	Mediterranean type	309,840	33,336	33,336
Galápagos Islands	Xerophytic shrubland	7,882	4,931	7,278
Juan Fernández Islands	Temperate Forest	100		91
Total		**17,452,038**	**2,142,839**	**888,789**

km² remaining in intact condition. *This amounts to just 1.44% of the land sur-face of the planet*, a relatively very small area that is roughly equivalent in size to Alaska and Texas combined. . . .

In spite of this small land area, the concentration of terrestrial biodiversity in these 25 hotspots is amazingly high. Indeed, if we look first and foremost at plants, our principal hotspot criterion, *we find that a staggering 131,399 vascu-lar plants are endemic to the 25 hotspots, representing 43.8% of all plants on Earth.* Although it is much more difficult to come up with an estimate of total plant diversity in the hotspots (endemics + non-endemics) because of extensive overlap with other hotspots and with adjacent non-hotspot areas, we very con-servatively estimate that the non-endemics would add at least 50% to the total. . . . *This means that at least 65.7% and more likely 70% or more of all vascular plants occur within the 1.44% of Earth's land surface occupied by the hotspots.*

If we look at vertebrate endemism, we find that the numbers for birds, mam-mals, reptiles, and amphibians are comparable. . . .

These figures . . . clearly reaffirm the tremendous global importance of these areas in international efforts to maintain biodiversity. *If 60% or more of all ter-restrial biodiversity occurs in the most threatened 1.44% of the land surface of the planet, it is difficult to avoid the conclusion that these areas deserve a lion's share of our attention over the next few decades.*

Indeed, if, as many experts suggest, we are at risk of losing between one third and two thirds of all species

> **"In spite of . . . [their] small land area, the concentration of terrestrial biodiversity in these 25 hotspots is amazingly high."**

within the foreseeable future, and if almost two thirds of at least the terrestrial species are in the hotspots, then its seems fairly obvious that we may make a major dent in the entire endangered species/mass extinction problem by placing very heavy emphasis on the hotspots. . . .

Although so much has already been lost, the hotspots continue to be under siege with many different land-use practices threatening their long-term in-tegrity. Nonetheless, the degree of biodiversity impact varies considerably from one threat to another. The worst and most-enduring often come under the broad banner of agriculture, both large-scale commercial agriculture and smallholder plots usually referred to as shifting agriculture or slash-and-burn. The rural poor continue to encroach upon remaining natural areas for simple survival, employing slash-and-burn agricultural practices that are unsustainable at high population levels and result in a continual rollback of forest. Large-scale com-mercial agriculture (*e.g.*, sugar cane, soybeans, oil palm, etc.) is often the most destructive activity in that it results in total clearance of extensive areas without any hope of near-term regeneration. In spite of the fact that very little natural forest remains in most of the hotspots, logging continues to be a threat in many areas. What is more, it is often carried out in the name of sustainability and funded by some of the same major financial institutions that help to support biodiversity conservation—a well-intentioned but misguided practice that often fails to take into account the fact that true sustainable forest management does not really exist anywhere in the tropics. As bad as logging in the tropics can be, it rarely involves the practice of wholesale clear-cutting, common in temperate forests. Regeneration is often possible, especially if areas are "high-graded" to remove only the most valuable species and then abandoned. A more insidious threat from logging often comes from the road networks that are created, providing easy access to land-hungry peasants that engage in the more destructive practices mentioned above. Other extractive industries like mining and oil and gas can also result in significant degradation of hotspot ecosystems, and in fact are increasing in some areas. However, these industries are becoming increasingly conscientious, and are starting to adopt "best practices" to mitigate impacts. They are also more site-specific than agriculture and logging, meaning that they are usually restricted to much smaller geographic areas and potentially, their impacts are more easily monitored and controlled.

Aside from these obvious threats to biodiversity, a number of others may be at least as important and may present an even greater risk to biodiversity over the long term. These include invasive species, both plants and animals, which can be very difficult to control and can have devastating impacts on restricted-range endemic species, and bushmeat hunting for both local consumption and commercial sale. The impact of the latter is beginning to receive much more international attention, and is particularly severe in places like the Guinean Forests of West Africa and Indo-Burma, where hunting traditions are deep-seated, pervasive, and locally significant in economic terms. However, with increasing human population and the upsurge of commercial trade in bushmeat, the effects of this activity are becoming more and more damaging on target species, especially those that are dependent on relatively undisturbed habitats that have already been severely fragmented by other land-use activities.

The good news is that there are positive signs on the horizon. The advent of many new technologies is improving our capacity to monitor and understand land-use practices, and ultimately to put in place more effective protective measures. New technologies such as the Landsat "Thematic Mapper" and various radar-based satellites allow for much more accurate documentation of activities like deforestation and precise identification of pressure points within particular regions than was possible in the past. They also allow for better protected area monitoring and maintenance, and prevention of encroachment and other activities that threaten the long-term viability of parks and reserves. Growing awareness on the part of corporations that biodiversity loss is indeed a globally important issue, and one that they can and should have an impact in helping to resolve, is also leading to more widespread adoption of corporate responsibility in extractive industries and even direct support for on-the-ground conservation activities. . . .

As indicated in the preceding pages, and emphasized again and again throughout this book, the 25 biodiversity hotspots are absolutely critical to maintaining life on Earth and to ensuring that our planet's rich biodiversity is not eroded over the first few decades of the new millennium. To ensure this, it is not enough just to do good science, to establish more parks and reserves, and to carry out more education and public awareness campaigns about the importance of biodiversity, as necessary as all of these may be. It is also essential that we adopt a new biodiversity philosophy, set a new "beacon on the hill," define a new "moral high ground" relating to this critical issue and especially to the hotspots. Put another way, *we have to create a value system that recognizes maintenance of the full range of life on Earth as simply "the right thing to do," and the only really appropriate behavior for civilized twenty-first-century society.* So little remains in the hotspots, and what does persist represents so small a portion (1.44%) of the land surface of our planet, that we can no longer rationalize and make excuses for continued destructive exploitation in these areas, be it for timber extraction, mining, or anything else that produces short-term gain for the few to the long-term detriment of the many.

> *"It seems fairly obvious that we may make a major dent in the entire . . . mass extinction problem by placing a very heavy emphasis on the hotspots."*

If we allow a "biotic holocaust" to take place, what we know from the five great mass extinction episodes of the prehistoric past is that it will take at least 5 million years possibly much longer to repair the damage. Just that 5 million year figure is about 20 times longer than *Homo sapiens* has been a species. If we don't do enough to prevent this mass extinction episode and let several million species disappear from the face of the Earth within the next few decades, this will be far and away the biggest "decision" ever made by one generation for future generations. Conversely, if we were to take the decisive action necessary to save our planet's magnificent biodiversity, this would surely rank as the most "responsible" initiative ever taken by one human generation in support of those that will come after us and will certainly be remembered in historic terms as the most momentous decision made by twentieth-century society. If ever morality at a grand scale was an issue in human history, this is surely the time par excellence. *If we are wise enough the seize the opportunities presented by the hotspots strategy and a handful of others, we will be regarded by future generations as true giants of the human condition. The choice seems straightforward. Either we recognize the great responsibility that lies before us and make this momentous historical decision to maintain the rest of life on Earth, or the likelihood is that we will be regarded as perhaps the most irresponsible generation in the history of this planet.*

Conservation Efforts Should Not Focus on Biodiversity "Hotspots"

by G. Carleton Ray

About the author: *G. Carleton Ray is a research professor in the Department of Environmental Science at the University of Virginia in Charlottesville.*

Petruchio's impassioned speech to Katharina in [William Shakespeare's] *Taming of the Shrew* (Act IV, Scene iii) encapsulates a conservation dilemma: "What, is the jay more precious than the lark, / Because his feathers are more beautiful? / Or is the adder better than the eel, / Because his painted skin contents the eye?"

Is conservation in the eye of the beholder? Is the song of the lark more to be valued than the silence of a rose? Should the richness of the painted coral reef take precedence over the reefs formed by the succulent and possibly endangered oyster? What portion of the landscape can be defined as rich? Do little things run the world or is it the big things that really matter?

Earth or Sea?

Does our evolution as giant land animals cloud our view? Human terrestrial evolution has caused this blue, water-planet to be called Earth, a slip of mind over matter that can lead to egregious bias. For example, we have been told that the 7 percent of land that is tropical forests houses more species than any other place. With images of forests being torn and burnt before our eyes, these places have rightly gained high conservation priority. But behind this choice is an ironic process of rejection. The October 1994 cover of *Bioscience* displays striking images of postagricultural changes of the terrestrial earth at human hands, over the title, "Where in the *World* Are the Conservation Crises" (emphasis mine). The accompanying article, by Stanford University's Center for Conservation Biology, purports to be a "global analysis of the distribution of biodiversity and the expansion of the human enterprise." Yet their globe is one without water, fresh or salt.

Which systems are really most diverse, and by what measure? Although most *described* species are terrestrial—no surprise there—the greatest phyletic, thus also genetic, diversity is marine. The terrestrial realm is occupied by only 11 phyla (only one, perhaps, endemic, the status of the Onychophora being arguable). This compares with about 28 marine (13 endemic), 17 symbiotic (4 endemic), and 14 freshwater (none endemic). Put in more tangible terms, a single clump of oysters in the Chesapeake Bay may host, attached to its shells, more animal phyla than all of the land, worldwide.

More specifically, P.H. Gleick offers that of all the world's water, 97.6 percent is salty and only 0.0093 percent fresh, translating to a teaspoon in a bathtub. Yet 12 percent of all animal species live in this small, freshwater piece of the globe, which contains a proportion of biodiversity to space that is exceeded nowhere else. If that were not enough, consider that freshwater extinction rates are probably higher than for any other Earth system and that depletion of freshwater resources continues to be catastrophic. Gleick reminds us that even in "healthy" North America, 30 percent of fish species are threatened, endangered, or of special concern, and of the 108 species of mussels in the Ohio River basin alone, 39 percent are either extinct or endangered.

What does the logic of naming this planet Earth seemingly omit? Merely water, where life originated, where it is richest, and where it may be most endangered. It appears that our problem is perception. We earthly creatures can witness the depletion and destruction of the land before our eyes. The seas present an umbral surface into which we peer only with difficulty, and usually with ignorance. As I have previously said, "The last fallen mahogany would lie perceptibly on the landscape, and the last black rhino would be obvious in its loneliness, but a marine species may disappear beneath the waves unobserved and the sea would seem to roll on the same as always." Furthermore, on the land we have long observed the massive depletion of Earth's biological capital, notably of soils, forests, and large mammals, but only recently have worldwide increases of "dead," anoxic zones and toxic phytoplankton blooms become obvious in the sea.

We still can only guess what the effects might be of the "strip-mining" of marine fishes, which may be at least the equal of deforestation in its effect on biodiversity. In sum, what is gone we may not know, and what seems healthy may not be so.

"We have no consistent way to establish one place or species over another as highest in priority, other than bias and familiarity."

I do not bring these matters to attention to exacerbate a terrestrial–marine competition or to question whether the harpy eagle or the whale is more to be valued, or even to suggest that we rename our planet Sea. The whole world is too rich and interdependent for that.

But we must admit that we have no consistent way to establish one place or species over another as highest in priority, other than bias and familiarity. Even the data for extinction are highly uncertain. It seems that unless we devise priorities on a sound scientific basis, Petruchio will remain with us.

Seeking the Magic Bullet

New discoveries of species and the facts and fears of extinction have recently brought the diversity of life on our small planet into critical, worldwide focus. We have been brought to astonishment by the discovery of seemingly unending life forms, including those within the ocean's depths. Because loss of species is so tangibly tragic and permanent, conservation of species, particularly the charismatic and endangered, has become an end in itself. From this perspective, it follows that we should identify hot spots for protection of maximal species diversity.

Hot-spot criteria appear in many conservation publications (e.g., species richness, high endemism, and critical habitats for reproduction, nurseries, feeding, or other biological and ecological processes). An outstanding example of the application of the species-richness criterion is provided by the International Council for Bird Preservation (ICBP), whose contention is that birds have "dispersed to, and diversified in, all regions of the world" and "occur in virtually all habitat types and attitudinal zones." Therefore, birds are assumed to be surrogates for biodiversity in general. There are two serious problems with this approach. First, the general assumption behind hot spots is ecological stasis, which is to say that environmental change is not sufficiently considered. All places will inevitably change location and character, probably in a shorter time than we may think. Second, the ICBP's own analysis shows clearly that birds are not surrogates for other vertebrates, such as reptiles and amphibians. Further, J.R. Prendergast et al. found that in Britain, where data are probably as good as can be found anywhere, only 12% of the bird and butterfly hot spots coincide. Interestingly, in their analysis, "cold spots" do not coincide either.

> *"Every portion of Earth has become critical habitat for some form of life."*

Does it not seem obvious that if hot spots were to be identified for *all* taxa—ants, termites, nematodes, plants, and the rest—the entire earth would be included, probably more than once over? Put in reverse, there are no walruses in the Amazon, no parrots in Greenland, no snow "fleas" (springtails of the order Collembola) on the desert, no mighty oaks in the sea's abyss, and no flashlight fishes in the lofty Alps. That is, through more than four billion years of biological evolution, from prokaryotes to monkeys and whales, every portion of Earth has become critical habitat for some form of life. Clearly, a different conservation paradigm is required.

The Oyster or the Pearl?

Most people, including scientists, are drawn inexorably to warm and user-friendly places, where species are presumably most varied and beautiful. Thus the tropics have become almost synonymous with richness, productivity, the good life, and diversity. But some of us are just as drawn to the cool clarity, color, and diversity of the higher latitudes. As E.T. Seton said for arctic prairies, "I never before saw such a realm of exquisite flowers so exquisitely displayed, and the effect at every turn throughout the land was colour, colour, colour. . . . What Nature can do only in October, elsewhere, she does here all season through, as though when she set out to paint the world she began on the Barrens with a full palette and when she reached the tropics had nothing left but green."

Or, consider the lowly, brainless, songless oyster, about which Jonathan Swift remarked early in the eighteenth century, "He was a bold man that first eat an oyster." More optimistically, Richard Sheridan declared, once eaten, "An oyster may be crossed in love." Even Shakespeare was ambivalent about oysters: "Rich honesty dwells like a miser, sir, in a poor house, as your pearl in your foul oyster" (*As You Like It*) or "Why, the world's mine oyster, / Which I with sword will open" (*Hamlet*). In more modern times, oysters have made fortunes, as have oyster pearls. Of course, it must be noted that temperate oysters produce the flesh and a tropical oyster, blessed with a nacre-producing organ, produces the pearl. But both molluscs have been valued principally as products, with little thought given to the environments that support them.

Oysters filter and clarify water. They also build reefs, which are as important structural components of estuaries as coral reefs are to tropical waters. Through their activities, oysters can change the very nature of the estuaries in which they live. Thus they have the potential to influence the metapopulation dynamics of fishes and invertebrates, both of estuaries and throughout the near-shore coastal zone. We hypothesize that in the continuum of watershed and estuarine dynamics, in which this creature plays such an important ecological and economic role, the oyster is key. It is the metaphoric, ecological pearl. Yet following two centuries of overharvest, greed, and mismanagement (or "dismanagement") the oysters of many estuaries have become insignificant, both economically and ecologically. We now know that the oyster-rich Chesapeake Bay of John Smith was a very different place than now exists.

The Chesapeake Bay has become, over much of its expanse, nearly oyster-less, a murky, erosion-prone body (a cause–effect relationship is suspected, but not proven). Surely, the bay still produces much and still bears semblances of richness and

"Hot-spot conservation tactics . . . [have] fatal flaws."

solitude. It is still valued for commerce and remains a playground for boaters and for swimmers, except during the summertime of stinging nettles. Seen only from a modern perspective, there is much value left, but the historical retrospect is dismal. This signifies that a principal culprit for the demise of marine living resources and biodiversity over the centuries is not merely greed, politics, and indecision, but also science itself. Fishery science has been devised to serve commerce and remains largely driven by output-side yield models, That is, the input-side, the ecosystem itself, still receives too little attention. . . .

We urgently need to reexamine our biases and apply the rapidly growing knowledge of both species natural history and ecosystem dynamics, and to look beyond the narrowly bounded traditions of conservation toward entire regional ecosystems to achieve our conservation goals.

Two Flaws of Hot-Spot Conservation

I contend that hot-spot conservation tactics reveal two fatal flaws. The first is the way we tend to think. An insight into Petruchio's questions may lie in Alfred North Whitehead's notion of the "fallacy of misplaced concreteness [that] flourishes because the disciplinary organization of knowledge requires a high level of abstraction." In this case, the abstraction is the species. The second flaw is the way conservation often operates. We can hardly know how fast extinction is progressing, especially because we do not know how many species exist. Despite this limitation, we must accept the ubiquity of critical habitat. The obvious way out of this problem is to look beyond species to ecosystem management, defined by J.F. Franklin as "managing ecosystems so as to assure their sustainability."

"Biological diversity is everywhere."

Ecosystem sustainability is key, as history tells us. Only a millennium or two ago, humans were inconsequentially fragmented over the land and the oceans were barely touched or known. Now, humans dominate the planet, ecosystems are fragmented, and the "Marine Revolution" is under way. Functionally impaired ecosystems are now less able to sustain the products, species, or ecological functions that constitute biodiversity or that contribute to human well-being. This recognition inevitably alters our management and conservation imperatives. Set-aside preservation is still essential for specific, narrow purposes, but much more comprehensive management and even hands-on restoration are now higher priorities. The conservationist's scope must expand, upscale and hierarchically, from species to land- and seascapes and to entire regions and biogeographic provinces. Furthermore, humans must be treated as part and parcel of the land and seascape.

Surely we dare not let go of condors, whales, or the Appalachian Blue Ridge, where fall colors and timber rattlesnakes can exist side by side. There is simply no excuse to eliminate a species knowingly, either by exploitationist development, social causes (jobs), conservation bias, or ignorance. The endangered species paradigm must remain, but with acknowledgment of what it can do and what it cannot. Nor can we ignore the need to take a broader view. Species and protected areas alike may hang on within a sea of pollution, people, and mis-guided environmental engineering. But the simple truth is that pockets of species and habitats are not viable in the long term unless major changes in so-cial and conservation perspectives occur.

Biodiversity is a very old portion of our intellectual history. . . . Despite this long lineage, scientists have only recently conjectured that sustainability will ultimately depend on knowledge of how nature works, which means how biodi-versity is distributed, how it originates, how it is maintained, and, most impor-tantly, what the relationship is between species and community diversity and ecological function.

Thus, while keeping a keen eye on species, we must also view biodiversity as more ecological than biological, more evolutionary than descriptive, and more dynamic than static. As G.A. Bartholomew reminded us, "Indifference to a phe-nomenon's natural context can result in a paralyzing mismatch between the problem and the questions put to it." I interpret this to mean that it is essential to recognize that ecosystems are what we must manage, not species one at a time, but together as functioning assemblages, interacting with their abiotic world.

Franklin is emphatic on this score: "Efforts to preserve biodiversity must fo-cus increasingly at the ecosystem level because of the immense number of species, the majority of which are currently unknown. . . . The ecosystem ap-proach is the only way to conserve organisms and processes in poorly known or unknown habitats and ecological subsystems." In other words, the sustainability of systems is the goal, encompassing all scales and based on concepts of adap-tive management. Not everyone agrees. C.R. Tracy and P.F. Brussard assert that the identification of umbrella species as "coarse filters" is the challenge, and besides, that it is "terrifically difficult to define an ecosystem." Franklin re-sponds, I think correctly, that umbrellas do not really work and that we must maintain as much as we can of biodiversity and "not simply those relatively few species that we choose to recognize."

Just on the face of the matter, it seems not logical, and certainly not eco-logical, to assume that a small-scale attribute (species) can cover a large-scale one (eco-system). For example, which oceanic species might we choose: a whale or a di-atom? What may each cover? In fact, species (great or small) do not necessarily travel from habitat to habitat via corridors, as the chosen species or umbrella de-sign often emphasizes, but have many ways to "percolate" through the land- or seascape. As for ecosystems, land- and seascape pattern is the surrogate for biodi-versity. Ecological pattern is describable in time and space, and biodiversity may be measured and its significance assessed within these dimensions. . . .

Biodiversity Is Everywhere

In conclusion, biological diversity is everywhere. Even city folk seem to crave it. I can think of no better expression of this than R.F. Dasmann's classic, *A Different Kind of Country:*

After spending an hour or more examining the wonders of this new city center I felt depressed—by the absence of people and of life except for trees, shrubs, and flowers growing in greater or lesser concrete pots. I moved to what was left of old Philadelphia, into the narrow streets, the dirty old converted town houses, the jumble of shops and theaters and the mixtures of older tall buildings. Here, and not in the new malls, was where the people were—crowding the sidewalks, moving into theaters or pubs, traveling to or from church, window-shopping. I ate lunch in the back of an old delicatessen and worried about the future.

Returning to Petruchio, perhaps if we can change our paradigm from "things" to higher-order patterns and process, from stasis to dynamics, and from an economic view of worth to a socioecological expression of value, then perhaps we can save biological diversity and, ultimately, ourselves. Biodiversity is not only a set-aside issue, but [Franklin writes] part of a larger task: "stewardship of *all* of the species on *all* of the landscape with every activity we undertake." The answer to Petruchio's paradox lies somewhere between the heart and head, and in the nexus of our caring for life on Earth–Sea and the understanding of ecological systems, wherein the beholder becomes the student and the policymaker the perpetrator.

The Convention on Biological Diversity Helps Protect Biodiversity Through Sustainable Development

by the Secretariat of the Convention on Biological Diversity

About the author: *The Secretariat of the Convention on Biological Diversity (CBD) is an organization created by the CBD to organize meetings, disseminate information, and in other ways assist national governments in implementing provisions of the convention.*

Biological diversity—or biodiversity—is the term given to the variety of life on Earth and the natural patterns it forms. The biodiversity we see today is the fruit of billions of years of evolution, shaped by natural processes and, increasingly, by the influence of humans. It forms the web of life of which we are an integral part and upon which we so fully depend.

This diversity is often understood in terms of the wide variety of plants, animals and microorganisms. So far, about 1.75 million species have been identified, mostly small creatures such as insects. Scientists reckon that there are actually about 13 million species, though estimates range from 3 to 100 million.

Biodiversity also includes genetic differences within each species—for example, between varieties of crops and breeds of livestock. Chromosomes, genes, and DNA—the building blocks of life—determine the uniqueness of each individual and each species.

Yet another aspect of biodiversity is the variety of ecosystems such as those that occur in deserts, forests, wetlands, mountains, lakes, rivers, and agricultural landscapes. In each ecosystem, living creatures, including humans, form a community, interacting with one another and with the air, water, and soil around them.

Excerpted from *Sustaining Life on Earth: How the Convention on Biological Diversity Promotes Nature and Human Well-Being*, by the Secretariat of the Convention on Biological Diversity (CBD), April 2000. Reprinted with permission.

It is the combination of life forms and their interactions with each other and with the rest of the environment that has made Earth a uniquely habitable place for humans. Biodiversity provides a large number of goods and services that sustain our lives.

At the 1992 Earth Summit in Rio de Janeiro, world leaders agreed on a comprehensive strategy for "sustainable development"—meeting our needs while ensuring that we leave a healthy and viable world for future generations. One of the key agreements adopted at Rio was the Convention on Biological Diversity. This pact among the vast majority of the world's governments sets out commitments for maintaining the world's ecological underpinnings as we go about the business of economic development. The Convention establishes three main goals: the conservation of biological diversity, the sustainable use of its components, and the fair and equitable sharing of the benefits from the use of genetic resources.

This [article] looks at the importance of biological diversity for the health of people and the planet. It explains the role of the Convention in protecting this biodiversity and ensuring that it is used for the benefit of all. . . .

The Value of Biodiversity

Protecting biodiversity is in our self-interest. Biological resources are the pillars upon which we build civilizations. Nature's products support such diverse industries as agriculture, cosmetics, pharmaceuticals, pulp and paper, horticulture, construction and waste treatment. The loss of biodiversity threatens our food supplies, opportunities for recreation and tourism, and sources of wood, medicines and energy. It also interferes with essential ecological functions.

Our need for pieces of nature we once ignored is often important and unpredictable. Time after time we have rushed back to nature's cupboard for cures to illnesses or for infusions of tough genes from wild plants to save our crops from pest outbreaks. What's more, the vast array of interactions among the various components of biodiversity makes the planet habitable for all species, including humans. Our personal health, and the health of our economy and human society, depends on the continuous supply of various ecological services that would be extremely costly or impossible to replace. These natural services are so varied as to be almost infinite. For example, it would be impractical to replace, to any large extent, services such as pest control performed by various creatures feeding on one another, or pollination performed by insects and birds going about their everyday business.

> *"Protecting biodiversity is in our self-interest."*

When most people think of the dangers besetting the natural world, they think of the threat to other creatures. Declines in the numbers of such charismatic animals as pandas, tigers, elephants, whales, and various species of birds, have drawn world attention to the problem of species at risk. Species have been disappearing at 50–100 times the natural rate, and this is predicted to rise dramatically. Based on current trends, an estimated 34,000 plant and 5,200 animal species—including one in eight of the world's bird species—face extinction.

For thousands of years we have been developing a vast array of domesticated plants and animals important for food. But this treasure house is shrinking as modern commercial agriculture focuses on relatively few crop varieties. And, about 30% of breeds of the main farm animal species are currently at high risk of extinction.

While the loss of individual species catches our attention, it is the fragmentation, degradation, and outright loss of forests, wetlands, coral reefs, and other ecosystems that poses the gravest threat to biological diversity. Forests are home to much of the known terrestrial biodiversity, but about 45 per cent of the Earth's original forests are gone, cleared mostly during the past century. Despite some regrowth, the world's total forests are still shrinking rapidly, particularly in the tropics. Up to 10 per cent of coral reefs—among the richest ecosystems—have been destroyed, and one third of the remainder face collapse over the next 10 to 20 years. Coastal mangroves, a vital nursery habitat for countless species, are also vulnerable, with half already gone. . . .

The loss of biodiversity often reduces the productivity of ecosystems, thereby shrinking nature's basket of goods and services, from which we constantly draw. It destabilizes ecosystems, and weakens their ability to deal with natural disasters such as floods, droughts, and hurricanes, and

> *"The Convention . . . deals with an issue so vital to humanity's future, that it stands as a landmark in international law."*

with human-caused stresses, such as pollution and climate change. . . .

The reduction in biodiversity also hurts us in other ways. Our cultural identity is deeply rooted in our biological environment. Plants and animals are symbols of our world, preserved in flags, sculptures, and other images that define us and our societies. We draw inspiration just from looking at nature's beauty and power.

While loss of species has always occurred as a natural phenomenon, the pace of extinction has accelerated dramatically as a result of human activity. Ecosystems are being fragmented or eliminated, and innumerable species are in decline or already extinct. We are creating the greatest extinction crisis since the natural disaster that wiped out the dinosaurs 65 million years ago. These extinctions are irreversible and, given our dependence on food crops, medicines and other biological resources, pose a threat to our own well-being. It is reckless if not downright dangerous to keep chipping away at our life support system. It is unethical to drive other forms of life to extinction, and thereby deprive present and future generations of options for their survival and development. . . .

Chapter 4

An Agreement for Action

While concern for the environment is constant in history, heightened concern about environmental destruction and loss of species and ecosystems in the 1970s led to concerted action.

In 1972, the United Nations Conference on the Human Environment (Stockholm) resolved to establish the United Nations Environment Programme (UNEP). Governments signed a number of regional and international agreements to tackle specific issues, such as protecting wetlands and regulating the international trade in endangered species. These agreements, along with controls on toxic chemicals and pollution, have helped to slow the tide of destruction but have not reversed it. For example, an international ban and restrictions on the taking and selling of certain animals and plants have helped to reduce over-harvesting and poaching.

> *"Under the Convention, governments undertake to conserve and sustainably use biodiversity."*

In addition, many endangered species survive in zoos and botanical gardens, and key ecosystems are preserved through the adoption of protective measures. However, these are stopgap actions. The long-term viability of species and ecosystems depends on their being free to evolve in natural conditions. This means that humans have to learn how to use biological resources in a way that minimizes their depletion. The challenge is to find economic policies that motivate conservation and sustainable use by creating financial incentives for those who would otherwise over-use or damage the resource.

In 1987, the World Commission on Environment and Development (the Brundtland Commission) concluded that economic development must become less ecologically destructive. In its landmark report, Our Common Future, it said that: "Humanity has the ability to make development sustainable—to ensure that it meets needs of the present without compromising the ability of future generations to meet their own needs". It also called for "a new era of environmentally sound economic development".

The Convention on Biological Diversity

In 1992, the largest-ever meeting of world leaders took place at the United Nations Conference on Environment and Development in Rio de Janeiro, Brazil. An historic set of agreements was signed at the "Earth Summit", including two binding agreements, the Convention on Climate Change, which targets industrial and other emissions of greenhouse gases such as carbon dioxide, and the Convention on Biological Diversity, the first global agreement on the conservation and sustainable use of biological diversity. The biodiversity treaty gained rapid and widespread acceptance. Over 150 governments signed the document at the Rio conference, and since then more than 175 countries have ratified the agreement.

The Convention has three main goals:
- The conservation of biodiversity,
- Sustainable use of the components of biodiversity, and
- Sharing the benefits arising from the commercial and other utilization of genetic resources in a fair and equitable way.

The Convention is comprehensive in its goals, and deals with an issue so vital to humanity's future, that it stands as a landmark in international law. It recognizes—for the first time—that the conservation of biological diversity is "a common concern of humankind" and is an integral part of the development process. The agreement covers all ecosystems, species, and genetic resources. It links traditional conservation efforts to the economic goal of using biological resources sustainably. It sets principles for the fair and equitable sharing of the benefits arising from the use of genetic resources, notably those destined for commercial use. It also covers the rapidly expanding field of biotechnology, addressing technology development and transfer, benefit-sharing and biosafety. Importantly, the Convention is legally binding; countries that join it are obliged to implement its provisions.

The Convention reminds decision-makers that natural resources are not infinite and sets out a new philosophy for the 21st century, that of sustainable use. While past conservation efforts were aimed at protecting particular species and habitats, the Convention recognizes that ecosystems, species and genes must be used for the benefit of humans. However, this should be done in a way and at a rate that does not lead to the long-term decline of biological diversity.

> *"There are many examples of initiatives to integrate the objectives of conservation and sustainable use."*

The Convention also offers decision-makers guidance based on the precautionary principle that where there is a threat of significant reduction or loss of biological diversity, lack of full scientific certainty should not be used as a reason for postponing measures to avoid or minimize such a threat.

The Convention acknowledges that substantial investments are required to conserve biological diversity. It argues, however, that conservation will bring us significant environmental, economic and social benefits in return.

National Action

The Convention on Biological Diversity, as an international treaty, identifies a common problem, sets overall goals and policies and general obligations, and organizes technical and financial cooperation. However, the responsibility for achieving its goals rests largely with the countries themselves.

Private companies, landowners, fishermen, and farmers take most of the actions that affect biodiversity. Governments need to provide the critical role of leadership, particularly by setting rules that guide the use of natural resources, and by protecting biodiversity where they have direct control over the land and water.

Under the Convention, governments undertake to conserve and sustainably use biodiversity. They are required to develop national biodiversity strategies and action plans, and to integrate these into broader national plans for environment and development. This is particularly important for such sectors as forestry, agriculture, fisheries, energy, transportation and urban planning. Other treaty commitments include:

- Identifying and monitoring the important components of biological diversity that need to be conserved and used sustainably.
- Establishing protected areas to conserve biological diversity while promoting environmentally sound development around these areas.
- Rehabilitating and restoring degraded ecosystems and promoting the recovery of threatened species in collaboration with local residents.
- Respecting, preserving and maintaining traditional knowledge of the sustainable use of biological diversity with the involvement of indigenous peoples and local communities.
- Preventing the introduction of, controlling, and eradicating alien species that could threaten ecosystems, habitats or species.
- Controlling the risks posed by organisms modified by biotechnology.
- Promoting public participation, particularly when it comes to assessing the environmental impacts of development projects that threaten biological diversity.
- Educating people and raising awareness about the importance of biological diversity and the need to conserve it.
- Reporting on how each country is meeting its biodiversity goals.

Conservation and Sustainable Use

The conservation of each country's biological diversity can be achieved in various ways. "In-situ" conservation—the primary means of conservation—focuses on conserving genes, species, and ecosystems in their natural surroundings, for example by establishing protected areas, rehabilitating degraded ecosystems, and adopting legislation to protect threatened species. "Ex-situ" conservation uses zoos, botanical gardens and gene banks to conserve species.

Promoting the sustainable use of biodiversity will be of growing importance for maintaining biodiversity in the years and decades to come. Under the Convention, the "ecosystem approach to the conservation and sustainable use of biodiversity" is being used as a framework for action, in which all the goods and services provided by the biodiversity in ecosystems are considered. The Convention is promoting activities to ensure that everyone benefits from such goods and services in an equitable way.

There are many examples of initiatives to integrate the objectives of conservation and sustainable use:

- In 1994, Uganda adopted a programme under which protected wildlife areas shared part of their tourism revenues with local people. This approach is now being used in several African countries.

• In recognition of the environmental services that forests provide to the nation, Costa Rica's 1996 Forestry Law includes provisions to compensate private landowners and forest managers who maintain or increase the area of forest within their properties.

> *"The Convention has already accomplished a great deal . . . by transforming the international community's approach to biodiversity."*

• In different parts of the world, farmers are raising crops within mixed ecosystems. In Mexico, they are growing "shade coffee," putting coffee trees in a mixed tropical forest rather than in monoculture plantations that reduce biodiversity. These farmers then rely entirely on natural predators common to an intact ecosystem rather than on chemical pesticides.

• Tourists, attracted in large numbers by the spectacular beauty of marine and coastal diversity of the Soufrière area of St. Lucia, had a negative impact on the age-old and thriving fishing industry. In 1992, several institutions joined with fishers and other groups with an interest in conservation and sustainable management of the resources and, together, established the Soufrière Marine Management Area. Within this framework, problems are dealt with on a participatory basis with the involvement of all stakeholders.

• Through weekly "farmer field schools," rice farmers in several Asian countries have developed their understanding of the functioning of the tropical rice ecosystem—including the interactions between insect pests of rice, their natural enemies, fish farmed in the rice paddies, and the crop itself—to improve their crop management practices. This way they have increased their crop yields, while at the same time almost eliminating insecticide use with positive benefits in terms of environmental and human health. About 2 million farmers have benefited from this approach.

• In Tanzania, problems surrounding the sustainable use of Lake Manyara, a large freshwater lake, arose following increased usage in recent decades. The formation of the Lake Manyara Biosphere Reserve to combine both conservation of the Lake and surrounding high value forests with sustainable use of the wetlands area and low-input agriculture has brought together key users to set management goals. The Biosphere Reserve has fostered studies for the sustainable management of the wetlands, including monitoring the ground water and the chemistry of the escarpment water source.

• Clayoquot Sound on the western coast of Vancouver Island, Canada, encompasses forests and marine and coastal systems. The establishment of adaptive management to implement the ecosystem approach at the local level is currently under development with the involvement of indigenous communities, with a view to ensuring rational use of the forest and marine resources.

• Sian Ka'an Biosphere Reserve in Mexico has great cultural value with its 23 recorded Mayan and other archaeological sites while also being the home of some 800 people, mainly of Mayan descent. The reserve forms part of the extensive barrier reef system along the eastern coastline of Central America and includes coastal dunes, mangroves, marshes and inundated and upland forests. The inclusion of local people in its management helps maintain the balance between pure conservation and the need for sustainable use of resources by the local community.

Each government that joins the Convention is to report on what it has done to implement the accord, and how effective this is in meeting the objectives of the Convention. These reports are submitted to the Conference of the Parties (COP)—the governing body that brings together all countries that have ratified the Convention. The reports can be viewed by the citizens of all nations. The Convention secretariat works with national governments to help strengthen reporting and to make the reports of various countries more consistent and comparable, so that the world community can get a clearer picture of the big trends. Part of that work involves developing indicators for measuring trends in biodiversity, particularly the effects of human actions and decisions on the conservation and sustainable use of biodiversity. The national reports, particularly when seen together, are one of the key tools for tracking progress in meeting the Convention's objectives.

The Convention's success depends on the combined efforts of the world's nations. The responsibility to implement the Convention lies with the individual countries and, to a large extent, compliance will depend on informed self-interest and peer pressure from other countries and from public opinion. . . .

Sharing the Benefits of Genetic Resources

An important part of the biodiversity debate involves access to and sharing of the benefits arising out of the commercial and other utilization of genetic material, such as pharmaceutical products. Most of the world's biodiversity is found in developing countries, which consider it a resource for fueling their economic and social development. Historically, plant genetic resources were collected for commercial use outside their region of origin or as inputs in plant breeding. Foreign bioprospectors have searched for natural substances to develop new commercial products, such [as] drugs. Often, the products would be sold and protected by patents or other intellectual property rights, without fair benefits to the source countries.

> *"The passage of the Earth's biodiversity through the coming century will be its most severe test."*

The treaty recognizes national sovereignty over all genetic resources, and provides that access to valuable biological resources be carried out on "mutually agreed terms" and subject to the "prior informed consent" of the country of origin. When a microorganism, plant, or animal is used for a commercial application, the country from which it came has the right to benefit. Such benefits can include cash, samples of what is collected, the participation or training of national researchers, the transfer of biotechnology equipment and know-how, and shares of any profits from the use of the resources.

Work has begun to translate this concept into reality and there are already examples of benefit-sharing arrangements. At least a dozen countries have established controls over access to their genetic resources, and an equal number of nations are developing such controls. . . .

Future Challenge

Economic development is essential to meeting human needs and to eliminating the poverty that affects so many people around the world. The sustainable use of nature is essential for the long-term success of development strategies. A major challenge for the 21st century will be making the conservation and sustainable use of biodiversity a compelling basis for development policies, business decisions, and consumer desires.

The Convention has already accomplished a great deal on the road to sustainable development by transforming the international community's approach to biodiversity. This progress has been driven by the Convention's inherent strengths of near universal membership, a comprehensive and science-driven mandate, international financial support for national projects, world-class scientific and technological advice, and the political involvement of governments. It has brought together, for the first time, people with very different interests. It offers hope for the future by forging a new deal between governments, economic interests, environmentalists, indigenous peoples and local communities, and the concerned citizen.

However, many challenges still lie ahead. After a surge of interest in the wake of the Rio Summit, many observers are disappointed by the slow progress towards sustainable development during the 1990s. Attention to environmental problems was distracted by a series of economic crises, budget deficits, and local and regional conflicts. Despite the promise of Rio, economic growth without adequate environmental safeguards is still the rule rather than the exception.

The Convention on Biological Diversity and its underlying concepts can be difficult to communicate to politicians and to the general public. Nearly a decade after the Convention first acknowledged the lack of information and knowledge regarding biological diversity, it remains an issue that few people understand. There is little public discussion of how to make sustainable use of biodiversity part of economic development.

The greatest crunch in sustainable development decisions is the short—versus the long-term time frame. Sadly, it often still pays to exploit the environment now by harvesting as much as possible as fast as possible because economic rules do little to protect long-term interests.

Truly sustainable development requires countries to redefine their policies on land use, food, water, energy, employment, development, conservation, economics, and trade. Biodiversity protection and sustainable use requires the participation of ministries responsible for such areas as agriculture, forestry, fisheries, energy, tourism, trade and finance.

The challenge facing governments, businesses, and citizens is to forge transition strategies leading to long-term sustainable development. It means negotiating trade-offs even as people are clamoring for more land and businesses are pressing for concessions to expand their harvests. The longer we wait, the fewer options we will have.

Information, Education, and Training

The transition to sustainable development requires a shift in public attitudes as to what is an acceptable use of nature. This can only happen if people have the right information, skills, and organizations for understanding and dealing with biodiversity issues. Governments and the business community need to invest in staff and training, and they need to support organizations, including scientific bodies, that can deal with and advise on biodiversity issues.

We also need a long-term process of public education to bring about changes in behaviour and lifestyles, and to prepare societies for the changes needed for sustainability. Better biodiversity education would meet one of the goals set out in the Convention. . . .

Take Action Now

Although still in its infancy, the Convention on Biological Diversity is already making itself felt. The philosophy of sustainable development, the ecosystem approach, and the emphasis on building partnerships are all helping to shape global action on biodiversity. The data and reports that governments are gathering and sharing with each other are providing a sound basis for understanding the challenges and collaborating on the solutions.

Much, much more needs to be done. The passage of the Earth's biodiversity through the coming century will be its most severe test. With human population expected to rise dramatically, particularly in developing countries, and the consumer revolution set for exponential expansion—not to mention the worsening stresses of climate change, ozone depletion, and hazardous chemicals—species and ecosystems will face ever more serious threats. Unless we take action now, children born today will live in an impoverished world.

The Convention offers a comprehensive, global strategy for preventing such a tragedy. A richer future is possible. If governments and all sectors of society apply the concepts embodied in the Convention and make the conservation and sustainable use of biological diversity a real priority, we can ensure a new and sustainable relationship between humanity and the natural world for the generations to come.

The Convention on Biological Diversity Is Extremist and Harmful

by Michael Coffman

About the author: *Michael Coffman is chief executive officer of Sovereignty International, an educational organization that seeks to promote national sovereignty and individual freedom against what it considers to be threatening initiatives of the United Nations and other international organizations.*

Before the white man brought civilization to North America, wolves, bears and other roving wildlife moved unobstructed from Mexico to the Hudson Bay. Although few people are aware of it, America came very close to allowing wolves and other carnivores to once again have supreme right of movement across America—by mandate of a warm, fuzzy treaty called the Convention on Biological Diversity.

Clothed in innocence, the treaty is in fact designed to radically transform Western Civilization into a society where wolves and other entities of nature have more rights than humans. Irrefutable evidence of this agenda was covertly obtained from the United Nations and made available to the Senate in a cliff-hanger race to the wire during the waning hours of the 103rd [1993–94] Congress.

White Man's Cities

Environmentalists have long asserted that white man's cities, highways, intensive agriculture, forest harvesting, and other activities have disrupted and fragmented natural ecosystems. According to environmental theology, earth's so called fragile web of life is being destroyed as species become extinct by the thousands, and biodiversity, critical to the web's survival, vanishes. As the 1980s dawned, a new age dream of sustainability and a world treaty to protect biodiversity began to take shape in the minds of those who would return us to nature.

The dream culminated in the 1992 United Nations Conference on the Envi-

Reprinted, with permission, from "Biodiversity Treaty More Than Senate Willing to Pay," (by Michael Coffman), a 1997 online article of Sovereignty International at http://epi.freedom.org/biodiversity.htm. Reprinted with permission.

ronment, otherwise known as the Earth Summit, held in Rio de Janeiro. Hosted by none other than proclaimed new age and United Nations leader Maurice Strong, the Summit gave birth to what was called the Convention on Biological Diversity. Less than thirty pages long, this treaty was promoted as a crowning achievement for man that would save the earth by protecting biodiversity through the application of vaguely scribed principles and theology.

But a horrible thing happened on the way to the signing ceremony at the Summit. President George Bush balked. He believed it left the United States unprotected with too many critical issues undefined. In spite of global catcalls and hoots of disdain from the press, Bush stuck to his convictions and the United States refrained from signing this otherwise beguiling document.

Such mundane concerns were lost on the presidential green team that succeeded Bush. Overnight the treaty went from being a dangerous document to one destined to save the earth. With little fanfare, President Bill Clinton signed the treaty in July 1993, and the convention disappeared into the bowels of the Senate Foreign Relations Committee for a full review.

The Senate Considers Ratification

A year later . . . the treaty was very quietly reported out of committee, with a recommendation to the Senate for ratification. For a treaty environmentalists had repeatedly claimed to be the most important ever, almost no mention was made of it in either environmental literature or in the popular press. The silence for such an auspicious occasion was deafening.

Only one Senator in the Senate Foreign Relations Committee, Jesse Helms (R-NC), opposed the treaty. His concern centered on the troubling fact that the actual enabling and binding protocol for the treaty would be written after the Senate had ratified it. Furthermore, the treaty had no provision for additional Senate review once the protocol was written. The Senate would be, in effect, signing a blank check.

Worse, the draft enabling protocol was to be written by NGOs (Non-Governmental Organizations). Made up of primarily environmental and socialist organizations, NGOs are hardly the type of institutions that instill confidence in anyone who is pro-humanity and for economic develop-

> *"Clothed in innocence, the treaty is in fact designed to radically transform Western Civilization into a society where wolves . . . have more rights than humans."*

ment. Even so, by the time Senate Majority Leader George Mitchell scheduled the ratification vote for Monday, August 8, [1994] Helms only had four other Senate allies.

Senator Mitchell had expected no opposition to the treaty and doubtless he and other Senators were stunned when the Senate was buried in an avalanche of letters, faxes, and phone calls to Senators protesting the treaty. The staggering response was the result of an awesome fax campaign led by the Maine Conservation Rights Institute through the Alliance for America. While the Alliance has had numerous fax campaigns before, this time calls were coming in from every walk of life.

It quickly became obvious that the effort to stop the biodiversity treaty had taken on a life of its own as citizens throughout America copied and re-faxed the faxes to their frustrated friends. Phone lines into Senate offices were jammed for four days.

Although the enormous backlash to the treaty received little press, it got

> *"The treaty would open a Pandora's box of litigation and legislation by environmental groups and federal agencies."*

action in Washington. The American Farm Bureau and National Cattleman's Association worked with Minority Leader Dole to convince thirty-five Republican Senators to sign a letter to postpone the vote. Since any treaty must be ratified by two-thirds majority, thirty-five Senators was a mandate.

In spite of a frantic lobbying effort by environmentalists, accompanied by a massive effort by the State Department to assure the Senators that there was nothing in the treaty to cause concern, Mitchell postponed the ratification process until after the Senate reconvened in September.

The Global Biodiversity Assessment

The extra time permitted the National Wilderness Institute to commission Constitutional lawyer Mark Pollot to write a legal brief on the treaty's implications. Although the brief was conservative, the implications were horrifying. Not only would the Senate be signing a blank check, the treaty would open a Pandora's box of litigation and legislation by environmental groups and federal agencies seeking to use the Supremacy Clause of the Constitution to meet the provisions of the treaty's as yet unwritten protocol.

Pollot's brief made it imperative to define what form the enabling and binding protocol would take. The United Nation's *Global Biodiversity Assessment* (GBA) was supposed to provide this information. The United States had already contributed $430 million for the treaty, so it was only reasonable for the Senate to want to see what it had paid for. But the only response the Senate received from the UN was a curt reply that the GBA did not exist.

Senators still had no supporting documentation when Senator Mitchell rescheduled the ratification for Monday, October 3. So once again the fax machines were put into action and once again Senate phones were jammed with calls from citizens outraged by the threat this treaty imposed.

The smoking gun surfaced on Thursday, September 29 when the American Sheep Industry [Association] covertly got a copy of Section 10 of the United Nations GBA. Copies were forwarded to the Senate Republican Policy Committee the following day.

As suspected, Section 10 of the GBA detailed an incredible set of plans to reorganize western civilization around nature. Property rights and other civil rights would be limited to only those activities that would do no harm to biodiversity. Political jurisdictions would be defined by bioregions. Unbelievable oversight powers were given to NGOs.

Worst of all, the basis for protecting biodiversity and ecosystems was to be centered on what is known as the Wildlands Project. This draconian plan calls for setting aside vast areas (about 50 percent) of America into reserve wilderness areas, interconnecting corridors, and human buffer zones where human use would be eliminated or severely restricted. According to the June 25, 1993 issue of *Science* magazine, such a system of reserves and corridors would create "an archipelago of human-inhabited islands surrounded by natural areas."

The same Friday morning that Section 10 of the GBA was delivered to the Senate, the *Chicago Tribune* published a scathing front page article quoting the United Nations' claim that the GBA did not even exist. The article also attacked the Sheep Industry, Republicans, and grass-root citizens for their paranoia.

In the meantime, unaware of the damning evidence now in Republican hands, Senator Mitchell brought the tension to a fevered pitch by notifying Senator Robert Dole of his intent to petition to cloture the treaty that afternoon. If Mitchell was successful it would effectively eliminate debate on the treaty.

Race Against Time

Stunning color maps graphically illustrating the enormity of the Wildlands Project were already available through the Maine Conservation Rights Institute (MECRI), and the maps arrived in the Senate simultaneously with Section 10 of the GBA. It became a race against time as the Republicans put together this evidence before Senator Mitchell went to the floor to petition for cloture. Armed with a full set of four by six foot posters of these maps in one hand, and key excerpts from Section 10 in the other, Senator Kay Bailey Hutchison (R-TX) marched onto the Senate floor on Friday afternoon, September 30 and dropped the bombshell on the treaty's supporters—with devastating effect.

Senator Mitchell, who by now had also received a set of maps from MECRI, wisely withdrew his intent to petition to cloture the treaty. The Senate adjourned without ever voting on the treaty. Vice President Al Gore's dream of reinventing the government around nature was dead—at least for now.

Reason has prevailed and our Constitution remains unencumbered. Humans will continue to be more important than wolves and grizzlies, and perhaps—just perhaps—if we manage to survive the next legislative session we will finally listen to those traditional resource scientists who are finding that we can preserve and enhance biodiversity by using sound natural resource management techniques. We don't have to give half of America back to the wolves to save the earth after all.

Sustainable Development and Biodiversity Preservation Are Incompatible Goals

by Kent H. Redford and Brian Richter

About the authors: *Kent H. Redford works for the International Program of the Wildlife Conservation Society. Brian Richter is a hydrologist for the Nature Conservancy.*

Over the last decade biodiversity conservation has become an objective of international conventions, national governments, state agencies, non-governmental organizations, local communities, school clubs, and individuals. Unfortunately, while becoming a common objective, the true meaning of biodiversity conservation has been pulled from its roots in the biological sciences, becoming a political concept with as many meanings as it has advocates. This confusion of meanings can frustrate efforts to mobilize conservation action, because successful conservation relies on clear goals laid out with specific and commonly understood definitions and assumptions.

Of the many confusing concepts associated with biodiversity conservation, few demand greater definition and scrutiny than "conservation through use," sometimes known as "compatible" or "sustainable" use. At face value these terms suggest that certain types or levels of human use are ecologically benign, incurring little or no loss of biodiversity. In fact, it was the promise that such human use would serve as the basis for conservation that brought so many different interest groups to agree on the importance of biodiversity conservation. Advocates of compatible use have suggested that substituting a compatible use for an incompatible one, or helping to perpetuate an existing use deemed as being compatible, is a reasonable strategy for conserving biodiversity. But strong warnings have been issued by conservation biologists such as Curtis H. Freese: "Human

Excerpted from Kent H. Redford and Brian Richter, "Conservation of Biodiversity in a World of Use," *Wild Earth*, vol. 10, no. 2 (802-434-4077; www.wild-earth.org). This article was adapted from a longer, more technical article in *Conservation Biology*, vol. 13, pp. 1246–56. Reprinted by permission of *Wild Earth*, the authors, and Blackwell Science, Inc.

intervention in an ecosystem for commercial purposes inevitably alters and generally simplifies, at some scale, ecosystem structure, composition, and function."

We maintain that compatibility between human use and biodiversity conservation cannot be stated in binary terms as a "yes" or "no" condition. All use has consequences. Different kinds and intensities of human use affect various aspects or components of biodiversity to differing degrees. Further, individual or societal decisions about the degree of biodiversity impact that is deemed "compatible" are value dependent and should be recognized as such. In reality, the incidence, the source, and the effects of many changes are often unclear, and that lack of clarity impedes action on both political and practical levels.

A Biodiversity Framework

Because the interaction between biodiversity and human use results in such complex impacts and variable degrees of conservation, we believe that some means of measuring the success of biodiversity conservation efforts is desperately needed. In that spirit, we have proposed a heuristic framework for measuring the consequences of human use for biodiversity. This framework builds from a matrix presented by Reed F. Noss and draws from a very specific definition of biodiversity.

Biodiversity refers to the *natural* variety and variability among living organisms, the ecological complexes in which they naturally occur, and the ways in which they interact with each other and with the physical environment. Biodiversity has three different components: genetic, population/species, and community/ecosystem. Each of these components has compositional, structural, and functional attributes. *Composition* refers to the identity and variety of elements in each of the biodiversity components. *Structure* refers to the physical organization or pattern of the elements. *Function* refers to ecological or evolutionary processes acting among the elements.

We suggest that the effects of human use or alteration on biodiversity can be assessed with our framework by determining how different types and intensities of resource use affect both the components of biodiversity and their attributes as defined above. In order to test the application of the framework, we examined conservation efforts at two sites where The Nature Conservancy has been working: the Roanoke River in North Carolina and the Pantanal in Brazil. We then additionally tested the framework against illustrative examples of human resource use from the literature.

> *"Of the many confusing concepts associated with biodiversity conservation, few demand greater definition and scrutiny than . . . 'sustainable' use."*

The results of our assessments demonstrate that the full range and expression of biodiversity components and attributes can be conserved only in ecological systems that are altered either very little or not at all. In those systems in which human impacts are more pronounced, the different biodiversity components and attributes are often affected. Some of these components and attributes are more sensitive to human use, while others are more robust. For example, genetic effects appear under much lighter regimes of use than do changes in ecosystem function.

Biodiversity and Human Use

We found that all consumptive use affects biodiversity in some attribute or component, commonly affecting not only the target component but other components as well. For example, the genetic component has been shown to be adversely affected by harvesting, be it fishing, logging, or trophy hunting. The population/species component is most commonly understood to be affected by human uses, and much work has demonstrated this, although subtle effects are often missed. Of increasing importance is an understanding of how the community/ecosystem component has been and is being affected by human activities. The extent to which the different attributes are affected by use remains a little understood and important topic for further research.

The primary points we gained from our analyses are that:
• different degrees of human use or alteration result in different negative effects on biodiversity;
• some components and attributes of biodiversity are more sensitive than other components to human use or alteration; and
• only extremely limited use or virtually no alteration will protect all components.

In our daily work we confront the discordance between the view that humans can use biodiversity without causing any harm, and our experience, shared by many of our peers, that this is not possible.

We follow in a long history of those who advocate that all biological entities and their environments have intrinsic value independent of their usefulness to humans. This value applies not just to species, or communities, or ecosystems, but to the complex intertwined web of life that has come to be called biodiversity. In such a value system, the preservation of biodiversity for its own sake, in its entirety and in its component parts, is a legitimate objective in and of itself. Our analysis suggested that biodiversity in its entirety can be conserved only in areas of very limited or no human use. But the vast majority of both the terrestrial and aquatic world have been, and will continue to be, vital sources of resources for the human population. We live in a world of use. But we must accept the undeniable fact that we cannot fully conserve the biodiversity of this planet through compatible or sustainable resource use strategies alone. All comprehensive biodiversity conservation strategies must be rooted in large protected areas in both the terrestrial and the marine realm.

Stabilizing Human Population Growth Would Help Preserve Biodiversity

by Richard Cincotta and Robert Engelman

About the authors: *Richard Cincotta is an ecologist and researcher for Population Action International (PAI), a Washington, D.C.–based organization that advocates policies to slow human population growth. Robert Engelman directs the Population and Environment Program at PAI.*

The world's biological wealth is dwindling. Earth—the only location in the universe that we know supports life—is being transformed into a world that is genetically poorer. The loss is irretrievable, and its roots lie in the spectacular success of a single species: us, *Homo sapiens*. The disappearance of species, proceeding thousands of times faster today than in the pre-human past, is still accelerating and is likely to advance even more rapidly in the 21st century. No one can know when the process will end, or what the world of nature will look like when it does.

Hopeful signs do brighten this dark prospect, however. Among the most hopeful is that human population may well reach a plateau or peak by the middle of the 21st century. The pressure of human activities on remaining habitats could reach a maximum around the same time—and then, perhaps, begin to subside.

Among the most pressing questions are: Does human population growth really matter to species loss? Can policies and programs significantly influence human population trends, and can they do this while upholding the basic human right of couples and individuals to make their own decisions about reproduction, free from interference? The evidence shows that the answer to all these questions is yes.

Scientists are becoming increasingly convinced that human beings have caused ecosystem change and species extinction almost since our own species emerged. Between 50,000 and 10,000 years ago, as early populations of hu-

Reprinted from an online summary of the book *Nature's Place: Human Population and the Future of Biological Diversity*, by Richard Cincotta and Robert Engelman, published by Population Action International, 2000, at www.populationaction.org/pubs/biodiv00/html/summary3.htm. Reprinted with permission.

mans expanded across the continents, more than 200 species of large animals disappeared forever. Then, between 1,500 and 500 years ago, as human populations reached the farthest oceanic islands, over 1,000 species of island birds went extinct. Today's wave of extinctions, however, is even more extensive. Moreover, it is fundamentally different from its two predecessors in ways that relate strongly to the pervasiveness and size of today's human population:

- *For the first time, human activities are affecting species of all types and habits, at all points of the globe, and pushing many toward extinction.* Scientists project that at least half of all living species could ultimately disappear due to habitat loss alone, creating a mass extinction on a scale comparable to those that have ended past geologic eras.

> *"Population growth is among a handful of underlying conditions determining the type and intensity of human activities that lead to biodiversity loss."*

- *Apart from habitat loss, other agents of human-caused extinction are now at work.* Even more species could disappear as a result of pollution, overhunting, overfishing and inadvertent introduction of exotic species into weakened ecosystems. Hanging over the future of all life is the puzzle of how global climate will change in coming centuries as a result of human influences, and how these changes will affect ecosystems and the species they support.

- *Not all species are at risk, however.* Evolution is resilient. A small percentage of species—from pigeons, to weeds, to microbial parasites—have proliferated beyond their pre-human numbers or ranges. Rapidly evolving pests and disease-causing organisms could swell their ranks. Humanity itself, with more than 30 times the population density it ever could have achieved without agriculture, now appears to have become the central organizing reality around which non-human life will evolve.

Population and Biodiversity

The full range of connections between local population growth, the influence of distant consumers, changing ecosystems and the loss of species is complex, controversial and in need of more research. Nonetheless, biologists agree on several key points:

- *Population growth is among a handful of underlying conditions determining the type and intensity of human activities that lead to biodiversity loss.* Population size itself is an important determinant of the *scale* of humanity's use of natural resources—resources upon which other species depend, as well. Population growth, along with increasing per capita consumption, has played a key role in the development of *human-dominated ecosystems* in which the survival of wild species is often precarious. And recent population growth has made biological conservation efforts more difficult, more expensive and more likely to conflict with human needs.

- *The growth of our species' numbers is tightly coupled to rising demand for food and shelter.* Increasing the supply of these essentials, by whatever means, affects biodiversity. Agricultural expansion and urban sprawl play the largest discernible roles in the loss and fragmentation of the world's forests and wetlands, and contribute significantly to river and coral reef siltation. Intensified agriculture and urban concentration are leading contributors to water-borne pollution. And jointly, agriculture and domestic activities account for over three-quarters of all water withdrawn for use from reservoirs and aquifers. These are also the primary beneficiaries of dam-building, which is one of the top two causes (along with biological invasions) of freshwater species extinctions.

- *When considering human population growth, analysts tend to overlook the parallel growth and proliferation of populations of organisms that are closely associated with our species.* These organisms, which include domestic and other species that thrive in human-dominated ecosystems, are themselves often principal agents of ecological disruption and biodiversity loss.

Early stabilization of human population would not by itself act as a breakwater against the current wave of extinctions. Nonetheless, it is arguably a necessary condition for saving more than 10 percent of the earth's natural ecosystems in perpetuity. And that achievement, ecologists argue, will be needed to avoid losing more than half of the planet's remaining plant and animal species.

Population Pressures in the Most Biodiverse Places

The emerging technology of *geographic information systems* (GIS) opens up new possibilities for analyzing the distribution and richness of species, including our own species. Several key findings emerge in this first-ever effort to utilize this technology in a Population Action International report:

- *More than 1.1 billion people now live within the 25 global biodiversity hotspots, described by ecologists as the most threatened species-rich regions on Earth.* In 19 of these hotspots, population is growing more rapidly than in the world as a whole. In one hotspot (the Caucasus), population is decreasing moderately. While the hotspots extend across some 12 percent of the planet's land surface, by 1995 they were home to about 20 percent of the world's population.

> *"More than 1.1 billion people now live within the 25 global biodiversity hotspots."*

- *Around 75 million people, or 1.3 percent of the world's population, live within the three major tropical wilderness areas: the Upper Amazonia and Guyana Shield, the Congo River Basin, and the New Guinea-Melanesia complex of islands.* All together, these areas cover around 6 percent of Earth's land surface. Population in the tropical wilderness areas is, on average, growing at an annual rate of 3.1 percent, over twice the world's average rate of growth—a product of rapid migration and high rural fertility rates in these regions.

- *In most hotspots located in developed countries, populations are projected to grow for several decades to come.* Past and present migration into these areas is the major factor in this continued growth, specifically in the U.S. states of California, Florida and Hawaii, and in western Australia and in New Zealand. Much of this migration is internal, with more people moving to warmer climates and coastal areas. Significant international migration has also been involved, to varying degrees, much of it with origins in developing countries. Much of what society and conservationists will need to accomplish to save species will have little to do directly with population change. Population analysis can, however, provide a measure of the risks that most species will face. For as population grows and as additional land, water and waste-absorbing sinks are needed to support these individuals, some conservation options necessarily fall by the wayside.

Population and Hope

The evidence of recent demographic research suggests that couples the world over, and especially younger women, today desire later childbirths and fewer children than ever before. Both desires—if put into effect—contribute powerfully to the slowing of population growth, now averaging 1.6 percent annually for less developed regions of the world and 0.3 percent for the developed regions. *The growth of our species, once the object of environmental fears, has instead shown itself in the past decade to be among the more resolvable of environmental concerns.*

A plateau or peak in human population by the middle of the new century is possible. But this is likely to occur only if developed and developing countries renew their commitments to the principles—and the shared investments—agreed to in 1994 at the International Conference on Population and Development in Cairo.

An early halt to human population growth will not end human-caused extinctions. Conservationists will continue to contend with our species' unprecedented densities, its geographic range and mobility, its need for natural resources and ways to dispose of wastes, and its use of technologies. The possibility of world population stabilization, in combination with modest decline in some regions, nonetheless offers among the greatest hopes for the future of species and ecosystem conservation on a human-dominated planet.

Governments Should Reduce Resource Exploitation

by Gary Kline

About the author: *Gary Kline is a professor of political science at Georgia Southwestern State University.*

Occupying a position at the top of the trophic pyramid, human beings necessarily impact the environment. Greater numbers mean a more significant impact. Human beings take up space, food, and other resources. The twentieth century has witnessed a population explosion—from approximately a billion people in 1900 to a projected six billion in the year 2000 and ten billion by the first quarter of the Twenty-first Century. Against natural ecosystems, humans may win the struggle for space, but only temporarily. The base of the trophic pyramid must remain broad enough to support the top, so population growth cannot be indefinitely sustained. Edward Wilson has written:

> Human demographic success has brought the world to this crisis of biodiversity. Human beings—mammals of the 50-kilogram weight class and members of a group, the primates, otherwise noted for scarcity—have become a hundred times more numerous than any other land animal of comparable size in the history of life. By every conceivable measure, humanity is ecologically abnormal. Our species appropriates between 20 and 40 percent, of the solar energy captured in organic material by land plants. There is no way that we can draw upon the resources of the planet to such a degree without drastically reducing the state of most other species.

The problem of population growth is exacerbated by the legacy of colonialism and the maldistribution of resources, especially land, and of political power. Colonial and post-colonial policies have steadily contributed to a polarization of rich and poor. The primarily agrarian developing countries have experienced an immense concentration of land ownership with a consequent dispossession

Excerpted from Gary Kline, "Biodiversity and Development," *Journal of Third World Studies*, Spring 1998. Reprinted by permission.

of many millions. Rather than face revolution or genuine land reforms, Third World governments have frequently opted for opening the fragile ecosystems of the tropics to settlement by the poor. Cary Fowler and Pat Mooney warn that "thousands of people left landless and jobless in the aftermath of the plantation economy are invading the tropical forest." The case of the Amazonian rain forest come readily to mind.

The United Nations Food and Agriculture Organization estimates the rate of destruction of tropical rain forests alone at some fifteen million hectares (or about thirty-seven million acres) annually, an area larger than that of Ireland. Indeed, it is these areas of greatest diversity and fragility which are most threatened today. At best, however, this is an ephemeral solution to such social problems because the poor soil of the rain forests can be farmed for only a few years before it is effete. The rich biodiversity of these ecosystems is decimated in the bargain. Unfortunately, these are also the areas with the highest rates of population growth.

Development and the Environment

Population pressures and interrelated factors have placed ecosystems everywhere under siege. Over-population in and of itself will lead to over-exploitation of biological resources. But in market systems, where the incentive of material profit governs, over-exploitation is encouraged as a matter of policy. The materialistic standards of the industrialized North, especially the U.S., are insinuated globally in the guise of "modernization," "progress," or "development." The countries of the North are especially discordant with Nature, though their technological superiority has allowed them to exercise hegemony. Traditional folkways and naturalistic religions and cultures which formerly helped protect Nature from the potential ravages of humankind have been consistently disparaged. An ethos of domination has supplanted one of reverence for the Earth.

Notions of development have been intertwined with such activities as clearing land, logging, paving and building, draining wetlands, application of chemicals, urbanization, industrialization, and a manifold of forces destructive of the environment. National policies generally calculate the value of natural resources in terms of their exploitation and discount their indirect value. This is the most insidious threat to biodiversity. It has been assumed that development entails an

> *"The problem of population growth is exacerbated by . . . the maldistribution of resources."*

increasing material standard—higher levels of production and energy usage, more intensive exploitation of natural resources, spiralling rates of consumption, waste and so forth.

In fact, if it could be adopted worldwide (which for a variety of reasons is not feasible) a material standard of living comparable to that of the U.S. would literally precipitate a collapse of the global environment. The industrialized agriculture of the U.S. provides the best illustration. . . . Were this industrial monoculture adopted globally, all known reserves of petroleum would be depleted in less than two decades. As it is, petroleum will be exhausted before the close of the 21st century, bad news indeed for industry and agriculture as we know it. Low-input crops will be a necessity.

The engineered crop varieties which require so much energy to yield their potential abundance will be in great need of the traditional mechanisms of defense and production: genetic diversity. Uniformity is a serious threat to sustainable agriculture, though a requisite for patenting seeds. Nevertheless, the corporate world continues to produce and push these narrowed varieties. Pressures to produce cash crops and displacement of traditional varieties by high-yield varieties (HYVs) are contributing to an alarming level of gene loss. It is estimated that more than ninety-five percent of the plant varieties which once graced American farms and gardens is now lost. "The new varieties are destroying—by replacing in the farmers' fields—the 'seed corn' of genetic diversity on which the newer varieties must be built," according to Raymond Nicholas.

The U.N. Food and Agriculture Organization claims that the "improved" varieties have eliminated about seventy-five percent of agricultural diversity worldwide. The pattern is reinforced by government policies, which subsidize particular kinds of crops and farm methods, by lenders, who choose the farmers and the

> *"We must hope . . . that our precious legacy of biodiversity will not be . . . decimated by human 'progress.'"*

crops that will receive loans, and by processors and marketers, who favor large producers, uniform produce, appearance, etc. Cultural tastes have followed these forces and presently constitute a further obstacle to any needed adjustments.

Centers of Biodiversity

We must hope, then, that our precious legacy of biodiversity will not be so decimated by human "progress" and "development" that insufficient remains to sustain life. Ironically, the rich countries of the North have the least biodiversity while the poor and developing countries of the South have the most. During the Ice Age, plant life was literally frozen in the temperate zones, while in the warmer tropical zones plant life flourished. The great Russian biologist Nikolai Vavilov first noted the unevenness of plant biodiversity and began to map the global pattern. More recent studies have refined the picture, but the areas of greatest biodiversity are still referred to as Vavilovian Centers. These are the original homes of the plants we rely on most. In truth, the thirty plant crops which together provide ninety-five percent of the food Humankind consumes came from Asia, Africa, and Latin America. The value of germplasm from the South to the farmers of the industrialized North is inestimable.

The countries of the North are now more cognizant of the value of the biodiversity of these centers. But the Third World is engulfed in debt even as it has virtually given away its genetic wealth to the North. The U.S. has argued that this biodiversity constitutes a "common heritage" of humanity which should be freely available to those (corporate) interests who wish to work with it. Nevertheless, the U.S. has argued that the corporations which are engineering seeds commercially and relying on these genetic materials to do so should be allowed to patent (and thus control) and profit from them. Meanwhile, in these areas of "economic underdevelopment" and biological richness, peoples are under great pressure to exploit their resources more rapidly and extensively in order to earn foreign exchange; and at the same time they have the fewest resources for programs of conservation and protection of biodiversity. The stakes are high, indeed. It is in the interests of all creatures, then, to find ways of preserving the Earth's biodiversity.

> *"Those who conserve our biological wealth deserve more of the benefits and more control over their lives and communities."*

Biodiversity: How Do We Protect It?

Biological diversity is a product of a tremendous variety of environmental conditions. This provides a clue to how to preserve it: our strategies and methods must also be diverse. Strength lies in variety, as we have seen. In agriculture, the great diversity of landraces was the result of many millions of individual farmers who over millennia saved seeds, selected plants, evaluated, and crossbred them. The essential role and vast contributions of these small, traditional farmers has too often been ignored. Any attempt to preserve biodiversity in agriculture necessarily must include these unsung and beleaguered heroes. Indigenous peoples have a wealth of knowledge and detail which will be critical to conservation of remaining plant species and varieties and the wider ecosystems in which they are embedded. They must be involved and rewarded; we cannot afford to allow agribusiness and financial institutions to eliminate this key sector of society, upon which all others ultimately rest. Biodiversity is essential to agriculture, and farmers and agrarian communities are essential to the conservation of biodiversity.

Simply put, those who conserve our biological wealth deserve more of the benefits and more control over their lives and communities. The landraces and genes taken by seed corporations from Third World farmers, and which are critical to the bioengineering of new varieties of plant crops, should not be used now to undermine small-scale agriculture and impoverish the very farmers who have developed and conserved these valuable biological resources. Traditional farmers had also developed methods and techniques of agriculture that allowed them to secure yields which were sustainable. But management has increas-

202

ingly been removed from these farmers and turned over in reality to remote government policy-makers or corporations. Conservation policies must begin with land reform and a healthy, new respect for local traditions, customs, and values. Insofar as possible, community-based institutions should be given responsibility for managing local conservation measures and policies.

National-level policies should be consonant and supportive. They must provide incentives to conserve rather than exploit biological resources. The world's traditional farmers must first be enlisted, encouraged to participate by rewarding use of their capital, labor, and land in ways that protect biodiversity. Currently, those who exploit are favored by most policies. Exploiters of biological resources benefit especially because the true costs of resource depletion are not calculated in most national policies. The real costs are surreptitiously passed along to society or to future generations. Glaring examples abound even in the U.S. where national lands, supposedly set aside for the future, are ranched or mined or logged at bargain-basement prices. Government policies must increasingly take into consideration the effects on biological resources and ecosystems. Advocates of "development" must understand that over-exploitation is far more costly than sustainable resource usage. Restoring ecosystems is, indeed, often impossible at any price. Conservation should be part of the definition of development and sustainability should be its cornerstone. Future generations are at stake; we have a moral responsibility to think of them.

Species and genes are best protected by protecting ecosystems. So many conservation efforts should be in situ. Traditional farmers should be subsidized to grow landraces, for example, because these are valuable for agriculture; but growing them puts the farmer at a disadvantage vis-a-vis those practicing industrial monoculture. Nations also need to set aside large tracts of land rich in biodiversity and strictly prohibit human interference,. Nature must have her places to work her will, which is beyond our powers. Ex situ conservation will also play a major role since so many ecosystems are already vitiated or terminal. There is a massive task ahead merely trying to identify and describe the characteristics of species. Plants and animals must then be kept viable, another monumental task requiring substantial funding. Plant gene banks should strive to preserve as many remaining landraces and "wild and weedy relatives of food crops" as possible.

"We must learn to appreciate and respect the diversity of life."

Because biodiversity is a world treasure, and because it is threatened by powerful economic, political, and social forces, the costs of conservation must be borne by all nations. Why, indeed, should not the North, which has prospered so handsomely in large part due to the biological wealth appropriated during colonial and neo-colonial periods, help bear the costs of conservation efforts which are so acutely needed in the South, where most of the wealth originated and yet remains? All of humanity will benefit. The future of the North is bound intimately with that of the South: the more affluent countries should lend assistance in the form of loans and grants, information, technical assistance, equipment, subsidies, and the like. Third World debt must be mitigated through constructive arrangements like the "debt-for-Natural swaps," but on a larger scale than at present.

Changing a Gluttonous Culture

The most important contribution the North could make, however, would be to reign in its materialistic culture and gluttonous appetite for energy and other resources. This, of course, would entail not merely material changes, but also profound changes in the dominant Western attitude toward Nature. As it is, we may be acting out on a grand scale a classic Greek tragedy in which hubris is the fatal flaw of the hero. We are deluding ourselves that we can dominate and endlessly manipulate Nature for our convenience. We cannot. Our prideful anthropocentric perspective must be tempered by reality before it is too late. Human survival depends upon our recognition that Nature's laws apply to us unequivocally. Development is not primarily about resource exploitation or domination, but about mastering our selves and living in harmony with Nature and in society with one another.

It is the task of education to help bring about greater awareness, as opposed to merely more technical knowledge. Many professions and disciplines must be enlisted and must cooperate. It makes no sense for political decisions to be made without regard for the environmental impacts of policy; or for economics to ignore the laws of physics and of ecology. We must learn to appreciate and respect the diversity of life, within the human community and without. In the words of Senegalese conservationist Baba Dioum, "In the end, we will conserve only what we love, we will love only what we understand, we will understand only what we are taught."

Preserving Cultural and Linguistic Diversity Can Help Protect Biological Diversity

by David Harmon

About the author: *David Harmon is executive director of the George Wright Society, a professional association of people who work with cultural and natural parks and reserves. He is a co-founder of Terralingua.*

Life's variety—its scope, depth and meaning—is one of the great story lines throughout history. Much of the world's visual and performing arts, its folklore and literature, can be interpreted as a coming-to-grips with difference. For many people, diversity is engaged through their experience of fellow human beings. "Know then thyself, presume not God to scan / The proper study of mankind is man," advised Alexander Pope in a famous couplet. For others, though, the wondrous profusion of nature is itself a kind of poetry, engendering passion and abiding interest:

> For centuries the diversity of living things has been a major interest of mankind. Not only are the multitude of the distinct 'kinds' or species of organisms and the variety of their structures seemingly endless, but there is no uniformity within species. . . . From remotest times, attempts have been made to understand the causes and significance of organic diversity. To many minds the problem possesses an irresistible aesthetic appeal, and inasmuch as scientific inquiry is a form of aesthetic endeavor, biology owes its existence in part to this appeal.

Theodosius Dobzhansky used these words to begin his *Genetics and the Origin of Species,* one of this century's major works of biology, a cornerstone of the "modern synthesis" of genetics and evolution.

Reprinted from David Harmon, "Sameness and Silence: Language Extinctions and the Dawning of a Biocultural Approach to Diversity," *Global Diversity*, vol. 8, no. 3 (Winter 1998), by permission of the author and the Canadian Museum of Nature, Ottawa, Canada.

Two Realms of Diversity

The two great realms of living diversity are cultural and biological. Today both are in peril, and it is no coincidence. The core of the biodiversity crisis is that we have placed our needs at the centre of the world, eclipsing those of all other species. Having done that, we now seem bent on reducing civilization to a single archetype, that of Western (largely U.S.) industrialized society—a kind of Global America.

The real story is not nearly so simple as this sweeping summary, of course. The grandiloquent "we" is still a rich plurality. Many indigenous peoples, for example, espouse biocentric world views, and exhibit none of the hubris to which the technologically sure-footed West seems all too susceptible. Moreover, the fast rise to prominence of the biodiversity issue within conservation and academic biology is, on one level, a collective statement of dissent against the dominant social and economic paradigm. Despite the long-standing interest recognized by Dobzhansky, it is only in the last twenty years [prior to 1998] that global biological diversity has come to be analyzed in depth. This period has seen the birth of the term "biodiversity" and of the discipline of conservation biology. More recently, two major global studies, by the World Conservation Monitoring Centre and the United Nations Environment Programme, have synthesized massive amounts of information on Earth's biological riches, both terrestrial and marine. Scores of scholarly books, several new journals, and countless specialist articles have been produced.

Why the flood of activity, and why now? We know the answer, though some may feel ashamed to admit it. The urgency comes from a feeling of dread of an impending crisis, of a looming threshold of biotic impoverishment—that Rubicon of extinction whose crossing humans might survive physically, but not spiritually. Dobzhansky was right: at the bottom of biology is the question of diversity's significance. Nothing in the discipline's theory—and now, nothing in its practice—is more important.

The same urgency has taken hold in anthropology and linguistics, the two social sciences most interested in cultural diversity. Their concern is globalization, whose foundations go back to the beginnings of European imperial-colonial ambition. Today, globalization runs in overdrive, fired by one advance after another in telecommunications and information processing, orchestrated by transnational corporations determined to develop a seamless global market-

> *"The two great realms of living diversity are cultural and biological."*

place. National governments have generally converged with the private sector on a market-based ideology that values uniformity and consistency (to deliver products) and devalues variety and uncertainty (as barriers to trade and investment). This is "perhaps the fundamental problem," as Jeffrey McNeely, IUCN's [World Conservation Union] chief biodiversity officer, sees it. The world . . .

has become a single global trading system, bringing new technologies, new approaches and new pressures for exploiting resources, . . . [overwhelming] resource management measures that local communities had developed from their long experience of surviving in an uncertain world. [These] highly diverse and often localized adaptations to local environmental conditions [are being replaced by] a world culture increasingly characterized by very high levels of material consumption, at least for a privileged minority.

Comparing Species and Languages

McNeely is one of a growing number of scientists and conservationists who have begun to analyze biological and cultural diversity in an integrated way. It is not a new approach: comparing species and languages, for example, has a venerable history. In biology; it goes back at least to Charles Darwin, whose enthusiasm is evident both in the *Origin of Species* and *The Descent of Man,* as well as in his praise of Sir Charles Lyell's chapter comparing species and languages in the great geologist's *Antiquity of Man.* This is because the two are fundamental units whose existence and importance seem self-evident. Yet each is hard to define in practice because it is not easy separating discrete from continuous variation at the margins, where species blend into other species (or subspecies) and languages into languages (or dialects). The standard defining criteria—that is, reproductive isolation for species,

> *"A growing number of scientists and conservationists . . . have begun to analyze biological and cultural diversity in an integrated way."*

and mutual intelligibility for languages—explain things quite well in many instances, but neither is authoritative. In nature, there are numerous exceptions to the classic biological species concept; while in linguistics, there are many examples where speech forms considered to be dialects of a single language are mutually unintelligible.

The process governing the formation of species and languages is similarly complex. In most cases, it follows prolonged geographic isolation resulting from the separation of a community of plants or animals or the migration of a community of speakers. Geographic isolation allows for—though does not necessarily produce—reproductive isolation (for species) or communicative isolation (for languages). If they do occur, a new species or language is born. Yet sympatric speciation (that occurring in the same area) is common, as are cases of "sympatric" language genesis: Aboriginal Australia is an excellent example where separate languages (over 250) apparently formed without long-term isolation, but rather through cultural interchange. This alternative mode of language development requires a relatively stable social equilibrium to be successful.

The elimination of conditions that allow for the isolation of species or languages threatens the continuation of large-scale speciation and language development. Just as the habitats of native flora and fauna are threatened by invasive species, languages can be threatened by disruptions to the cultural and economic settings in which they have evolved. Just as modern transport allows invasive species to travel all over the world, global telecommunications means that economically dominant languages are now heard daily in the remotest regions. Geographic isolation no longer results in either communicative isolation or the stable social equilibrium needed for mutual cultural enrichment.

Gauging Cultural Diversity

Cultures cannot be distinguished on the basis of one facet. Nonetheless, broad trends in cultural diversity can be tracked by gauging trends in linguistic diversity, the range of variation exhibited across languages. This is difficult to measure because, as any linguist can tell you, there are vehement disagreements over the taxonomy of the world's languages. So, just as species richness serves as the most common standard of global biodiversity, language richness, or the number of distinct languages in use, signifies linguistic diversity.

Language richness also conveniently indicates cultural diversity as a whole. Not only is language the carrier of many cultural differences (and is considered by many to be emblematic of distinctive world views), it is the best proxy measure because it allows a comprehensible division of the world's peoples into constituent groups. If we could on a single day ask each person on the planet to name his or her native language, the results would be an approximation of the world's cultural diversity at that moment.

Even if this were possible, such a census would not capture the nuances of language use. For example, if "mother tongue" is defined as a person's "first language," then it follows that even a person raised in a bilingual or multilingual household can have only one mother tongue. This may be true in a strict sense, but the daily experience of millions of people includes the equally effective use of two (or more) languages, usually in different spheres: one at home, another at work or the market, perhaps a third at worship, and so forth.

The Scope of Language Extinction

Such multilingualism may well have been the norm throughout most of history, but it likely will not be much longer. Every linguist who has seriously studied the situation believes that large numbers of the world's languages are threatened with extinction in the decades to come. As with species extinction projections, the evidence for this derives not from accurate empirical data, but from extrapolations—in this case, extrapolations from what is known about the process of language extinction among smaller languages for which linguists have obtained detailed demographic information. The crucial question is whether a language is becoming moribund. This occurs when it is no longer being passed on to the younger generations of the speech community. The failure of intergenerational transmission in a language is analogous to the loss of reproductive capacity in a species.

We know that the great majority of indigenous languages in North America are in trouble. Probably 80% of those in the USA are moribund and the general situation in Canada and Mexico is very poor, Leanne Hinton's 1994 review of the situation in California paints a typical picture. Of the 50 contemporary indigenous languages in the state (at least 50 others existed before Europeans arrived), more than 15 are recently extinct and many others have fewer than 10 speakers (all elders). Only two or three have as many as 150 or 200 speakers. The pages of linguistic journals, papers presented at conferences, and postings to the ENDANGERED LANGUAGES e-mail list are filled with similar examples. Even in Europe (where European Union (EU) recognition of language rights is relatively strong compared with the rest of the world), almost every regional language is haunted by incipient or possible moribundity.

To assess the global situation, . . . I analyzed data from *Ethnologue: Languages of the World* (the standard reference) with endangerment factors in mind. . . . Of the roughly 6,500 living languages listed, the 10 largest account for just under half of the world's population. By contrast, between 3,400 and 4,000 languages (52%–60% of the global total) are spoken by no more than 10,000 people. Most of these are indigenous languages, and they are the mother tongues of roughly 8 million people only, or far less than 1% of the world's population. The overwhelming dominance of the "big ten," [the ten largest languages, which cover 49% of the world's population] the disparity between the great number of small languages and the tiny proportion of the world's population they represent, and the globalization pressures discussed above are the three macro-factors that point to a probable mass extinction of languages in the coming century.

> *"The great majority of indigenous languages in North America are in trouble."*

It seems likely that the overall percentage of linguistic extinctions during the 21st century will far exceed current estimates of species extinctions, which put global species loss at 1–10% per decade. Michael Krauss thinks that perhaps 50% of the world's languages are already moribund, and that 20–50% will likely become extinct during the next hundred years, with as many as 90% becoming so moribund as to be committed to extinction. Peter Mühlhäusler believes that more than 95% of all languages are endangered, and RMW Dixon estimates that at least 75% will become extinct. I think it is reasonable to predict that, during the next century, at least 50% of the world's languages will become extinct (or irreversibly moribund) as mother tongues. At worst the percentage could be far higher.

Why even try to preserve this raft of tiny languages, these relics of a bygone era which will never be of any economic or political importance, and whose existence was always precarious anyway? Let me try answering with an analogy.

A couple of years ago, I was listening to a radio news story about U.S. government efforts to protect grizzly bears in the greater Yellowstone region. The reporter interviewed a local rancher who said, "Why are we wasting money on this? Our grandparents spent a lot of time and effort cleaning bears out of this country so our children, livestock and homes would be safe." The unspoken argument is that free-ranging grizzlies—potentially deadly, with next to no commercial value in comparison with sheep or cattle—are obsolete within the context of a modern, agricultural landscape. The counter-argument is that grizzly bears are important to a vital, intact ecosystem, and the ecosystem is to be valued in its entirety, whatever inconveniences, dangers or economic hardships its individual components may pose to humans.

This is essentially the same argument that must be made for preserving languages and the other components of cultural diversity. Though an individual language may be economically and demographically insignificant on a global scale, each one is a unique expression of human creativity. There is no such thing as a "primitive" language. [Dixon writes that] modern linguistics shows that "all languages are roughly equal in terms of overall complexity" and that, "by examining the ways meanings are organised in some little-known language," linguists may "evolve some new mode of thinking that could help to deal with problems in the modern world." This is very like Aldo Leopold's famous injunction about natural resource management: the first rule of intelligent tinkering is to keep all the parts. Whether in nature or culture, it is diversity as a whole and the processes that created it, not just the individual products of those processes, which must be valued.

Another reason biologists should care about cultural diversity is because endemism and richness in species and languages coincide on a national scale, and this is strongly suggestive of a substantive relationship between the two. Over 80% of the world's languages are endemic to a single country, and those countries with the highest number of endemic languages are also among the highest in endemic species. Of the 25 countries with the most endemic languages, 16 are also in the top 25 in endemic vertebrate species, and 12 appear on the list of the 19 countries with the most Endemic Bird Areas as identified by BirdLife International. In addition, 17 are in the top 25 for higher (flowering) plants, including non-endemics. Finally, 10 of the 12 "megadiversity countries" are also among the top 25 in endemic languages.

"Endemism and richness in species and languages coincide on a national scale."

Three biogeographical principles help explain these patterns of concurrence. First, large countries with highly varied terrain, climate and ecosystems tend to have high numbers of endemic species simply because of their size and biophysical diversity. These same factors, operating at the lower population levels that prevailed before European expansion, also fostered communicative isolation, thus allowing many small autonomous languages to evolve. Second, island countries tend to have higher numbers (and often a high density) of endemics because of their physical isolation from continental land masses. Islands that in addition have broken terrain or some other significant physical barriers to ease of movement also tend to have more endemic languages than similar continental countries. Third, tropical countries tend to have more species than others. These countries also tend to have more endemic languages because their species richness made it possible for small hunter-gatherer bands to flourish before the advent of concentrated agriculture. With these small cultural groups came many endemic languages. Examples of the first factor include Mexico, USA, India and China; of the second, Papua New Guinea and Philippines; and of the third, Cameroon and Tanzania. Where all three factors coincide, as in Indonesia, the possibility exists for extremely high endemic richness in both species and languages. Indigenous knowledge is also a window on those species that science has not yet described taxonomically or ecologically.

> *"Proponents of biological and cultural diversity are fighting the same battle."*

A final reason biologists should care is that proponents of biological and cultural diversity are fighting the same battle. If biodiversity is to be preserved, a fundamental shift in attitudes will have to take place. Today's dominant socio-economic view is inimical to biodiversity because it devalues the total range of biotic variation in favor of the very narrow portions of it that are currently commercially viable. The whole movement to elevate biodiversity to a central place, not just in conservation but in workaday life, depends on getting people to recognize that all living processes and their components are valuable, not just those that happen to be of use to humans. There are models that begin to show the way, but they are found primarily among indigenous peoples whose cultures and languages are threatened by wholesale, unmoderated change.

It is not a question of idealizing indigenous people or of locking them into a bygone lifestyle. Many of them wish to realize aspects of modern life: not just technology, but access to national political institutions, formal education, etc. At present, however, it is next to impossible for tribal people to integrate modern institutions and traditional culture. Instead, they are forced to abandon or repudiate their traditions to gain full access to modern institutions. There is no intrinsic reason why this should be a Hobson's choice. It is possible for modernity to engage bearers of tradition so that the result is additive and accepting rather than annihilating. Consider the hard economic proof offered by the growing popularity of heritage tourism which, at its best, respects the integrity of the host culture without undermining its authenticity. In its motives, heritage tourism is closely allied with ecotourism, and both have the potential to be positive forces on behalf of diversity.

Is Extinction Inevitable?

One can fairly ask whether the extinction of large numbers of languages is inevitable. Some linguists think so, and argue that salvage linguistics—documenting languages before they disappear—is the only useful thing that can be done. But more endangered-language communities increasingly are refusing to accept this. There are language retention and rejuvenation activities popping up all over the world. In New Zealand, children can take part in Maori immersion programs. In California, a master-apprentice program pairs elder speakers with younger learners of the remaining native languages of the state. In the Hebrides and Highlands, speakers of Scottish Gaelic have formed Comann an Luchd Ionnsachaidh, an adult learner's society. In Botswana, organizations support Shiyeyi, Ikalanga and other tribal languages by publishing workbooks and holding classes. Several new international nongovernmental organizations also have taken up the cause of linguistic diversity.

The enactment of Article 8(j) of the Convention on Biological Diversity is one of a growing number of international activities that adopts a biocultural perspective. Article 8(j) calls for preserving, maintaining and promoting the "knowledge, innovations and practices of indigenous and local communities embodying traditional lifestyles relevant for the conservation and sustainable use of biological diversity." While the implementation of 8(j) is still decidedly a work in progress, the article's very existence, and the fact that indigenous representatives are taking an active role in shaping it, are highly significant.

The dawning of a biocultural approach signals a new chapter in humankind's age-old fascination with diversity. Luisa Maffi is a linguistic anthropologist and president of Terralingua, a new international organization dedicated to integrating the understanding and protection of linguistic, cultural and biological diversity. She has observed that "questions about the consequences of loss of linguistic and cultural diversity have been raised mostly in terms of ethics and social justice, and of maintaining the human heritage from the past—and rightly so. . . .

> However, when we consider the interrelationships between linguistic, cultural, and biological diversity, we may begin to ask these questions also as questions about the future—as related to the continued viability of humanity on earth. We may ask whether linguistic and cultural diversity and diversification may not share substantive characteristics with biological diversity and diversification, characteristics that are ultimately those of all life on earth.

Maffi is asking the right questions, because the answers will help to determine the fate of Earth's living variety in the years to come.

Glossary

Biodiversity   the full range of variety within and among **genes, species,** and **ecosystems** of the world.

Ecosystem   a dynamic complex of living organizations and their nonliving environment interacting as a functional unit.

Endemic   found only in a specified locality.

***Ex situ* conservation**   conservation of elements of **biodiversity** outside their natural habitat.

Gene   the functional unit of hereditary found in the DNA molecule; it is responsible for inherited characteristics of organisms.

Genetic diversity   variation in genetic composition of individuals within populations of a **species.**

Hotspot   area of unusually high **species richness** or **endemism.**

***In situ* conservation**   conservation of elements of **biodiversity** within their natural habitats and **ecosystems.**

Landraces   cultivated genetic varieties of domesticated plants or animal breeds; typically refers to products of traditional agriculture rather than of modern breeding practices or biotechnology.

Species   the basic unit of classification of living organisms; members of a species are naturally capable of interbreeding with each other but not with members of other species.

Species richness   the number of **species** (especially native species) within a defined region.

Taxonomy   the study and classification of living forms of life.

Vascular plants   plants with a vascular system that transports water and other nutrients throughout the plant body, as opposed to plants such as liverworts or mosses that lack this ability. Vascular plants are frequently utilized by scientists as an indicator to determine a region's **biodiversity** or **species richness.**

Bibliography

Books

Yvonne Baskin — *The Work of Nature: How the Diversity of Life Sustains Us.* Washington, DC: Island Press, 1997.

Joel Cracraft and Francesca T. Grifo, eds. — *The Living Planet in Crisis: Biodiversity Science and Policy.* New York: Columbia University Press, 1999.

Niles Eldredge — *Life in the Balance: Humanity and the Biodiversity Crisis.* Princeton, NJ: Princeton University Press, 1998.

Kevin J. Gaston and John I. Spicer — *Biodiversity: An Introduction.* Malden, ME: Blackwell Science, 1998.

Randall Kramer, Carel van Schaik, and Julie Johnson — *Last Stand: Protected Areas and the Defense of Tropical Biodiversity.* New York: Oxford University Press, 1997.

National Research Council — *Perspectives on Biodiversity: Valuing Its Role in an Everchanging World.* Washington, DC: National Academy Press, 1999.

Sheila Peck — *Planning for Biodiversity: Issues and Examples.* Washington, DC: Island Press, 1998.

Clifford J. Sherry — *Endangered Species: A Reference Handbook.* Santa Barbara, CA: ABC-CLIO, 1998.

Vandana Shiva — *Biopiracy: The Plunder of Nature and Knowledge.* Boston: South End Press, 1997.

Bruce A. Stein, Lynn S. Kutner, and Jonathan S. Adams, eds. — *Precious Heritage: The Status of Biodiversity in the United States.* New York: Oxford University Press, 2000.

Timothy M. Swanson — *Global Action for Biodiversity: An International Framework for Implementing the Convention on Biological Diversity.* London, UK: Earthscan, 1997.

Paul M. Wood — *Biodiversity and Democracy: Rethinking Society and Nature.* Vancouver: UBC Press, 2000.

Bibliography

Periodicals

Catherine Badgley — "Can Agriculture and Biodiversity Coexist?" *Wild Earth*, Fall 1998.

Christopher Bright — "Invasive Species: Pathogens of Globalization," *Foreign Policy*, Fall 1999.

Michael S. Coffman — "Globalized Grizzlies," *New American*, August 18, 1997.

Indur M. Goklany — "Saving Habitat and Conserving Biodiversity on a Crowded Planet," *BioScience*, November 1998.

M.A. Hutson et al. — "No Consistent Effect of Plant Diversity on Productivity," *Science*, August 25, 2000.

International Wildlife — "Plundering the Planet's Species," September/October 1999.

Alexander N. James et al. — "Balancing the Earth's Accounts," *Nature*, September 23, 1999.

William F. Jasper — "Global Master Plan," *New American*, October 25, 1999.

Jocelyn Kaiser — "Rift over Biodiversity Divides Scientists," *Science*, August 25, 2000.

Edward J. Maruska — "The Pace of Extinction," *World & I*, May 1999.

Jack McClintock — "Twenty Species We May Lose in the Next Twenty Years," *Discover*, October 2000.

Bill McKibben — "Interview with E.O. Wilson," *Audobon*, January/February 1996.

Norman Myers — "What We Must Do to Counter the Biotic Holocaust," *International Wildlife*, March 1999.

Scott Norris — "A Year for Biodiversity," *BioScience*, February 2000.

Elizabeth Pennisi — "Taxonomic Revival," *Science*, September 29, 2000.

Stuart L. Pimm and Peter Raven — "Biodiversity: Extinction by Numbers," *Nature*, February 24, 2000.

David Quammen — "Planet of Weeds," *Harper's*, October 1998.

Richard E. Rice et al. — "Can Sustainable Management Save Tropical Forests?" *Scientific American*, April 1997.

Don C. Schmitz and Daniel Simberloff — "Biological Invasions: A Growing Threat," *Issues in Science and Technology*, Summer 1997.

Science News — "Hey, We're Richer than We Thought!" April 1, 2000.

Douglas H. Shedd — "Into Thin Air," *Forum for Applied Research and Public Policy*, Fall 2000.

Bob Wildfong — "Saving Seeds," *Alternatives Journal*, Winter 1999.

215

Organizations to Contact

The editors have compiled the following list of organizations and websites concerned with the issues debated in this book. The descriptions are derived from materials provided by the organizations. All have publications or information available for interested readers. The list was compiled on the date of publication of the present volume; the information provided here may change. Be aware that many organizations take several weeks or longer to respond to inquiries, so allow as much time as possible.

American Livestock Breeds Conservancy (ALBC)
PO Box 477, Pittsboro, NC 27312
(919) 542-5704 • fax: (919) 545-0022
e-mail: albc@albc-usa.org • website: www.albc-usa.org

ALBC works to prevent the extinction of rare breeds of American livestock. The conservancy believes that conservation is necessary to protect the genetic range and survival ability of these species. ALBC provides general information about the importance of saving rare breeds as well as specific guidelines for individuals interested in raising rare breeds. It sells *A Conservation Breeding Handbook* and other books on breeding and caring for farm animals.

Biotechnology Industry Organization (BIO)
1625 K St. NW, Suite 1100, Washington, DC 20006
(202) 857-0244 • fax: (202) 857-0237
e-mail: info@bio.org • website: www.bio.org

BIO represents biotechnology companies, academic institutions, and state biotechnology centers engaged in the development of products and services in the areas of biomedicine, agriculture, and environmental applications. It conducts workshops and produces educational activities aimed at increasing public understanding of biotechnology. Its publications include the bimonthly newsletter *BIO Bulletin*, the periodic *BIO News*, and the book *Biotech for All*.

Canadian Forestry Association (CFA)
185 Somerset St. W, Suite 203, Ottawa, ON K2P 0J2 Canada
(613) 232-1815 • fax: (613) 232-4210
website: www.canadian-forests.com

CFA works for improved forest management that would satisfy the economic, social, and environmental demands on Canadian forests. The association explores conflicting perspectives on forestry-related topics in its biannual *Forest Forum*.

Conservation International (CI)
2501 M St. NW, Suite 200, Washington, DC 20037
(202) 429-5660 • fax (202) 887-0193
e-mail: info@conservation.org • website: www.conservation.org

CI works to preserve and promote awareness about the world's most endangered biodiversity through scientific programs, local awareness campaigns, and economic initiatives. It publishes fact sheets, reports, and occasional papers on biodiversity conservation program such as *Encouraging Private Sector Support for Biodiversity Conservation: The Use of Economic Incentives and Legal Tools.*

Defenders of Wildlife
1101 14th St. NW, Suite 1400, Washington, DC 20005
(202) 682-9400
e-mail: info@defenders.org • website: www.defenders.org

Defenders of Wildlife is dedicated to the protection of all native wild animals and plants in their natural communities. The organization focuses on the accelerating rate of extinction of species and the associated loss of biodiversity, and habitat alteration and destruction. The organization publishes *Defenders* magazine.

National Audobon Society
700 Broadway, New York, NY 10003
(212) 979-3000 • fax: (212) 979-3188
e-mail: webmaster@list.audobon.org • website: www.audobon.org

The society seeks to conserve and restore natural ecosystems, focusing on birds and other wildlife for the benefit of humanity and the earth's biological diversity. It publishes *Audubon* magazine and the WatchList, which identifies North American bird species that are at risk of becoming endangered.

Political Economy Research Center (PERC)
502 S. 19th Ave., Bozeman, MT 59718
(406) 587-9591 • fax: (406) 586-7555
e-mail: perc@perc.org • website: www.perc.org

PERC is a research center that provides solutions to environmental problems based on free market principles and the importance of property rights. PERC publications include the quarterly newsletter *PERC Report* and papers in the *PERC Policy Series* dealing with environmental issues including biodiversity conservation.

Rainforest Action Network (RAN)
221 Pine St., Suite 500, San Francisco, CA 94104
(415) 398-4404 • fax: (415) 398-2732
e-mail: rainforest@ran.org • website: www.ran.org

RAN works to preserve the world's rain forests and protect the rights of native forest-dwelling peoples. The network sponsors letter-writing campaigns, boycotts, and demonstrations in response to environmental concerns. It publishes miscellaneous fact sheets, the monthly *Action Alert Bulletin*, and the quarterly *World Rainforest Report.*

Rural Advancement Foundation International (RAFI)
110 Osborne St., Suite 202, Winnipeg, MB R3L 1Y5 Canada
(204) 453-5259 • fax: (204) 925-8034
e-mail: rafi@rafi.org • website: www.rafi.org

RAFI is an international nongovernmental organization dedicated to the conservation of genetic diversity in agriculture and the responsible development of rural communities. Its primary publication *Communique*, published four to six times a year, features articles on biodiversity and intellectual property. RAFI's other publications include the report *The Seed Giants: Who Owns Whom?*

Secretariat of the Convention on Biological Diversity
393 St. Jacques, Suite 300, Montreal, Quebec, H2Y 1N9 Canada
(514) 288-2220 • fax: (514) 288-6588

e-mail: secretariat@biodiv.org • website: www.biodiv.org

The Secretariat of the Convention on Biological Diversity promotes scientific cooperation between the signatories of the 1992 biodiversity treaty. It produces newsletters and brochures; its website disseminates numerous documents and studies pertaining to biodiversity.

World Resources Institute (WRI)
10 G St. NE, Suite 800, Washington, DC 20006
(202) 729-7600 • fax: (202) 729-7610
website: www.wri.org

The WRI is an independent center for policy research on natural resources and the environment. Its publications include *Balancing the Scales: Guidelines for Increasing Biodiversity's Chances Through Bioregional Management* and other reports on environmental protection.

Worldwatch Institute
1776 Massachusetts Ave. NW, Washington, DC 20036-1904
(202) 452-1999 • fax: (202) 296-7365
e-mail: worldwatch@worldwatch.org • website: www.worldwatch.org

Worldwatch is a research organization that analyzes and calls attention to global environmental and resource problems. It compiles the annual *State of the World* and *Vital Signs* anthologies and publishes the bimonthly *Worldwatch* magazine. Its Worldwatch Papers series include two publications on biodiversity: *Nature's Cornucopia* and *Losing Strands in the Web of Life*.

World Wildlife Fund (WWF)
1250 24th St. NW, PO Box 97180, Washington, DC 20077-7180
(800) 225-5993
website: www.worldwildlife.org

WWF works to save endangered species, to conduct wildlife research, and to improve the natural environment. It publishes an endangered species list, the bimonthly newsletter *Focus*, and a variety of books on the environment.

Websites

IUCN Red List of Endangered Species
www.redlist.org

The Red List is a searchable database of plant and animal species that are threatened by extinction. It was created by the World Conservation Union (IUCN), a global environmental organization.

The Virtual Library of Ecology and Biodiversity
http://conbio.net/vl/

The Virtual Library features a searchable index of electronic resources on biological diversity.

Index

Index

ethics
  in biodiversity conservation, 56, 170
  and biodiversity loss, 27, 180
  of commercial farming practices, 121
Ethnologue: Languages of the World, 209
exotic species. *See* species, invasive
Exotic Wildlife Association, 147
extinctions
  concerns about, are overstated, 19
  on Hawaii, 44–45
  human activities are causing, 12
  and human settlements
    in North America, 70–71
    in Polynesia, 68–70
  language, 208–11
  inevitability of, 212
  mass
    current, 15, 29
    and alien species, 39–40
    effects of, 16–17
    and human population growth, 196
    and human survival, 23
    rates of, 16, 25, 49–50, 156, 163, 180
    in Southern Africa, 49–50
  previous
    causes of, 23
    recovery from, 26, 170
    species benefiting from, 93
extremophiles, 24

Featheringill, Linda, 125
ferrets, 22
fertilizers
  as conservation tools, 141
  increase in use of, 115
  and industrial agriculture, 117–18
fire regimes, 76
Fish and Wildlife Service, U.S., 16, 81
fisheries, 104–105
Florida, 41–42
Flynn, Tim, 41, 42
Forum on Nature and Human Society, 153
Fowler, Cary, 200
Franklin, J.F., 175
Freese, Curtis H., 192

Gaelic Earth Liberation Front, 133
Gaston, Kevin J., 48
genetic diversity, 11
  and biodiversity, 25
  and criteria for endangered status, 51–52
  of farm animals, 120–24
  and hybridization, 114–55
  of livestock, decline in, 115
  loss of, in agricultural crops, 108
  as measure for biodiversity, 53
  and seed hybridization, 114
  sharing benefits of, 185–86
genetic engineering, 131, 142–44
Genetics and the Origin of Species (Dobzhansky), 205
Genetix Snowball movement, 133
Giffin, Jon, 47
Gilpin, Michael, 19
Glazer, Steve, 101
Gleick, P.H., 172

Glen Canyon Dam, 100–101
Global Biodiversity Assessment (United Nations), 190
global warming
  data does not support, 86
  see also climate change
Gore, Al, 89, 191
governments
  opposition to regulation by, 18
  role of, in biodiversity preservation, 182–83
  should reduce resource exploitation, 199–204
Grace, Michelle, 40
Grant, V., 54
grass, 38–39
Gray, Vincent, 87
green revolution, 108, 116–17
  has helped preserve wildlife, 136
Gregg, Bill, 39, 40
Grime, Phil, 57, 59
Grumbine, R. Edward, 12
"Guidelines for the Preservation of Biodiversity Loss by Alien Invasive Species"
  criticism of, 62–63
Guterman, Lila, 56

habitat
  fragmentation of, 92–93
  loss of,
    and atmospheric CO_2, 84
    categories of, 75–76
      ranking, 76–77
    is major cause of extinctions, 17, 75, 156
    threatens biodiversity in U.S., 73–81
Harmon, David, 205
Hawaii
  biodiversity loss in, 43–47
  and brown tree snake, 39
  human settlement of, 69–70
Hawksworth, David, 154, 155, 160
Heartland Institute, 85
Hector, Andy, 59
Helms, Jesse, 189
Hench, Jayne, 40
Hi-Bred Corn Company, 114–15
Hinton, Leanne, 209
Hooper, David U., 60
Hosansky, David, 15
hot spots, 28, 44, 157
  agricultural, 111–12
  conservation efforts should focus on, 161–70
    con, 171–77
  criteria for, 173
  human population in, 197
  identification of, 166–67
  terrestrial biodiversity in, 168
  threats to, 168–70
Hotspots: Earth's Biologically Richest and Most Endangered Terrestrial Ecoregions (Mittermeier et al.), 161
humans
  activities of, do not affect global warming, 85–89
    con, 84
  effects of biodiversity loss on, 26–27, 51
  and species extinction, 12, 25
    effects on climate-induced migrations, 83
    historical and contemporary threats, 77–78
    in Polynesia, 68–70

Index